The Baseball Film

Screening Sports

Series Editors: Lester D. Friedman, Emeritus Professor of Media and Society, Hobart and William Smith Colleges, and Aaron Baker, Professor of Film and Media Studies, Arizona State University

Sports and media have had a long and productive relationship. Media have transformed sports into a global obsession, while sports in turn have provided a constant flow of events to cover and stories to tell. This symbiosis with media has both sold sports as entertainment and enabled them to comment on issues and identities in contemporary culture. Movies tell some of the most insightful stories about sports, which have also been defined throughout their history by a convergent media landscape that includes print, radio, television, and digital technologies. Books in the Screening Sports series will focus on the relationship between sports, film, and other media forms and the social and culture issues raised by that complex collaboration.

The Baseball Film

A Cultural and Transmedia History

AARON BAKER

Rutgers University Press

New Brunswick, Camden, and Newark, New Jersey, and London

Library of Congress Cataloging-in-Publication Data

Names: Baker, Aaron, author.
Title: The baseball film : a cultural and transmedia history / Aaron Baker.
Description: New Brunswick : Rutgers University Press, [2022] |
    Includes bibliographical references and index.
Identifiers: LCCN 2021015685 | ISBN 9780813596891 (hardcover) |
    ISBN 9780813596884 (paperback) | ISBN 9780813596907 (epub) |
    ISBN 9780813596914 (mobi) | ISBN 9780813596921 (pdf)
Subjects: LCSH: Baseball films—United States—History and criticism. |
    Baseball—Social aspects--United States. | Baseball in motion pictures. |
    National characteristics, American, in motion pictures.
Classification: LCC PN1995.9.B28 B35 2022 | DDC 791.43/6579—dc23
LC record available at https://lccn.loc.gov/2021015685

A British Cataloging-in-Publication record for this book is available from the British Library.

References to internet websites (URLs) were accurate at the time of writing. Neither the author
nor Rutgers University Press is responsible for URLs that may have expired or changed since the
manuscript was prepared.

♾ The paper used in this publication meets the requirements of the American National
Standard for Information Sciences—Permanence of Paper for Printed Library Materials,
ANSI Z39.48-1992.

www.rutgersuniversitypress.org

Manufactured in the United States of America

For Number 23

Contents

The Baseball Film

Introduction

• • • • • • • • • • • • • • • • • • • •

The Baseball Film:
Nostalgia and Innovation

Anyone with even a casual knowledge of baseball has probably heard the sport referred to as the national pastime. On a literal level that phrase points to a time from the late nineteenth century through the 1970s when baseball was the most popular professional sport in the United States. Yet even as Major League Baseball (MLB) has given way to the National Football League in fan interest and profitability, the former sport's status as the national pastime has endured, becoming more symbolic than actual by invoking the idea that it represents the core of American identity. Conservative commentator George Will offers an eloquent explanation of this idea when he states that MLB, with its slow pace and extended schedule, "requires patience" like the democratic process central to American society. Will also asserts that baseball like democracy demands compromise, what he calls "the slow politics of the half loaf." He notes that during its long season that lasts from spring to fall "the best team is gonna get beaten a third of the time, the worst team's gonna win a third of the time, the argument, over 162 games, is that middle third." Summing up his comparison of baseball with democracy, Will states: "It's a game you can't like if winning's everything, and democracy is that way too."[1]

Yet American national identity based on promises of democracy and economic opportunity has been compromised in recent decades with the outsourcing of jobs, consolidation of wealth at the top of the society, voter suppression, resistance to immigration, and tolerance of racism in the justice system. Vivian Sobchack argues that when the American dream is challenged by such selfish forces, the division and conflict they create are sometimes avoided through escape into nostalgia, back to a time of imagined community before the complexities of the present, and that baseball exemplifies that retreat.[2] Documentary filmmaker Ken Burns, who has been anointed as the guardian of baseball's collective memory, acknowledges that "the national pastime . . . as emblematic of 'America'" reflects both the opportunities and the shortcomings of the country's history. In the filmmaker's words, baseball is "about race, . . . it's about wealth, it's about labor and its tensions. This is a metaphor for the entire country."[3]

Although Burns alludes to how race has been the basis for who gets an opportunity and who doesn't, as well as to the fact that players and owners have consistently feuded over dividing up MLB's earnings, he makes no mention of how women have rarely even been allowed into the game that is supposed to represent their nation. Throughout most of its time at the pinnacle of American sporting life, professional baseball was just for White males. While baseball has always taken pride in how it broke the color barrier when Jackie Robinson joined the Brooklyn Dodgers in 1947, the subsequent opportunities for African Americans in the sport were limited and have declined in recent decades. Globalization has brought more Latino and Asian players to MLB, but Whites still control almost two-thirds of the spots and own and run just about all the teams.

However, for the most part film and TV representation of baseball ignores this contradiction between the game calling itself the national pastime but yet, at its highest level, refusing to give fair opportunity to everyone in the society. Such lack of inclusion will present an increasing challenge to MLB as the makeup of the United States becomes more diverse and as women increasingly insist on their right to access in the world of sports. A few movies and some television coverage have begun to acknowledge this need for progressive change, yet there is still the strong tendency in media representation of baseball to hang onto the tradition of nostalgic stories about the sport. Such backwardness offers denial of and protection from change, be it the economic impact of globalization, the influence of computers on what we know and how we know it, or cultural shifts in the makeup of American society. Not surprisingly, movies most stubbornly hang on to this nostalgic view of baseball, while TV and representation of the sport online are more open to either cultural change or new ways to assess performance. Yet whether representing the past or the future, media portrayal of baseball frequently offers the game as a means of social connection. The 1989 film *Field of Dreams* concludes with the main character Ray Kinsella (Kevin Costner) charging twenty dollars to visit the ball field he built on his Iowa farm, an ending that Sobchack describes as an example of selling the dream of an imagined community.[4] Be it looking back nostalgically to the past or boldly engaging with where the game and American society are going, most of the media representations of baseball analyzed in this book offer a similar promise of joining the right team.

Chapter 1 focuses on five films that exemplify the contrasting nostalgic and progressive tendencies in Hollywood baseball movies. The first, *The Natural* (1984), is perhaps the most paradigmatic example of a monocultural filmic portrayal of baseball in which White men define the game and rely on their hard work and self-reliance to play it well. The second film discussed in this chapter, *The Pride of the Yankees* (1942), likewise offers a celebration of White masculinity but also reveals how baseball intersects with the history of immigration in the United States and therefore presents a less exclusive idea of the sport inflected by class and ethnicity. *A League of Their Own* (1992) and *42* (2013) tell the important stories of how women first played professional baseball and Jackie Robinson became the first African American in the major leagues in more than half a century. Both films attracted large audiences because they present the inspiring history of women and Blacks succeeding in the American national pastime that has too rarely given them central roles. The last movie discussed in chapter 1, *The Catcher Was a Spy* (2018), offers another example of how there is room in baseball for social difference by telling the true story of Moe Berg, who was Jewish, bisexual, a major league catcher for sixteen seasons, and also an American hero for his military service in the Second World War.

Chapter 2 traces how two Babe Ruth biopics, *The Babe Ruth Story* (1948) and *The Babe* (1992), ask us to enjoy the spectacle provided by the Yankee slugger while the home runs and wild lifestyle lasted, but ignore how owners took advantage of his dysfunction to make large profits off his stardom. The 2011 HBO documentary *The Curious Case of Curt Flood* tells the sad but significant story of how the all-star outfielder referred to in the title sacrificed his career to help players get fairer compensation for their talents. Another baseball film from 2011, *Moneyball*, celebrates the use of new methods of analysis to give the small-market teams a chance, yet MLB owners also use such advanced metrics to roll back the salary gains that players have made. Movies and TV representation of baseball in the minor leagues like *Time in the Minors* (2010), *The Battered Bastards of Baseball* (2014), and the TV series *Brockmire* (2017–2020) offer an even sadder story of unfair pay. In sum, all the narratives analyzed in chapter 2 raise questions about how much baseball has really delivered on its celebrated promise that players' hard work and achievement lead to the financial rewards of the American dream. Yet while the films discussed in this chapter illustrate the struggle between players and owners over the profits they generate, I trace as well how the sport's synergy with newspapers, radio, and television has both been a major source of that revenue and also defined a representational style that celebrates an individual heroism that Hollywood films about the sport have adopted to support their ideology of self-reliance.

Chapter 3 looks at movie and television representations of baseball's attempts to achieve greater social diversity. The 1994 film about Ty Cobb shows how he was accepted as a major star despite his racism, misogyny, and violent temper because he represented the idea of dominant White masculinity. It was that world of White privilege that Jackie Robinson entered, and as much as his opportunity to play for the Dodgers was about selling MLB to Black fans and helping Brooklyn put a stronger team on the field, his presence also seemed to get baseball closer to fulfilling the promise of opportunity for all that it had always claimed to represent and that made it America's national game. Mitchell Nathanson writes that, from its origins in the nineteenth century, the "creed" of the sport has been "offering baseball as a way to acculturate into mainstream American life."[5] However, Nathanson notes that such a promise has often been more a "cultural fiction" than a reality.[6] That it took more than a decade after Robinson joined the Dodgers for every MLB team to hire at least one Black player and that no African American managed until Frank Robinson took over the Cleveland Indians in 1975 showed that baseball was more intent on limiting than facilitating Black access.

Today, as African American opportunities in baseball are again in question, economic incentives might help move the game toward greater inclusion. As Hua Hsu points out, in the United States "the culture is being remade in the image of white America's multiethnic, multicolored heirs."[7] Baseball's need to be hipper and Blacker to attract a new generation of fans recalls how Robinson gave a big boost to newspaper circulation when he arrived with the Dodgers and Brooklyn and five other National League teams set attendance records in his first season.[8] As Robinson himself commented: "They hadn't changed because they liked me any better; they had changed because I could help fill their wallets."[9]

As much as the history of African American participation in MLB has been about White control and restriction, access for women to professional baseball has been much more limited. Jennifer Ring makes a strong case for how part of the justification for keeping women out of baseball has involved denying the history of their involvement in the game. She traces the origins of this omission to early characterizations of baseball that viewed the game as defining normative masculinity.[10] By contrast, three movies about girls' and women's baseball, *Blue Skies Again* (1983), *A League of Their Own* (1992), and *I Throw Like a Girl* (2014), as well as Jessica Mendoza's commentary on ESPN telecasts demonstrate their ability on the field and to explain the game, yet also show the ideas and actions that have limited their access.

In recent decades baseball as a business has followed the trends of globalization in regard to pursuing less expensive player labor overseas and looking to grow international markets. But because the sport has been played in Latin America and Asia since the nineteenth century, MLB's globalization has not been entirely about imposing a North American game on the rest of the world. Chapter 4 employs Roland Robertson's idea of glocalization, the notion that globalization involves both a combination of external economic and cultural hegemony along with the retention of local practices and values, to describe how America's national pastime functions in other parts of the world. Films like *Mr. Baseball* (1992), *Kokoyakyu* (2006), *Roberto Clemente* (2008), and *Sugar* (2008) show this glocalized version of baseball in Japan, Puerto Rico, and the Dominican Republic and how the culture of the game from those places has influenced the sport in North America.

Chapter 5 traces how, while players, team management, and the media are quick to admit that organized baseball couldn't exist without the money that fans spend on the game, there is a long history of portraying them in film and television as disillusioned, obsessed, silly, angry, and even dangerous. Films like *The Fan* (1996), *Bull Durham* (1988), *Fever Pitch* (2005), and *Fernando Nation* (2010) follow this pattern, yet with the exception of the first movie they also reveal how baseball fans empower themselves through their knowledge of the game, creating a capacity for learning and analysis that may help them in other parts of their lives and to build social connections. Like the fandom shown in these films, fantasy baseball has rapidly developed as a way for lovers of the sport to show their admiration for their favorite players, yet it also empowers its participants by giving them control over the assemblage and maintenance of the teams in competition. The internet has been a huge boon for fantasy baseball, giving players a way to research their teams and communicate and play with friends. As it has been increasingly monetized by the development of platforms to play for cash prizes, fantasy baseball has also helped grow fan interest in the sport shown on television and the internet.

While most baseball films focus on adults excelling at the game to embody models of heroism, a few movies instead show the sport as an activity to form the identities of young people. In chapter 6 I analyze two films about kids' baseball and two more about how the game figures in the relationship between children and their fathers. *The Bad News Bears* (1976) foregrounds the influence of the 1960s counterculture to challenge the idea that competition in Little League baseball offers kids a positive learning experience. Another film about kids' baseball, *The Sandlot* (1993), shows a group of boys who play on their own, yet the adults in their lives still model ideas of gender that influence their developing identities.

The Disney biopic *The Rookie* (2002) and Clint Eastwood's *Trouble with the Curve* (2012) are both movies about adult main characters using baseball to repair strained relationships with their fathers. Mainly because he is the central character whose agency drives the narrative, Jimmy Morris (Dennis Quaid) in *The Rookie* succeeds in fixing his relationship with his father Jim Sr. (Brian Cox) by making it to the big leagues and showing the older man the error of his authoritarian parenting. By contrast, in the Eastwood film his star image built on a gruff, controlling masculinity so defines his lead role as Atlanta Braves scout Gus Lobel that his grown daughter Mickey (Amy Adams) has to adjust to him to make their relationship work, in part through her ability to navigate the male-dominated world of professional baseball.

Throughout the book I capitalize "White," and "Black" when they refer to racial groups. My justification for doing so is well stated by Kwame Anthony Appiah when he writes that a good reason to capitalize the racial designation Black is that it "is not a natural category but a social one—a collective identity—with a particular history."[11] The same justification applies as well for White. While Richard Dyer points out that part of the privilege that White people have enjoyed has been the assumption that "whites are not of a certain race, they're just the human race," in fact, just as Appiah says about Blacks, Whites have an identity with a history, and capitalization of White refers to that fact.[12]

1

Hollywood Baseball Films

● ● ● ● ● ● ● ● ● ● ● ● ● ● ● ● ● ● ● ●

Nostalgic White Masculinity
or the National Pastime?

Combining the conventions of how print, radio, TV and the internet represent the sports world with its talent for affirmative stories and happy endings, Hollywood has made hundreds of films about athletes who dream big and are determined to win. Baseball has been the subject of many of those films, and such movies have often endorsed the idea that success in the United States comes from the same hard work, self-discipline, and team collaboration needed to prevail on the field.

However, not all baseball films recognize such symbolic meaning for the sport as testament to an inclusive notion of the American dream. While some movies about the game locate it within the history of how diversity and opportunity have strengthened American society, most prefer stories that construct a more monocultural image of baseball as defined only by the achievements of White males. The first kind of baseball movie aspires to represent the sport with all its complexities of social difference, but also the resulting opportunities it has offered to more people for participation and enjoyment as spectators and fans. The latter more nostalgic baseball film presents the game as symbolic of an American society before the value of diversity was understood and acknowledged. Yet even the most utopian Hollywood baseball movie, which assumes that hard work and playing by the rules produce success and that White men have best exemplified that truth, also has the need to appeal to lovers of the game with a degree of plausibility based on resemblance to the real sports world. The presence of such realism often injects historical contradictions and social difference into the baseball film in ways that complicate its narrative otherwise focused on White characters as its causal agents.

Sports historian Ben Rader has documented how by the late 1970s the National Football League (NFL) had outgrown Major League Baseball (MLB) and become the most popular sport in America.[1] Moreover, baseball may continue to lose popularity moving into the future, in part because the languid pace of the game doesn't fit into the ever faster lifestyles of our contemporary digital world. As America has grown more polarized with wealth and influence consolidated in fewer hands, the force and violence of football better mirror the society's inclination to pursue domination rather than equal opportunity. Former major league player and manager Davey Johnson summed this up when he stated that "the American way is to dominate somebody."[2] The recent increased emphasis in baseball on power pitchers and launch angle, strike outs and home runs is an attempt to make the game fit such a winner-take-all contemporary mindset. However, MLB and the films and other media that show it also seem to be demonstrating some increased awareness of the need to include greater diversity in their representation of the sport, in part to rebuild its shrinking fan base, but also in the process moving closer to living up to the promise of the American dream for all that allows it to claim the honor of being the national pastime.

Baseball, the American Dream, and Nostalgia

Lawrence Samuel writes about the American dream that "no other idea . . . has as much influence on our individual and collective lives, with the Dream one of the precious few things in this country that we all share."[3] Central to this notion of the American dream is what Samuel calls "its grounding in the ideal of equal opportunity," the promise that a better life in the United States is available to everyone and is a "meritocracy," "earned rather than inherited," using traits such as self-reliance, resourcefulness, and optimism.[4] Samuel mentions exemplars of the American dream from the first half of the twentieth century like Babe Ruth and Henry Ford as well as more recent figures who embody it such as Oprah Winfrey and Barack Obama.[5] However, rather than Samuel's assumption of "equal opportunity" for all, Jennifer L. Hochschild posits instead the more qualified notion of "a significant likelihood . . . of reaching their goals" to persuade Americans to strive for a better life.[6] She writes therefore that the dream is "the promise that all Americans have a reasonable chance to achieve success as they define it—material or otherwise—through their own efforts."[7]

Both Hollywood movies and baseball have long been important vehicles for communicating and endorsing such ideas of the American dream. Robert Sklar has written about "Hollywood's capacity to purvey America's myths and dreams," and certainly the paradigmatic Hollywood story in which main characters achieve what they want if they believe and try hard enough fulfills this promise.[8] Along with movies, commercial sports are among the most prominent cultural activities that affirm our belief in equal opportunity based on merit and the acquisition of productive skills, hence the widespread use of the expression "a level playing field." Baseball in particular, long the most popular and still one of the main sports in American life, has played a major role in symbolizing the possibility of success. Samuel goes so far as to write that "as America's game, baseball is the American Dream incarnate."[9]

Samuel adds that home ownership has also been an important part of defining the American dream as material success by imagining the place where a better life would be enjoyed. Jim Cullen agrees, noting that "a great many people" in the United States have pursued the goal of "a place they could call their own."[10] Samuel traces the emphasis on owning a home to the cultures of European immigrants who brought with them a "love of the freestanding house . . . where land ownership conveyed status, security and wealth," particularly when located in rural settings with "the absence of the city's poverty, crime, overcrowding and bad hygiene understandably making the house in the country seem like utopia."[11] Besides how it celebrates the hard work, development of productive skills, and determination needed for upward mobility, baseball, with its field that symbolizes a pastoral landscape and its ultimate goal of returning home, fits neatly into this affirmation of the ideal location of the American dream. Two of the most iconic baseball films, *The Natural* (1984) and *Field of Dreams* (1989), arrive at happy endings defined by the protagonists living, and playing ball, on rural home-steads. Samuel sums up this product of the intersection of America's pas-time and film when he concludes that "baseball, the movies and the single-family house ... were the clearest expressions of the American Dream."[12]

While Samuel and Hochschild are clear about what the American dream promises, Robert Elias adds that such opportunity for success should be accessible "for natives and newcomers alike ... regardless of one's class, gen-der, religion and ethnicity."[13] Professional baseball in fact has a history of access to those who could make the grade regardless of class or ethnicity. In that sense it has been an avenue for success for immigrants or at least the sons of immigrant families. David Voigt notes that, before the Second World War, baseball was "a primary vehicle of assimilation for immigrants into American society," and Harold Seymour has explained that "the argot of baseball supplied a common means of communication and strengthened the bond [for] ... immigrants living in the anonymity ... of large industrial cities ... baseball gave to many the feeling of belonging."[14] The 1942 biopic of Yankees star Lou Gehrig, *The Pride of the Yankees*, offers a gently humor-ous representation of the slugger's German immigrant mother initially dis-missing and misunderstanding baseball. Yet when she sees her son's success with the Yankees, it reaffirms her optimistic American identity, and the film shows her excited celebrations with her husband, friends, and neighbors after Lou hits two home runs in a 1928 World Series game.

More recently, Latin American and Asian players have replaced working-class White ethnics as the new arrivals in MLB, matching how their com-munities have become the largest immigrant groups coming to the United States since federal legislation in 1965 that emphasized reuniting families and skilled labor gave them access similar to that previously offered to Euro-peans. However, it's important to note again that women have never been given as much opportunity in professional baseball as working-class and eth-nic men, and the percentage of non-White players, despite the much-trumpeted success of Robinson and the African American, Latino, and Asian players who followed him, has been carefully limited. Such contin-ued gender and racial exclusion has been justified by pointing to the highly competitive nature of MLB determined by the limited number of spots and the many aspirants. In this sense, MLB represents how the American dream, as Elias states, is "held out for all but satisfied by only the select few who have the requisite skills and determination."[15]

Its lack of rush, the iconic tools made of wood and leather that symbolize America's pastoral past, and the inclination to celebrate the heroes of its storied history all testify to the nostalgic nature of baseball. Svetlana Boym describes the concept of nostalgia as itself having a long history, first appearing in seventeenth-century medical discourse to refer to the disease of being obsessed with the past and unable to accept the present reality. The challenges created by the rapid changes of modernity prompted this desire for escape into the past, what Boym calls "a longing for a home that no longer exists or has never existed."[16] She points to contemporary popular culture as full of such nostalgic visions of the past "longing for continuity in a fragmented world . . . a defense mechanism in a time of accelerated rhythms of life and historical upheavals."[17]

While some fans certainly are drawn to baseball's celebration of the past, Susan Jacoby also blames this nostalgic tendency for its recent decline in popularity. In 1954 French cultural historian Jacques Barzun observed that "whoever wants to know the heart . . . of America had better learn baseball."[18] Today searching for baseball in the chest of the American body politic might turn up a pacemaker. Jacoby points out that the game has the oldest and Whitest fan base of any of the major sports. Only 25 percent of viewers who watch baseball on television are under age thirty-five, and six out of ten in that same demographic are White men over fifty-five.[19] She attributes this older fan base to the changing attention spans brought on by digital technology. Baseball is a sport that moves deliberately and requires patience and therefore in Jacoby's view doesn't fit the quick return of the culture of the internet and the smartphone.[20] However, while its slow pace is seen as a barrier to appealing to younger fans, Elias also notes the potential value such time for reflection allows. Just as in the first half of the twentieth century baseball offered immigrants a way to connect to American life and find community through fandom in "alienated urban centers," he comments that its mindfulness "in the postmodern world perhaps . . . can help us make sense of [the] . . . fast-paced information age."[21]

Besides his observations about how baseball limits and critiques as well as endorses the American dream, Elias also comments on the nostalgic quality of the sport. Like Boym, he cautions that "the danger" of nostalgia "comes when [it] . . . is used to sanitize the past and divert us from present realities."[22] Elias also quotes Michael Kammen, who calls nostalgia "heritage by consumption" "whereby the memory business serves emotional, business and political interests."[23] This statement describes well how the nostalgia so prominent in baseball can function: while some older fans may see the sport as a positive reminder of good memories they have of playing in their youth or how the game helped them connect with a parent in a way that has emotional resonance, baseball is also a consumer product that creates profits from such feelings. Not only does *Field of Dreams* sell us the emotional power of baseball to relive the past, but such commodification of nostalgia is even celebrated within the movie's narrative, as its main character, Ray Kinsella (Kevin Costner), saves his Iowa farm by charging visitors twenty dollars to see the diamond he has built in a cornfield. *Field of Dreams* also exemplifies Kammen's statement about how nostalgia can serve "political interests" in how the film uses the sport to reaffirm the centrality of Kinsella's White masculinity.

Although he agrees with Fredric Jameson that nostalgia in popular culture is in part a reversion to an idealized past as an evasion of how history influences the present, Paul Grainge also views it as commodification of the emotions and remembrance of experiences that the consumer seeks, what Frances Smith calls "nostalgia's return to a lost time, most frequently the time of one's youth."[24] Grainge cleverly explains such commodified nostalgic culture, what he terms "the heritage industry," as aimed at a baby boomer demographic while employing the new technologies of cable and streaming to make older films and television readily available.[25] This would certainly seem like a good description of the over-fifty fan base central to baseball and the Hollywood and historical films and programs about the sport aimed at them. Ken Burns's documentaries about the national pastime and some of the programming on MLB Network fit in this category of nostalgic popular culture.

Diversity and a Dream for the Future

The nostalgic tendency in baseball appears in its agrarian iconography, pacing, and historical focus but also in the sport's ambivalence toward the increasing diversity of the United States. Despite the significant contributions of African Americans, Latinos, and Asians to the game, nostalgic film narratives about baseball still often adhere strongly to the idea that Whites have defined the sport. While long celebrated for its inclusion of Jackie Robinson in 1947 as a precursor to the civil rights gains for African Americans in the 1950s and 1960s, baseball has slipped in the participation of Blacks.

From a high of 19 percent in 1986, the percentage of MLB players who are African American is now less than half that at 7.5 percent.[26] Jacoby believes that there are cost barriers that prevent many Black families from supporting their kids' involvement in baseball. To make it as a professional requires expensive equipment, lessons, and membership on club teams, not to mention that a very low percentage of college baseball scholarships go to African Americans. This impacts the popularity of the game with Black fans, as participation in a sport is one reliable way to generate interest.

However, both cultural critic Gerald Early and comedian and actor Chris Rock explain the decline in Black interest in baseball differently. Rock points out that young African Americans often find the money to buy expensive clothes, sneakers, and phones, so maybe the reason for Black disinterest in baseball lies elsewhere. "You can't tell me that Black kids can't afford baseball when everyone's buying Jordans for $300," comments Rock.[27] Both he and Early also agree that a better explanation has to do with baseball's nostalgic obsession with celebrating America's past, a mindset that the two men argue doesn't appeal to Blacks who prefer to look forward toward a time of equal opportunity rather than back to when they were marginalized as second-class citizens. The idea of America's agrarian past that baseball celebrates doesn't include equal status for African Americans. When baseball at the end of the nineteenth century was becoming established as America's national game, as Early puts it, "Blacks . . . were denigrated and degraded by the American pastoral myth, reinvented as the dream of the Southern plantation: in this vision they were loyal, know-your-place darkies."[28] Rock adds, "Black people don't like to look back," and he scoffs at MLB's interest in "fake, antique stadiums that are supposed to remind us of the good old days" with their "cheezy organ music at the games." "Where's the beats?" he asks. Rock's reference to the lack of rap music at major league games leads to his analysis of the importance of Black culture in defining the tastes of young Americans regardless of race. "You lose Black America and you lost young America," he points out before concluding, "We [Blacks] don't need baseball, but baseball needs us."[29]

Besides its declining appeal to African Americans, another challenge for baseball in regard to building its fan base is the need to include more women. Jennifer Ring points out that "the taunt 'You throw like a girl'" and "Pete Rose's remarkably honest assertion that he was grateful he was born a boy because otherwise he couldn't have played baseball" both exemplify the masculinist reality that "the national pastime has been declared the domain of only half the nation."[30] As Ring notes, in Burns's 1994 PBS documentary *Baseball*, often regarded as the most definitive about the sport, "there is no mention of the fact that women played professional baseball on all-women and mixed teams, against all-women teams, men's teams and mixed teams in the nineteenth century."[31] While Burns gives little attention to the role women have played in baseball history, Ring notes that "women have attempted to gain access to America's diamonds for as long as baseball has been played."[32] She recounts the example of how in 1931 seventeen-year-old minor league pitcher Jackie Mitchell struck out both Babe Ruth and Lou Gehrig in an exhibition game in Chattanooga, Tennessee, a performance that was dismissed as "bawdy publicity" by the *Sporting News* and prompted MLB commissioner Kenesaw Mountain Landis to void Mitchell's contract "on the grounds that 'professional baseball was too strenuous a game to be played by women.'"[33] Ring summarizes that throughout the history of baseball "white women were permitted to play when men went to war [a reference to the All-American Girls Professional Baseball League that operated from 1943 to 1954 and was celebrated in Penny Marshall's 1992 film *A League of Their Own*], and Black women [such as Mamie "Peanut" Johnson] were allowed to play when integration of Major League Baseball drained the Negro Leagues of their best players."[34] Yet Ring concludes that the "integration" for which Jackie Robinson was the celebrated pioneer is "incomplete" because "it does not include America's girls and women. . . . if baseball is the national pastime, the implication is that women are not part of the nation."[35]

Yet as much as baseball's preference for White masculinity limits opportunities for women and its popularity in an ever more diverse American society, Jacoby is still hopeful about the game's future. She points to how, throughout the history of baseball, the sport has responded to challenges in successful ways that have renewed its popularity. Jacoby notes the enormous stardom of Babe Ruth in the 1920s after the scandal of the 1919 World Series that was fixed by gamblers and the success of free agency in the 1970s that freed players from the economic tyranny of the reserve clause, by which they had no bargaining power with owners and had to accept whatever they were offered in salary. Ruth's experience coming from a reform school in Baltimore to become the biggest star in the game and the ability of the MLB players union to win the right to submit to outside arbitration after three years of big league service and earn free agency after six both demonstrate baseball's adherence to core American values of opportunity and reward for hard work. But as much as Jacoby wants to note baseball's central role in affirming the American dream, filmic representation of the game also shows the contradictions inherent in its history, how assertion of these egalitarian values has been accompanied by pushback from those who benefit from their denial.

While acknowledging such commercial and ideological meanings for baseball nostalgia, Elias, like Jacoby, also asserts the relevance of the game for the future of the American dream. He points out that the history of baseball has been distinguished by three major progressive successes: the All-American Girls Professional Baseball League, established in 1943 as the first professional sports league with women players; Robinson in 1947 breaking the unwritten agreement among team owners to exclude Blacks; and the challenge by St. Louis Cardinals outfielder Curt Flood of the reserve clause to the Supreme Court in 1972, leading to free agency, and better paychecks, for MLB players three years later. Encouraged by such progressive milestones as realizations of the promise of the American dream, Elias asserts that, regardless of its declining TV ratings and aging fan base and the criticism of how its nostalgic quality limits its ability to remain relevant, baseball still matters. Based on these past successes, Elias argues that "baseball could provide initiatives to help reform not only the national pastime but also American society."[36] He states that, based on the success of its players union in winning free agency, baseball "could lead the way on worker's rights and in revitalizing the labor movement"; building on Robinson's pioneering success, it "could promote genuine racial equality and improve race relations"; and, as the founders of the first professional sports league for women, baseball "could promote new breakthroughs in women's access to the game and to sports and American institutions."[37] Elias sums up such exhortations by concluding: "Baseball has within it the capacity to help make the American dream one that's more worth attaining, and to make it one that's far more accessible to far more people than the conventional American dream."[38]

The remainder of this chapter focuses on five films that exemplify both the conservative and the progressive tendencies in baseball described above. The first, *The Natural* (1984), is perhaps the most paradigmatic example of a nostalgic, monocultural filmic portrayal of baseball in which White men define the game and rely on their hard work and self-reliance to play it well. The second film discussed in this chapter, *The Pride of the Yankees* (1942), likewise offers a celebration of White masculinity, but also reveals how baseball intersects with the history of immigration in the United States and therefore presents a less monocultural ideal of the sport inflected by class and ethnicity. By contrast, *A League of Their Own* (1992) and *42* (2013), the two highest earning films about baseball, represent important moments in the sport's history when women and African Americans were included in the national game. Finally, *The Catcher Was a Spy* (2018) again shows that there is room in baseball for difference by telling the true story of Moe Berg, who was Jewish, bisexual, a major league catcher, and an American hero for his military service in the Second World War. Like *A League of Their Own* and *42*, *The Catcher Was a Spy* shows some of the more progressive moments in baseball's past without slipping into nostalgia.

Baseball Films and White Masculinity

Gender theorist R. W. Connell argues that sports play a major role in defining normative ideas of masculinity. In fact, she goes so far as to write that "sports has come to be the leading definer of masculinity in mass culture" and that the "superior force" and "superior skill" demonstrated by male athletes "have become a theme of backlash against feminism" and support patriarchal societies with "symbolic proof of men's superiority and right to rule."[39] In most sports films dominant masculinity gets reaffirmed not only by how men play 62 percent of the lead roles in Hollywood movies, but also by how they often perform in a utopian narrative typical of American cinema, whereby characters achieve success simply by trying hard and following the rules.[40] In such utopian stories the most often White athletic protagonist who succeeds through determination, self-reliance, and hard work "controls his own destiny . . . in free and fair competition offered as representative of an American society that promises rewards to the most deserving individuals."[41] In short, the male protagonist at the center of most sports film narratives is there because he has demonstrated himself worthy of our attention and admiration.

The 1984 film *The Natural* offers a good example of how the sports film affirms dominant masculinity in this way and how baseball movies often do so with a nostalgic story to avoid contemporary challenges to what Connell calls the assertion of "men's superiority and right to rule" as well as the intersecting privilege that Whiteness confers. Based on Bernard Malamud's 1952 novel in which a star ballplayer is corrupted by gamblers, *The Natural* was adapted by veteran Hollywood screenwriter Roger Towne and advertising executive Phil Dusenberry to change the downbeat ending of the book so that Roy Hobbs (Robert Redford) in the climactic scene hits a long home run to ruin the fix and win the pennant for his team, the New York Knights.

The movie's utopian reversal of the original story explains Hobbs's heroism as the result of a work ethic and self-reliance he gained growing up on a farm. It begins with Roy as a boy learning to play baseball from his father (Alan Fudge). After the father's sudden death from a heart attack that he suffers by a large oak, that same tree is struck by lightning and provides the wood Roy uses to make a bat that he calls Wonderboy. *The Natural* uses nine shots to show Roy carefully making the bat, an example of the work ethic the boy has learned that has also helped him become an outstanding ballplayer. Like the farm that he and his father worked, Roy's ability as a ballplayer comes as a product of industrious individualism within the agrarian environment that baseball symbolizes with its green fields and wood and leather tools. Despite the father's tragic death, it's no surprise that Roy as a young man of nineteen has the skill and courage to leave home in pursuit of a career as a ballplayer. Throughout the film we see Roy imbued with the qualities given him by his rural origins: not only the self-reliance and ability to work to achieve his goal, but a quiet confidence that Redford's understated acting communicates effectively.

In contrast to the rural environment that has formed Roy and given him these heroic qualities, the city where he goes to find fame and success as a ballplayer is filled with corruption, deception, and violence. Central to the danger of this urban environment are Roy's interactions with women. Just as *The Natural* is typical of Hollywood baseball narratives in how it centers its story around a White male protagonist, it also follows the common pattern in American film of portraying female characters as either supportive of the hero's goals or obstacles he must overcome. The first two women Roy encounters after he leaves home exemplify the latter type of antagonists. On the train to Chicago to try out for the Cubs, Roy meets a star ballplayer, the Whammer (Joe Don Baker), and accepts the slugger's challenge to pitch to him. During a layover the competition takes place in a field by the tracks, and Roy strikes the Whammer out on three pitches. Harriet Bird (Barbara Hershey), an attractive but mysterious woman dressed entirely in black, had been eyeing the established star but turns her attention instead to Roy after his pitching success. Once arrived in Chicago, Harriet lures Roy to her hotel room, where she shoots him before killing herself.

After that violent interruption of Roy's ambition, the story then jumps forward sixteen years to Hobbs, now thirty-five, attempting to return to his dream of playing professional baseball. Even after winning a spot as an outfielder with the New York Knights, he again encounters an attractive but dangerous woman, Memo Paris (Kim Basinger), who tries to lead him astray toward a gambler, Gus Sands (Darren McGavin), and the payoffs that marked the downfall of the title character in Malamud's novel. Besides these two sexualized femme fatales, the only other female character in *The Natural* is Hobbs's childhood sweetheart Iris (Glenn Close), who fits the stereotype for a supportive, "good" women in Hollywood films by returning near the end of the story to inspire Roy to reject the gamblers' bribe and hit the heroic home run.

Although *The Natural* is not a historical film, it attempts to build plausibility, and justify its celebration of White masculinity, by invoking real events, people, and spaces. Roy's shooting is based on the story of Eddie Waitkus, a first baseman for the Philadelphia Phillies who in 1949 was wounded by an obsessed fan, Ruth Ann Steinhagen, in a Chicago hotel room. Waitkus recovered and returned to baseball; his assailant was institutionalized. Malamud seems to have had Waitkus in mind when he wrote his 1952 novel, both because of the shooting he includes but also because sportswriters referred to the first baseman as "the natural" during his playing days.[42] Besides it's invocation of the Waitkus shooting, *The Natural* also adds a historical element to its story with the Whammer, a character who in the film recalls Babe Ruth. Joe Don Baker brings the same stocky body and extreme confidence the Babe had to the role, not to mention the Yankee star's appetite for casual sex. Harriet Bird knew that such promiscuity would give her access to the Whammer, and it is that plan that inadvertently leads her to Hobbs.

Yet, typical of the nostalgic baseball film, *The Natural*, except for its references to real ballplayers, makes little mention of historical conditions or social identities. Class difference comes up briefly when Roy and the Knights' greedy owner, the Judge (Robert Prosky), discuss the player's age, low salary, and opportunity for a big payoff if he cooperates with Gus's fix. Race is referred to only indirectly by the film in that no non-Whites ever appear. The world of professional baseball shown in *The Natural* is one in which the game is played exclusively by White men for White fans. Considering that the story is set in 1939 and that the integration of MLB wouldn't happen until 1947, this racial exclusivity is an accurate portrayal of big league baseball at the time.

The Natural therefore exemplifies how, as David J. Leonard notes, most sports films tell stories about the success of White male athletes and in the process marginalize women and non-White men.[43] Marjorie Kibby sees *The Natural* as one of a group of nostalgic sports films from the 1980s reacting to how "established norms of masculinity appeared increasingly difficult to live out."[44] She describes those 1980s films as a response to economic changes occurring in the 1970s that "introduced new groups to the workplace" in particular women, and how "rapid technological change revolutionized traditional competences," to reduce "the dominance of men in the workforce."[45] Kibby sees nostalgic sports films as presenting the attitude that "if in the eighties, the present was unsatisfactory and the future a threat then looking back to the past . . . was the best option." These nostalgic sports films were not history per se so much as what Kibby calls "a restructuring of that history in the hope of a revised future."[46] While the two female characters who seek to undermine Roy Hobbs (Harriet and Memo) present a threat that he overcomes, race as a challenge to his authority never overtly appears in the film. The world of professional baseball in *The Natural* allows only White men, and Hobbs as the heroic main character therefore enjoys what Leonard calls "whiteness as both wrapped up in privilege and unnoticed."[47]

Such privilege manifests itself in *The Natural* not only in how Hobbs as a White male has the opportunity to play at the highest level of professional baseball because of his race, but also in how the Whiteness he embodies, in the words of bell hooks, is "synonymous with goodness."[48] Of course none of the ballplayers in the film are as good as Hobbs; he is the best, the hero of the ballgames that structure its narrative. In this sense, the eponymous title of the film indirectly refers to how he epitomizes the Whiteness that pervades it. As Richard Dyer puts it, "As long as white people are not racially seen and named, they/we function as a human norm."[49] Hobbs is the best example of that norm, and the film's title, as it describes someone who is a perfect fit for what he does, refers to that fact.

While the Whites-only world of big league baseball in *The Natural* makes it historically accurate, the mise-en-scène in the film offers a more ideological position on race, valorizing Whiteness in the world it represents. Redford's heroic protagonist, and the only favorable representation of a female character in the film, Glenn Close's Iris, both frequently appear costumed

FIG. 1 Roy Hobbs (Robert Redford) symbolizes White masculinity in *The Natural* (1984).

in white and bathed in soft, golden light. By contrast, the characters representing corruption, greed, and violence—not only the two manipulative women, Harriet Bird and Memo Paris, but also the gambler Gus and his accomplice the Judge, are shown consistently in dark clothing or shadow. As the characters raised in a rural environment and who embody the positive values of work, self-reliance, modesty, and honesty, Roy and Iris are both blond, and the film's visual style emphasizes their Whiteness, while the characters who embody negative values and occupy urban spaces are associated with darkness and deception. We see striking examples of these racially coded visual patterns in the Chicago shadow-filled hotel room where Harriet Bird, dressed entirely in black, shoots Roy, wearing a white shirt and cardigan sweater, and in the New York nightclub filled with jazz music where the gambler with Memo's assistance is first introduced to Roy and tries to recruit him to accept a payoff to throw games. Probably the best example of the film's visual endorsement of Whiteness occurs in its final scene just after Hobbs's home run, when we return to the sunny wheat field in which the film opened with Roy playing catch with his dad. In this last scene, Roy wears a white shirt and throws a baseball to his blond son as Iris, also dressed in white, looks on approvingly.

The Natural's moral allegory had come to a climax in the previous scene in which Hobbs's long home run won the pennant for the Knights. His blast travels so high and far that it hits the light towers above the stands in right field, setting off a shower of sparks that resembles a Fourth of July fireworks display. The music swells dramatically while Hobbs rounds the bases as the culmination of a spectacular scene typical of the kind of blockbuster film-making that became increasingly common in 1980s Hollywood. In fact, Elias reads *The Natural* as the sort of conservative movie prominent in Reagan-era America, like the *Star Wars* sequels (1980, 1983), *Raiders of the Lost Ark* (1981), and *Top Gun* (1986), that offered nostalgic and/or spectac-ular distraction while economic changes consolidating wealth with a smaller and smaller percentage of the population were making life more difficult for many Americans. Elias describes the 1980s as a time when "the middle classes shrink and corporate values flourish . . . to compensate for the decline we were given baseball."[50] The 1980s saw the release of baseball films such as *The Comeback Kid* (1980), *Tiger Town* (1983), *The Slugger's Wife* (1985), *A Winner Never Quits* (1986), *Stealing Home* (1988), *Field of Dreams* (1989), and *Major League* (1989) with the same White male protagonist and nos-talgic quality that characterize *The Natural*.

As much as any of the 1980s baseball films, *Field of Dreams* most resem-bles *The Natural* in its affirmation of White masculinity. The Kevin Cost-ner lead character, Ray Kinsella, risks his Iowa farm and the economic security of his family by building a ball field on his land to fulfill the emo-tional needs of several characters—both real and magical—including him-self. The emotional reassurance of the field benefits the eight Chicago White Sox players who were banned from baseball for selling the 1919 World Series to gamblers but now have a way to return to the game. Such nostalgic revi-sion of baseball history allows the banned players to shed the derogatory Black Sox label that had been placed on them after the fix came to light. Giving the eight a place to play baseball again in *Field of Dreams* returns the focus to their ability as athletes and the self-reliance and discipline of Whiteness that created those skills. Even the one Black character in the film, writer Terrance Mann (James Earl Jones), uses baseball to affirm the agency of Whiteness by reimagining the past. While Chris Rock and Gerald Early may urge baseball to improve its appeal to Blacks by looking to a more multicultural future rather than celebrating a past in which African Americans were denied rights and opportunities, Mann, who had made a career voicing the counterculture's challenge to racism, individualism, and materialism, travels to Iowa from his home in Boston and tells Ray to hold on to the field he has built despite the threats from the bank to foreclose on his unprofitable farm. Mann promises Ray that people will come and pay for the privilege of watching the games there: "People will come Ray . . . as innocent as children, longing for the past. . . . watch the game . . . as if they dipped themselves in magic waters. The one constant through all the years, Ray, has been baseball. . . . This field, this game is a part of our past Ray. It reminds us of all that once was good and that could be again." In this soliloquy Mann celebrates baseball as part of an American past that was "good" and will hopefully return, ignoring the fact that part of that history was the denial to Blacks of the chance to play the game at the major league level where it best represented American opportunity. After this nostalgic speech Mann steps on the field with the White Sox, his disembodiment in the film's last scene as he disappears into the corn with them when they finish their game showing his acceptance of the self-reliance of Whiteness that Kinsella and the players affirm.

Mann's magical self-sacrifice, along with the scene soon after of Kinsella playing catch with the reincarnation of his father returned as a young ballplayer, contribute to a strong emotional emphasis at the end of *Field of Dreams.* Leonard comments that the conservative sports films of the 1980s use such "emotionalism as a hook, as a means to teach whiteness, masculinity and the American Dream, even as they deny their place in the narrative . . . stories that make even the most cynical race scholar well up with tears."[51] Baseball as a way for both Roy Hobbs and Ray Kinsella to end their stories with the reestablishment of a father/son bond by playing catch on the farm offers similar examples of such emotionalism to disarm analysis of the affirmation by the two films of White masculinity.

The Pride of the Yankees also centers around the heroism of a White male player, but unlike the 1980s films it is neither nostalgic nor utopian. Rather than celebrate the past to avoid the complexities of the present, *The Pride of the Yankees* was a film released during World War II that explains Lou Gehrig's terminal disease and premature death as a price worth paying for the opportunities he enjoyed growing up in American society. His experience is therefore offered by the film as a way to understand the losses suffered by Americans as a result of the war.

As much as it is known for Gary Cooper's re-creation of the star first baseman's emotional farewell speech to a Yankee Stadium crowd in 1939, *The Pride of the Yankees* is also the story of the son of working-class German immigrants finding great success on the baseball field and realizing the American dream. A New York native, Gehrig starred in both football and baseball at Columbia University before playing sixteen years for the Yankees. During his Hall of Fame career he won two Most Valuable Player awards and a Triple Crown for Yankee teams that took six World Series titles. Although the biopic culminates with his speech and points to Gehrig's death just two years later from amyotrophic lateral sclerosis (ALS) in 1941, most of the movie is an upbeat celebration of his success on the field and his close relationships with his parents and wife Eleanor (Teresa Wright).

The Pride of the Yankees opens with a statement about Gehrig by sportswriter and Hollywood screenwriter Damon Runyon, whom producer Samuel Goldwyn had hired "to write a patriotic forward to the film."[52] "He [Gehrig] faced death with that same valor and fortitude that has been displayed by thousands of young Americans on far-flung fields of battle," Runyon begins. He continues about Gehrig: "He left behind him a memory of courage and devotion that will ever be an inspiration." At several points in the film, Gehrig's German immigrant mother, who worked as a cook at Columbia, makes reference to the freedoms and opportunities that make American great and that she is happy her son enjoys. Such references to the chances for a better life explain the logic behind Gehrig's comment in his famous farewell speech at Yankee Stadium that, despite his terminal illness, he is "the luckiest man alive." During a 1943 USO tour that Cooper took to visit American troops in the South Pacific, servicemen asked him to recite the Yankee Stadium farewell. They had recently seen *The Pride of the Yankees* and "were moved by the selfless speech of a dying man."[53]

Robert Burgoyne uses Noel Ignatieff's concept of civic nationalism to explain how films set during wartime justify the sacrifices of combat and in the process demonstrate that they offer to all, "regardless of race, color, creed, gender, language or ethnicity," the opportunity for membership in that national community. Civic national identity for Ignatieff is therefore earned, through a contribution to the society such as service during wartime. Such identity is "called civic because it envisages the nation as a community of equal rights-bearing citizens, united in patriotic attachment to a shared set of political practices and values," Ignatieff writes.[54] As the son of a working-class immigrant family, Gehrig makes his contribution not only through his heroism playing the country's national pastime but also, as Runyon put it, in how he "faced death with that same valor and fortitude that has been displayed by thousands of young Americans on far-flung fields of battle." That its title character was a White ethnic helped the Gehrig biopic lessen any challenge its celebration of the immigration experience may have presented to the social status quo. Nonetheless, in addition to its wartime theme of accepting sacrifice as the price of opportunity, *The Pride of the Yankees* also emphasizes national identity as open to newcomers willing to work hard and contribute. Mama Gehrig's dream that Lou will go to Columbia to become an engineer (not a ballplayer) exemplifies the idea that national identity can be gained by contributing to, literally helping to build, American society. Before his stardom convinces her that baseball is a viable career, Mrs. Gehrig (Elsa Janssen) twice tells Lou "I want you to be somebody" by studying engineering to take advantage of his opportunity for a better life because "America is a wonderful country where everyone has a chance."

In contrast to such civic nationalism, Ignatieff also defines an ethnic national identity that looks to give unity to the community by defining it not through acceptance of diversity but as including only those with "preexisting ethnic characteristics" that are "inherited" rather than earned.[55] *The Natural* exemplifies this ethnic national identity in Roy Hobbs, who while he uses his work ethic learned on the farm to become a good ballplayer, also embodies an exclusive idea of Americanness that is passed on through baseball within the world of White men who populate the nostalgic, utopian film narratives about the game.

Producer Samuel Goldwyn, although he himself was an immigrant from Poland who had benefitted from the idea of civic national identity, and while he hired Runyon to give *The Pride of the Yankees* a patriotic resonance, was generally not interested in the social meanings of Gehrig's story. Richard Sandomir, in his exhaustive book about the making of the film, explains how Goldwyn wanted as little baseball as possible in the movie, favoring instead a romantic melodrama that centered around the relationship between Gehrig and his wife Eleanor. Nonetheless, at the time of the film's release, the producer linked its example of American opportunity with the movie's celebration of a great romance: "It's a love story. It's a success story.

It's the kind of story that could happen only in this land of equality and opportunity. It's a tender, moving, touching romance."[56] The idea of patriotic sacrifice as the price for Gehrig's success certainly made sense at the time, however, for Goldwyn it was most important that the romantic emphasis would attract more women to see the film and boost its earnings.[57]

The Pride of the Yankees was one of a group of World War II sports biopics films made in the early 1940s. Along with *Knute Rockne—All American* (1940), *Gentleman Jim* (1942), and *The Iron Major* (1943), it tells the story of the son of an immigrant, working-class family whose hard work and determination allow him to assimilate and achieve success in the sports world. Yet as much as these biopics present stories of success through hard work and following the rules as an endorsement of the opportunities in American society that made wartime service worthwhile, they also include issues of social difference that impact the characters' lives. In Lou Gehrig's case, he faces the challenge of class inequality during his time at Columbia, how he chose sports for his life's work in reaction to the restrictions placed on traditional masculinity by the social and economic forces of modernity, but also how, once he becomes a star, Eleanor and his parents are marginalized as the spectators and consumers of his sports heroism.

At Columbia Mama Gehrig works as a cook at a fraternity of upper-class brothers whose arrogance and sense of entitlement prompt them to make fun of Lou's earnestness and lack of sophistication. They invite him to a party where Myra (Virginia Gilmore), the girlfriend of one of the fraternity members, leads Lou on and they later tease him about his naïve words of affection for her. The film's central strategy of how to overcome class disadvantage is to work hard and develop a career that would enable social mobility. Mama Gehrig's dream for Lou to become an engineer exemplifies that strategy. However, her son's dedication to football and baseball leaves little time for study, and when his mother falls ill Lou takes the quicker route to money by signing with the Yankees. In place of his working-class disadvantage, *The Pride of the Yankees* shows Lou acquiring through sports a strong, self-determining masculinity—further enhanced by his embodiment of national identity defined by the common purpose of the war effort.

The Pride of the Yankees celebrates Gehrig's ideal masculinity for his strength, courage, self-discipline, hard work, and dedication to a cause; meanwhile, female characters like Eleanor and Mama Gehrig are defined as the dependent beneficiaries of Lou's economic success. Besides providing well for Eleanor, Gehrig buys his parents a house in suburban New Rochelle.

His strong and assertive mother, who worked so hard to raise him and put him through college, becomes his full-time fan, listening to his games on the radio and watching Lou play at Yankee Stadium. A key scene that shows Gehrig privilege his marriage with Eleanor over his relationship with his mother comes when the latter tries to choose the furniture and decorations for the newlyweds' home and Gehrig has to insist that his new wife have the privilege of making the purchases. If the promise offered to men in a wartime sports biopic like *The Pride of the Yankees* was the opportunity for upward mobility in return for the duty to defend America in wartime, women were assured the commodities that symbolized improved social status in exchange for their acceptance of supportive roles. While producer Goldwyn saw the film's emphasis on romance and family as attracting female viewers, it also fit into the advertising role that Charles Eckert describes Hollywood having taken on, beginning in the 1930s, whereby stars were associated with various products. According to Eckert, films like *The Pride of the Yankees* celebrated "the importance of the consumer and . . . the dominant role of women in purchasing."[58] If not the same degree of agency given the title character, such consumerism at least offered female viewers identification with women in the story who to some extent contributed to defining the Gehrig family's successful life. Ironically, male spectators of the film and of commercial sports have been offered a similar role, asked to buy a demonstration of physical strength and assertive self-determination denied to most of them in the industrial and postindustrial workplace.[59]

Women and African Americans Join the Game

In 1943, Philip Wrigley, owner of the Chicago Cubs, decided to establish the All-American Girls Professional Baseball League (AAGPBL) with teams in four midwestern cities as a way of maintaining interest in the game while many MLB stars were serving in the military. Wrigley was optimistic that a women's professional baseball league would build a sizeable fan base because of the established popularity of softball. In the mid-1940s the *New York Times* estimated that 150 million spectators turned out to see softball played by 600,000 teams, many of whom were made up of women.[60] Historian Susan Cahn states that "working-class women of the 1930s and 1940s joined softball teams in unprecedented numbers," and in 1941 four semipro teams in Chicago drew 234,000 paying spectators.[61]

But while Wrigley wanted to build on the acceptance and popularity of women playing softball, he was also intent that the AAGPBL be a baseball league. For the women skilled at softball, the shift to baseball was not an insurmountable challenge. Many of them had played baseball as well. However, the Cubs' owner also sought to get attention for the AAGPBL by recruiting players who embodied a contrast between normative ideas of feminine attractiveness and their ability to skillfully play what was thought by many to be an exclusively male game.[62] Such demonstration of athletic skill on a baseball field was not the only part of American life in which women took over jobs that men had traditionally held before the war. Cahn notes that during World War II women were required to do many kinds of work that had previously been done by men and baseball was just one of those areas where they were needed.[63]

To soften the shock of its revision of traditional gender roles, the AAGPBL enforced rules asserting the requirement that players present a feminine appearance that was conventionally attractive but not sexy. The players had to wear skirts on the field and were required to use makeup and not cut their hair too short.[64] Wrigley and his associate Arthur Meyerhoff also decided it would generate publicity with fans and give the league legitimacy as professional baseball if they hired former MLB players, like Hall of Famer Jimmie Foxx, to manage the teams.[65]

In addition to such requirements for feminine appearance and the presence of male authority on the field, there were also rules about the "respectable" behavior that the players had to adhere to off of it, including curfews, older female chaperones to supervise them, and no drinking or smoking.[66] Cahn explains that many of the former AAGPBL players she has interviewed regarded as silly such rules mandating femininity and "respectability" but were willing to put up with them if that was the price to play professional baseball.[67]

In 1944, once he saw that MLB baseball would not have to shut down and could continue during the war, Wrigley agreed to hand over control of the AAGPBL to Meyerhoff, who believed in the quality of the product and grew the league to ten teams. Although the AAGPBL received some national media attention in the form of a 1947 Movietone newsreel titled *Diamond Gals* as well as stories in magazines like *Colliers* and the *Saturday Evening Post*, owners found more success promoting their teams as part of the midwestern communities where they played. Cahn concludes that "AAGPBL teams fared best in medium sized cities like Rockford [Illinois] and Fort Wayne [Indiana]" where there was less competition from other professional sports.[68]

The popularity of the AAGPBL peaked in 1948 with 910,000 paying fans, but attendance declined in the next few years, and by the end of the 1953 season the league was down to five teams and discontinued operation in 1955.[69] While girls' and women's softball continued to thrive, because Little League and high school teams were limited to boys, it was difficult to develop enough female baseball players at the higher skill level the league had established. The AAGPBL also faced competition for fan attention from TV, which was aggressively growing the market for men's professional sports, particularly MLB and the NFL. Yet perhaps the biggest reason the AAGPBL lost fans in the 1950s was that after the war ideas of gender moved back in a more conservative direction to fit in with an increased emphasis on the traditional values of "home, family and marriage."[70] Cahn concludes that the tension between normative femininity and the athletic skill of the players in the AAGPBL therefore became "threatening" during this more conservative time in American society.[71]

Penny Marshall's 1992 film *A League of Their Own* does a good job following the historical record of the AAGPBL that Cahn describes. It foregrounds how the league marketed a contrast between the feminine appearance it insisted that the players present with the strong physicality of their baseball skills. Typical of a Hollywood style of storytelling focused on one or a few main characters, Dottie (Geena Davis) presents the primary embodiment of this contrast. A star catcher for the Rockford Peaches, not only is Dottie the most skilled player in the league, but from the time she joins the Peaches she always conforms to the rules of appearance and behavior, wearing feminine clothing and makeup, with her long, red hair carefully styled. Because she is therefore the ideal representative of the league's brand, Dottie becomes central to a publicity campaign launched by Ira Lowenstein (David Strathairn), the character based on Arthur Meyerhoff, who runs the league.

The scene that best exemplifies Dottie's combination of femininity and baseball skill occurs just after Lowenstein has told the players that the owners are considering shutting down the league because of weak attendance. During the game that day, Dottie creates some spectacle for a bored reporter and photographer whom she sees in the stands. On a ball hit in the air foul, she jumps up from her position behind the plate and does the splits as she slides to make the catch. The film quickly cuts to Peaches manager

FIG. 2 Dottie (Geena Davis) makes a spectacular play, and performs femininity, in *A League of Their Own* (1992).

Jimmy Dugan (Tom Hanks), showing his shocked expression as if to imply the reaction of those in attendance at the game—and the viewer. The play-by-play announcer in the stadium asks incredulously "What did she do?," and the photographer snaps a quick shot of Dottie's acrobatic position that accentuates her legs in the short skirt while the reporter asks Lowenstein, "What's her name?" This comic scene in *A League of Their Own* shows how the AAGPBL players like Dottie, a character based on seven-time all-star Dorothy Kamenshek, accepted performing femininity for men if it allowed them to play professionally.

Yet as much as *A League of Their Own* foregrounds the women's baseball skills and makes gentle fun of the requirement that they be feminine and attractive as they display them, it also accepts the return to values of marriage and family that will contribute to the end of the league. As with the tension between femininity and baseball ability, again it is Dottie who embodies these family values. The film opens with Dottie as a grandmother many years after she played just one season and then returned to her husband Bob (Bill Pullman) to have a family. As the film begins, she is depressed about Bob's recent death and reluctant to attend a celebration of the

FIG. 3 Branch Rickey (Harrison Ford) as White savior in *42* (2013).

AAGPBL at the Hall of Fame in Cooperstown until her daughter convinces
her to go by asking, "When are you gonna realize how special it was?" This
initial scene establishes, even before the film flashes back to her time as a
player and the league's successes on the baseball field, the importance of marriage and family for Dottie. We therefore aren't entirely surprised when
she makes the decision to give up baseball during her first season when Bob
returns home wounded from the war. The centrality of marriage and family
is reaffirmed again when, at the end of the film, its flashback ends with the
Hall of Fame celebration and we see Dottie's sister Kit (Lori Petty), who
had been so fiercely committed to playing baseball and resistant to compro-
mising with ideas of normative femininity when they were young, now
show up at the museum with her two children and six grandchildren.

While *A League of Their Own* celebrates the success of women playing
professional baseball but having to compromise with conservative ideas of
femininity, the 2013 biopic about Jackie Robinson, *42*, presents a similar
acceptance of White paternalism that he had to tolerate in return for his
opportunity. The latter film also shows the ugliness and hostility of the
racism that was directed at Robinson more explicitly than in the other movies that have been made about his experience. One example comes in an
extended sequence showing some of the worst abuse that Robison received
from Phillies manager Ben Chapman (Alan Tudyk) when Philadelphia and
Brooklyn played early in the 1947 season.

We hear Chapman repeatedly call Robinson the N-word, ask him "Why don't you go back to the cotton fields?," and finally yell "This is a White man's game. . . . Get that through your thick monkey skull!" Consistent with its emphasis on Robinson's heroism guided by Dodgers' executive Branch Rickey (Harrison Ford), *42* shows his response to this racist taunting as first restraint and then assertive action to help win the game against the Phillies. Director Brian Helgeland uses a dark, claustrophobic composition in the tunnel leading to the Dodger dugout where we see Robinson, angry about Chapman's abuse, breaking a bat against the wall. Rickey approaches and tells Jackie that to respond angrily would make people think "you're in over your head," and a better reaction is to "get on base and score . . . win this game for us," which in the subsequent scene is exactly what he does.

While Robinson's presence playing himself in the 1950 biopic, *The Jackie Robinson Story*, helped ensure the film's box office appeal and the realism of its action sequences, it also impacted the off-the-field scenes. Biographer Arnold Rampersad describes how Ruby Dee, who played his wife Rachel Robinson, found Jackie "friendly but tense" on the set, especially during the film's romantic moments. Rampersad explains that Robinson had "little personal experience with other women," and cites a magazine writer who noted "Jack's clear embarrassment . . . during 'a mildly romantic scene' with Dee" when Rachel was present during shooting.[72] By contrast, the actor who plays him in *42*, Chadwick Boseman, while he doesn't approximate the movements of a professional athlete, works for the film because he convincingly presents an assertive hip-hop masculinity appropriate for the time as well as sexual chemistry with the actress who plays Rachel Robinson in the 2013 movie, Nicole Beharie.

Former Negro League player Sammie Haynes in Burns's 1994 documentary comments that "Jackie had a terrific temper. He knew how to fight and he would fight." Rickey wanted the confidence that went with Robinson's ability to defend himself, but he also asked him initially not to respond with anger and violence to the racism he faced. From much practice in his first three years, Robinson does a great job presenting that restraint portraying himself in the 1950 film. Boseman in *42* generally plays Robinson with the same discipline and control, but also emphasizes the stress that for the Dodgers star holding back his anger compounded and at times demonstrates the defiance that he would show later in his career by infusing the role with intensity and attitude. In a scene from *42* in which the Dodgers are turned away from a Philadelphia hotel because of Robinson's presence, he and one of the team's southern players, Dixie Walker, argue after the latter asks Jackie to apologize for what he calls a "circus" situation. Todd Boyd's analysis of the transition from a civil rights to a hip-hop identity characterizes how Boseman's performance here differs from that of Jackie Robinson in the 1950 biopic. Boyd writes that "civil rights often imposed a certain unspoken code of moral behavior . . . that one should 'act right' so as not to offend . . . White society," whereas "hip hop could care less about what White people have to say."[73]

Matching Boseman's defiant attitude in the hotel scene is Jay-Z rapping "I Jack, I Rob, I Sin" in his song "Brooklyn, We Go Hard" on the film's soundtrack. These elements of hip-hop style prompt Dave Zirin to acknowledge the effectiveness of *42* in appealing to younger viewers when he comments: "I can understand why a teacher I know thinks it's a great primer for young people who don't know Jackie's story."[74] MLB evidently thought so as well, and in addition to collaborating in the production of the film by providing research and rights, it organized screenings for all thirty teams with players in attendance to show *42* to thousands of teens.[75]

Along with Boseman's assertive masculinity, *42* also bolsters its appeal to a younger audience by emphasizing the romance and sexual chemistry in Jackie's relationship with his wife Rachel. The film includes several scenes of the couple during private moments: the mutual joy of his proposal and her acceptance, a sexually charged scene on their wedding night, a goodbye kiss on the front porch in Pasadena when Jackie heads off to spring training with Billie Holiday singing "Lover Man" on the soundtrack, and a brief night scene of a bare-chested Jackie and Rachel in her nightgown exchanging a kiss as they look out at the skyline of Manhattan.

Yet, as much as *42* succeeds in employing elements of a hip-hop aesthetic to appeal to younger fans, it also follows established conventions of the Hollywood sports film that affirm more conservative ideas of race. Although historical references in *The Natural* and *Field of Dreams* function to justify the centrality of their White protagonists, as a film about a Black main character with racism as his antagonist, *42* positions the past as a narrative world marked by hate and bias to be overcome and left behind. As David Leonard points out, sports films about non-White athletes often seek to present sports competition, because of its insistence on fairness and impartial assessment of preparation and ability, as a way racism has been defeated.[76] He therefore interprets *42* as not only displacing the racism directed at

Robinson into the past but also showing how his ability to compete allowed MLB to move toward a present of more equal access.

Moreover, Leonard notes how the acts of racism shown in *42*, such as Chapman's tirade, are individualized. The film asserts that it is the racist individual who is the problem, not the institutional racism of the larger society. Besides Chapman, *42* in this way makes villains of the gas station worker who refuses to let Robinson use the bathroom, even after his Kansas City Monarchs Negro League team buys gas for their bus, and the airline employee who gives away Robinson's and Rachel's seats on a flight after she uses a "white only" bathroom. Similarly, the ability of sports to overcome racism in *42* is also based on self-reliance. Robinson's success is shown as resulting from his personal strength to deal with the pressure and racist abuse he faces after joining the Dodgers, and even more importantly as coming from the actions of the movie's White savior character, Rickey, who Leonard asserts acts to "redeem whiteness" in the film ostensibly focused on black heroism:

> *42* depicts Rickey as a visionary who because of his religious values, contempt of segregation, and business acumen decides that the Brooklyn Dodgers would sign Jackie Robinson and eventually bring down the walls of Jim Crow inside and outside MLB. He is not simply the decider but someone who facilitates the process by demanding that Jackie "turn the other cheek" and ignore the racism of other players and the press, which would derail their plans. In fact, he is depicted as someone who redeems and transforms Robinson from an angry, quick-tempered, and undisciplined Negro League player to a civil rights hero and baseball legend.[77]

While *42* may revert in certain ways to the Hollywood sports film conventions of emphasizing individualism and self-reliance and privileging White masculinity, it is also a movie that demonstrates an awareness of the need to brand baseball more in terms of racial diversity, specifically in this case by using hip-hop culture, as a strategy to attract younger and more multicultural fans.

The Catcher Was a Guy

Like *The Natural*, most Hollywood baseball movies celebrate the achievements of White male protagonists and look back nostalgically to a time when the sport was the national pastime and its promise of achieving success through hard work, self-determination, and belief in the rules of the game had yet to be complicated by recognition of the problem of social injustice and the value of cultural difference. Conservative commentator Joseph Sobran articulates this nostalgic mindset when he writes in the *National Review*: "Racial integration has worked better in baseball than in any other area of American life. The game has an unforced racial and ethnic balance. It succeeds because the rules are really impartial. Baseball is a refuge from 'social justice.' What it offers instead is simple fairness. There are no 'racist' balls and strikes, no 'affirmative action' balls and strikes, only balls and strikes."[78] Sobran's idea of baseball as an "impartial" opportunity for success informs most of the films about the sport that have been made in the history of American cinema, from the silent period (*The Busher* 1919, *Headin' Home* 1920, *Babe Comes Home* 1927), through the studio era (*Elmer the Great* 1933, *Pride of the Yankees* 1942, *The Babe Ruth Story* 1948, *The Stratton Story* 1949, *The Pride of St. Louis* 1952), and in particular since 1980 when movies like *The Natural, Field of Dreams, Major League* (1989), *Mr. Baseball* (1992), *The Sandlot* (1993), *For the Love of the Game* (1999), *The Rookie* (2002), *Moneyball* (2011), and *Trouble with the Curve* (2012) contributed to a sustained rejection of the countercultural values of the 1960s and 1970s. There have been fewer baseball films made about the challenges faced by women, Latino, African American, and working-class players, although those that have been produced, mostly in the last four decades, including *Eight Men Out* (1988), *A League of Their Own, Soul of the Game* (1996), *Mr. 3000* (2004), *Sugar* (2008), *Fernando Nation* (2010), *El Pelotero* (2011), and *42,* show the rich cultural diversity of the game's history to push back against the nostalgic cycle of baseball movies that started in the Reagan era.

A film like *The Catcher Was a Spy,* based on the Nicholas Dawidoff biography of Moe Berg, who was Jewish, had degrees from Princeton and Columbia, spoke several languages, played sixteen years in the major leagues, was bisexual, and during World War II worked as an American spy to assess how close the physicist Werner Heisenberg and the Nazis were to developing an atomic bomb, would seem to best fit in the latter category of more socially and historically aware stories. In fact, as a Hollywood production trying to pack the complexity of Berg's life into a biopic/war movie genre hybrid, it winds up combining both kinds of baseball movies.

In regard to screen time, *The Catcher Was a Spy* is actually less about baseball than about World War II. There are only three scenes of Berg playing ball: the first early on shows him catching for the Red Sox in 1934; we see him hitting a little later in the film during a tour of Japan that same year with a group of American all-stars; and then during the second half of the film that is dedicated to his wartime service he plays in a pick-up game with a group of GIs. Yet baseball, like Berg's heroics as a spy, is an essential part of the film's mission to redefine its main character as "tough and queer," a revisionist way of representing Jewish men that Nathan Abrams identifies in Hollywood films since the 1990s.[79]

Abrams describes the long-standing stereotype of Jewish men as intellectually strong but physically weak that Berg sought to revise through his career as a ballplayer and, along with hundreds of thousands of other American Jews, through his wartime service. Abrams describes this stereotype as the "'queer' or sissy diaspora Jew … intellectual yet … inadequately masculine Ashkenazi (Central and Easter European) males found in the diaspora." Abrams adds that this diasporic Jewish man "is feminized, … studious and delicate. He never uses his hands for manual labor, exercises or pays attention to maintaining his body."[80] Daniel Boyarin refers to this stereotypical definition of Jewish masculinity when he writes: "The Jew was queer and hysterical—and therefore not a man."[81]

The experience of World War II and the commitment of Jewish men to fight in the American military helped to modify this gender stereotype. As Deborah Moore points out, Jewish men sought to demonstrate their Americanness by enlisting to fight the Nazis.[82] In *The Catcher Was a Spy*, Berg (Paul Rudd) makes clear his commitment to this idea of American identity when he is interviewed for a job by General William Donovan (Jeff Daniels), head of the OSS, the intelligence agency that would become the CIA after the war. Berg tells Donovan that "I'm willing to die for my country." Such courage to fight combined with his success as an athlete show how Berg exemplified the new Jewish masculinity that Moore describes as "based on American military norms of virility" taken up by the half million Jews in uniform during World War II.[83]

While the film omits most of Berg's earlier life as a ballplayer, his biographer Nicholas Dawidoff, whose book was the main source for the movie, tells us that Moe's pharmacist father criticized his son's career as "just a sport, he doesn't have a profession."[84] Regardless of his father's disapproval, Moe as a young man was more concerned with rejecting the Jewish stereotype of weakness and lack of physicality by developing himself into a professional athlete. Dawidoff describes how Berg played basketball as well as baseball at Princeton and, by his senior year, had become "a fine athlete. . . . He had filled out to a willowy six foot one. . . . The varsity shortstop, he [had] started every game there for the Tigers" for the last three years.[85] When Berg entered the major leagues by signing with Brooklyn after his graduation in 1923, several teams, especially in New York, were looking for Jewish stars. In July of that year the *Jewish Tribune* reported that New York Giants manager John McGraw was offering $100,000 for a good Jewish player, but also quoted him on why there were so few to choose from: "The parents . . . influence them to not let anything interfere with their mental training for the future."[86] Berg, as both a good student and a strong athlete, offered another idea of success: "He was important to Jews because he confirmed that you could be intellectual and an athlete and an American, too," writes Dawidoff.[87]

The last scene of Berg playing baseball with a group of American GIs in Italy reaffirms this combination of baseball and military service to counter the stereotypes of Jewish men that the film seeks to revise. As this scene shows, the soldiers are somewhat awestruck and intimidated once they realize that a former major league ballplayer has joined their game. Although Berg reminds them that he was a marginal player who batted just .240 in his career in the big leagues, he doesn't disappoint the GIs by hitting a long home run.

However, as much as Berg was regarded as exemplifying Jewish intellectual excellence as well as a new athletic aptitude, he never really embraced his religious or ethnic identity to any great degree. Dawidoff notes that unlike Detroit Tigers slugger Hank Greenberg, who "assumed the burden of being a hero to the Jews, . . . Berg distanced himself from religion."[88] *The Catcher Was a Spy* touches on this secular mindset when he is asked by Jewish Dutch physicist Sam Goudsmit (Paul Giamatti) "You are a Jew?" and Berg shrugs before responding with indifference "Jew*ish*."

Just as *The Catcher Was a Spy* fits Abrams's analysis of the greater number of Hollywood movies since the 1990s that present Jewish men who embody an increasingly physical mainstream masculinity, Harry Benshoff and Sean Griffin describe a concurrent change in the filmic portrayal of gay and lesbian characters. Benshoff and Griffin note that gays and lesbians began to get greater representation in Hollywood movies starting in the 1990s, although they add that because these films were still primarily for straight audiences, they offered stories concerned less with accurate portrayals of queer identity and more with safer representations that avoided

FIGS. 4 AND 5 Moe Berg (Paul Rudd) as soldier and ballplayer in *The Catcher Was a Spy* (2018).

showing gays and lesbians engaging in sex or as part of larger communities. *The Catcher Was a Spy* fits that pattern by offering a more conventional, virile masculinity for its Jewish main character as part of keeping the film "resolutely heterosexual."[89]

To be fair, *The Catcher Was a Spy* matches Benshoff and Griffin's idea of a queer film in the sense that it portrays Berg beyond an either or "straight-gay binary."[90] The movie begins with a brief scene in Zurich setting up the 1944 climactic confrontation that Berg will have with Heisenberg (Mark Strong) about the state of the German atomic bomb. After just four minutes, however, the film jumps back eight years to Berg playing catcher for the Red Sox at Fenway Park, demonstrating his confidence and skill on the baseball field by throwing out a runner trying to steal second base. The following scene in the Red Sox clubhouse then introduces the idea of his sexuality when a young Sox player, Bill Dalton (Bobby Schofield), tells an older teammate, Lefty Grove (John Schwab), that "Berg seems strange, . . . odd. . . . I don't feel like showing my dick to a queer." The veteran player's response to Dalton, "Then don't show it to him," sums up the film's attitude toward Berg's sexuality: it won't be brought out as an important part of how the film defines him, but it also doesn't detract from the movie's celebration of his accomplishments as a ballplayer and spy. Berg himself affirms this closeted approach in the aforementioned interview for a job with General Donovan. When the general asks Berg point-blank, "Are you queer?" Berg responds without hesitation: "I'm very good at keeping secrets."

Beyond that exchange with Donovan, two additional scenes refer directly to Berg's sexuality. One comes immediately after the conversation in the Red Sox locker room, in which Berg visits a gay bar and, as he leaves, finds Dalton following him. Berg beats Dalton up for this intrusion on his privacy, spurred on by the latter calling him a "fuckin faggot." Like his baseball and spy work, this scene of justified violence affirms Berg's physical toughness and the resulting revision of stereotypical filmic representations of Jewish and queer men. The second scene is more nuanced. During his trip with a group of major league stars to play a series of games in Japan in 1934, Berg meets a Japanese history professor named Kawabata (Hiroyuki Sanada). The dialogue between Berg and Kawabata, their looks and affectionate gestures toward each other, and that they spend the night together in Berg's room all suggest the intimacy of their relationship. However, as Benshoff and Griffin point out, mainstream films like *The Catcher Was a Spy*, with a largely straight audience in mind, are careful not to show any queer sexual activity too explicitly, and as Suzanna Danuta Walters points out, they emphasize the ethos of self-reliance in Hollywood cinema to represent "individual gays, isolated from the 'sin' of gay community and politics and sexuality."[91]

By contrast, Berg's relationship with the one prominent female character in *The Catcher Was a Spy*, Estella (Sienna Miller), is much more explicit in its sexuality. Arriving late for dinner after the visit to the gay bar and run-in with Dalton, Berg almost attacks her as Estella plays the piano. The couple has passionate sex on top of the instrument, after which she asks Berg, "Where did that come from?" and he answers, "Any normal man would have done the same." After acknowledging the queer dimension of Berg's identity, this lovemaking scene with Estella begins the film's narrative arc toward what Benshoff and Griffin call "Hollywood's demand for happy heterosexual closure."[92] Even though we learn through a postscript that "Moe and Estella never reunited" after his return from war, Berg calls her from Zurich just before the climactic confrontation with Heisenberg and his Nazi bodyguards as if to affirm the centrality of their relationship. This endorsement of the romantic and emotional bond with Estella fits the continuing tendency for Hollywood movies to be fundamentally heterosexist. Benshoff and Griffin note that movies with "action and adventure film heroes" in particular insist that such characters "never be gay."[93]

Yet while *The Catcher Was a Spy* is quite clear about the heterosexist priorities in its representation of Moe Berg, the film's portrayal of his contribution to the revision of Jewish masculinity through his participation in baseball and in the war still presents a progressive pattern for the revision of how movies show queer men. While Berg the ballplayer and spy demonstrates that Jews can be manly in normative terms, portraying his sex life in the film asserts that such strong masculinity isn't limited to heterosexuals. *The Catcher Was a Spy* therefore rejects the usual pattern whereby queer men are represented in Hollywood films as less than masculine. Showing Berg as Jewish, bisexual, but also confident, physically strong, and capable fits the contemporary idea of queer identity that Benshoff and Griffin describe as "just as healthy, just as effective . . . just as capable . . . as any heterosexual."[94]

As much as individualism, Whiteness and conservative ideas about gender and sexuality establish roadblocks to the protagonists in *A League of Their Own*, *42*, and *The Catcher Was a Spy*, these three films nonetheless open baseball to women, African Americans, and queer men. This access moves the sport closer to realizing its promise of being the national pastime, of representing the American dream and its promise to all of the opportunity for success. Moreover, these three films are by no means the only signs that baseball sees itself as moving toward greater social inclusion and broadening its appeal. While a list of the "best" baseball movies on MLB .com includes *The Pride of the Yankees, The Natural, Field of Dreams, Major League, The Sandlot, For Love of the Game, 61** (2001), and *The Rookie* that celebrate White masculinity, since the 1970s there have also been popular baseball films made that shift toward a more inclusive idea of the game.[95]

Three films from that same best-of list signal the shift and celebrate female participation. *The Bad News Bears* (1976) offers a comic portrayal of a Southern California Little League team that includes a star pitcher who is a girl. *Bull Durham* (1988) features Susan Sarandon as Annie Savoy, a fan of the Durham Bulls minor league team who not only is well informed about the game but also advises its players on how to improve their performance on the field. The success of those two films and *A League of Their Own* in 1992 opened the way for more movies about women and baseball, such as the remake of *The Bad News Bears* in 2005, along with the release that same year of *Fever Pitch* with Jimmy Fallon as a Red Sox superfan and Drew Barrymore as his girlfriend who joins him in a love affair with the team. Documentaries about baseball have also acknowledged the role of women in the sport. In 2014 Spike Lee released *I Throw Like a Girl*, about Little League pitcher Mo'ne Davis, and in 2020 Netflix began streaming *A Secret Love*, a documentary about the lesbian relationship of former AAGPBL player Terry Donahue and her partner, Pat Henschel.

In addition, baseball movies have begun to recognize the globalization of its workforce. In 2008 when *Sugar* was released, the number of Latino players in MLB was at an all-time high of 27 percent. *Sugar* tells the story of a young Dominican player named Miguel "Sugar" Santos (Algenis Perez Soto), who works hard and braves the cultural dislocation of coming to the United States to try to make it to the major leagues to pay for a better life for him and his family back home. Along with their recognition of women's participation, documentaries on baseball have started to tell the stories of multicultural players, including *Roberto Clemente*, about the Puerto Rican outfielder, also released in 2008 and directed by Bernardo Ruiz for PBS. Two years later, the ESPN 30 for 30 documentary series included *Fernando Nation*, a film by Cruz Angeles telling the story of Mexican pitcher Fernando Valenzuela. Also in 2010 Ken Burns added *The Tenth Inning* to his epic 1994 documentary of baseball, four additional hours that included segments on the new arrivals from Latin America and about Japanese superstar Ichiro Suzuki.

Yet regardless of such a progressive tendency in baseball movies, these are filmic representations of the sport, not big league baseball itself. However, there are signs that MLB ownership has also become aware of the need to accept greater diversity: the number of Latino players continues to rise, and the commissioner's office has supported several initiatives to increase access to baseball for young Black players. When MLB resumed play in summer 2020 after the COVID-19 shutdown and nationwide protests in response to the killing of George Floyd, signs on the fields and clothing worn by players expressed support for the Black Lives Matter movement.

Nonetheless, MLB is also very much aware of its fan base made up of older White males. As a result, the big leagues seem to be simultaneously stuck in the past and looking toward a new future. The 2020 off-season saw the historic hiring of Kim Ng as the general manager of the Florida Marlins; she is the first woman to hold such an executive position in any men's professional sport. Yet Ng was the only non-White-male hire to a MLB management position in a year when hopes for greater inclusion were high. Like the filmmakers who portray the game in their movies, MLB has to decide if it wants to offer a nostalgic version of the sport or finally become the American national pastime for the twenty-first century.

2

The Business of Baseball

• •

While *The Natural* and *The Pride of the Yankees* celebrate strong athletic masculinity as a response to class disadvantage, independent filmmaker John Sayles's 1988 movie *Eight Men Out* sets the problem in a broader historical framework and doesn't equate baseball with empowerment. *Eight Men Out* tells the story of eight Chicago White Sox players, unhappy with how they are paid by team owner Charles Comiskey, who were accused of making a deal with gamblers to throw the 1919 World Series. Sayles's choice to emphasize the economic determinants of the fix makes his movie an example of Robert Rosenstone's assertion that historical films represent events in the past from the perspective of the time when they are made. Robert Elias reads nostalgic baseball films of the 1980s like *The Natural* and *Field of Dreams* as using a utopian narrative to avoid recognizing how greed and the power of big money—supported by the conservative policies of the Reagan administration—were making life increasingly difficult for working people in American society.[1] *Eight Men Out* by contrast looks back on the 1919 series from the 1980s to present an earlier historical example of ongoing class division in American society. Sayles therefore makes his movie an allegory of the financial forces of the 1980s, showing the underpaid White Sox players caught between their owner and the gamblers—both of whom wanted to exploit them, like working Americans at the time when the film was made caught between corporate greed and a complicit federal government. In an interview with historian Eric Foner, Sayles contrasted his film with the switch in *The Natural* from Roy Hobbs taking the gamblers' money in Malamud's novel to the hero in the movie who wins the pennant, explaining that the maker of the 1984 film "wanted to be more in tune with the Eighties. Or he may have meant, 'I want to make more money.'"[2]

Doug Rossinow states that during the 1980s in the United States "the big winners . . . were those already on top." What he calls the "winner-take-more society" during that period made it "the crucial decade within a longer history of wealth concentration" in the United States. Rossinow points out that "between 1946 and 1976, in an era of income equalization, the average income of the top 1 percent of . . . earners rose by less than 10 percent, while that of the bottom 90 percent increased by about 75 percent." Between 1976 and 2007, however, "the situation was dramatically different: the average income of the top 1 percent virtually tripled, while that of the bottom 90 percent increased only about 15 percent."[3]

Looking at the growth in economic inequality in the 1980s specifically, Rossinow documents that "20 percent of U.S. households with the lowest incomes saw, on average, no economic benefit between 1980 and 1990. The next 40 percent saw paltry gains, on average in the middling single digits." Those at the top did much better. Rossinow notes that "the total income share taken by the top 1 percent, which had grown by 10 percent during the 1970s, increased by almost 50 percent in the 1980s. The income share of the top one-hundredth of 1 percent had risen by an impressive 30 percent in the 1970s, but it spiked in the 1980s, climbing by more than 75 percent."[4]

Working during this time when wealth in American society was flowing to the top, Sayles tells the story of the 1919 fix as driven by the players' desire to get a fairer share of the money that their talent on the field generated. Baseball historian Bob Hoie, in his research about major league salaries, used "transaction cards," team documents obtained from the Hall of Fame that list player salary and bonuses, to show that in fact the White Sox in 1919 were "paid the prevailing . . . wage" for Major League Baseball.[5] Therefore, as much as Sayles's film may focus on Charles Comiskey's greed as the reason why eight of his best players colluded with gamblers, in fact the White Sox owner was typical of how teams shortchanged players under the reserve clause that suppressed salaries for most of the first century of the game. As the team that won the most games in the American League in 1919 and drew the second most paying fans, the White Sox players may have felt especially aggrieved at their salaries, yet as Hoie's research shows, except for a few top stars, lack of leverage in salary negotiations was the norm at the time in Major League Baseball. As Ben Rader points out, "The players bargained from a weak position." The reserve clause in all Major League contracts from 1890 until 1975 bound players to the team with which they had signed. Unless they were traded or their contract was sold to another club, they could not bargain with any other team. Rader specifies that players "had only three available responses to owner proposals: play for the salary offered, quit organized baseball, or hold out—refuse to play—until they received more generous terms."[6] In addition to this limited negotiating leverage for players there was also the fear that ownership would not offer them a contract at all or that their salary would be reduced from one year to the next. In 1918 attendance had dropped, and Eliot Asinof, whose book was the basis for the Sayles film, notes that the owners agreed on salary cuts across the board at their winter meeting: "During the 1918 season, the war [and flu pandemic] had cut into baseball's attendance figures. Wary of another financially difficult year . . . the club owners had agreed to cut the ballplayers' salaries to the bone. . . . Charles Comiskey . . . had been especially loyal to the agreement."[7]

As the film's exposition introduces those involved and sets the scene for the fix, Sayles presents several statements of the players' excellence and lack of fair pay. Discussing who might take a bribe, former player and now gambler Bill Burns (Christopher Lloyd) describes Sox second baseman Eddie Collins (Bill Irwin)—whose fifteen-thousand-dollar salary was second highest in the American League and almost double that of any of his teammates—as "the only one getting paid what's he's worth."[8] When another gambler, Sport Sullivan (Kevin Tighe), talks in a bar with first baseman Chick Gandil (Michael Rooker), he asks incredulously, "Seven men on the best ball club that ever took the field willing to throw the World Series?" To which Gandil responds, "You never played for Charlie Comiskey." Looking further at the salary data Hoie provides, they show that the two players whom the film presents as the leaders of the plan to conspire with gamblers, Gandil and Swede Risberg, were among the lowest paid on the club.[9] MLB players making deals with gamblers to supplement their salaries kept low by the reserve clause were not uncommon around the time of the 1919 fix. Statistician Bill James has documented how, in the period from 1917 to 1927, "thirty-eight players were either banished from baseball or at the least had serious charges brought against them for game-throwing."[10] In reaction, Rader explains that the owners, "terrified that disclosure might undermine public confidence in the game and result in the loss of valuable property (in the form of players), had tried to maintain a cloak of absolute secrecy while suppressing all evidence of game-fixing."[11]

Although Comiskey was reluctant to lose his star players, American League president Ban Johnson and the other club owners were anxious to limit the damage brought by the 1919 fix to the veracity of their product and so hired federal judge Kenesaw Mountain Landis and gave him unlimited power as commissioner of baseball to clean up the reputation of the game. Even after the eight White Sox players were exonerated on conspiracy charges by a Cook County grand jury in August 1921, the new commissioner banned them from organized baseball for life. "No player that throws a game; no player that sits in conference with a bunch of crooked players and gamblers . . . will ever play professional ball," Landis proclaimed.[12]

But while Sayles shows how Landis banished the players to protect the investments of the owners, the mode of storytelling in *Eight Men Out*, with its use of multiple points of view, also presents a more complicated form of narrative causality than the agency of a strong male protagonist that drives most biopics like *The Pride of the Yankees* or the heroic Hollywood stories that *The Natural* exemplifies. Sayles told historian Eric Foner that it took him eleven years from the time he wrote the script for *Eight Men Out* to get the movie made partly because of the cost of shooting a period film, but also because "I wanted to tell that story, *Eight Men Out*, Not *One Man Out*."[13] He explains that in most commercial films "it's very difficult for an audience to accept or follow more than three points of view. You have the omniscient point of view; then there's the protagonist point of view . . . and finally there's the antagonist point of view. . . . For an audience that's used to making an emotional connection with a film, it's very, very alienating to have too many points of view—and that fact mitigates against complexity."[14]

However, regardless of the challenge in presenting more than three points of view in a story, Sayles pursues the historical complexity needed to explain the complicated actors and events of the 1919 World Series fix with as many perspectives as there were banned ballplayers. On the White Sox there were two players, Buck Weaver (John Cusack) and Joe Jackson (D. B. Sweeney), who knew of the deal with gamblers but still played very well. Weaver hit .324 in the series, and Jackson led both teams with a .375 average. Catcher

Ray Schalk (Gordon Clapp) and Manager Kid Gleason (John Mahoney), see the fix unfold and in frustration exhort the crooked players to straighten up. These four represent the White Sox non-conspirators. A second point of view is that of the six players on the White Sox shown to be in on the deal. Sayles criticizes these conspirators for selling out their own teammates and manager who wanted to win and for making a deal that turned out to be disastrous in that it led to a lifetime ban for them as well as for Weaver and Jackson.

Sayles also represents competing interests among the gamblers that break down in terms of those who don't and those who do have money and therefore the ability to control the deal, a division reflective of the larger class politics of the story. Billy Maharg (Richard Edson) and Bill Burns come up with the plan to fix the series but are pushed aside by the money and muscle of gambling kingpin Arnold Rothstein (Michael Lerner). A fifth perspective in the film is that of the two journalists, Ring Lardner (Sayles) and Hugh Fullerton (Studs Terkel), who try to untangle what happened. Ben Rader explains that Maharg, whom he describes as "a small time Philadelphia gambler," was "embittered because he had not received his promised cut of the take from the 1919 fix" and therefore was a key source in revealing to the press that to lose the series "eight Chicago players had been promised $100,000, most of which they never received."[15] *Eight Men Out* shows that even in their fix with gamblers, the White Sox players again were underpaid.

In addition to the players, gamblers, and journalists, we also see the perspective of Chicago owner Charles Comiskey (Clifton James), at first trying to promote his first-place team to the sportswriters he wines and dines to help him drum up excitement and ticket sales for the series, and then increasingly glum and outraged as the Sox lose and the fix becomes apparent. A seventh point of view in the film is that of the new commissioner of Major League Baseball brought in to fix the problem. Judge Landis (John Anderson) seems at first eccentric and self-interested, but acts decisively to ban the eight White Sox players to protect the interests of the owners—with the exception of Comiskey—who need to defend the integrity of their sport. Rader describes Landis as "a 'skillful and ruthless cartel enforcer' who acted to protect the owners from each other and from outside foes."[16] Last and least empowered, we see the fix from the vantage point of the fans, represented poignantly by two young boys, Bucky (Tay Strathairn) and Scooter (Jess Vincent), who make such an effort to see their favorite team play. The boys represent the interest of loyal Sox fans whose belief in heroism is betrayed by the fix.

In addition to how he uses the Lardner and Fullerton characters to show the prominence of newspapers in revealing the fix, Sayles also includes a self-reflexive scene about the media's role in interpreting the game. After the World Series became established as a national event in 1905 scoreboards were often set up by newspapers in front of their offices or in large spaces such as armories or theaters, allowing crowds to follow the games represented with lights or icons of players and baseballs that moved to simulate the action. Historian Jules Tygiel notes that some viewed such scoreboard re-creations as portraying the essence of baseball without all the distractions offered at the park.[17] In *Eight Men Out*, we see a scene of gambler Arnold Rothstein watching a scoreboard set up in a hotel ballroom in New York in order to know that the first Cincinnati batter would be hit with a pitch by White Sox starter Eddie Cicotte, the agreed-on signal that the fix was in place. For Rothstein's interest the scoreboard indeed distilled the game to its essence: in this scene, and in *Eight Men Out* as a whole, that central meaning was money's impact on the game.

Besides his use of many characters to represent all the conflicting interests in the 1919 World Series fix, Sayles also directed the performances of his actors to effectively re-create the class politics of the story. In his interview with Foner, the director describes screening the fast-paced Jimmy Cagney film *City for Conquest* (1940) for his cast to help them develop the speed and tone of how the working-class urban ballplayers and gamblers would have spoken. Sayles said that he "told the actors—except the one who played Joe Jackson, because he was supposed to be from Georgia—'This is your rhythm. Spit it out.' That made a statement back then, spitting it out."[18]

Yet while D. B. Sweeney as Jackson may not have spoken with urban, working-class speed, his athletic skills, shown in two carefully executed tracking shots, helped Sayles bring realism and emotional power to the story of haves and have-nots. The effect of these compositions becomes apparent in the film's last scene, in which we see Jackson in 1925, four years after his ban from Major League Baseball, playing under an assumed name, Brown, for a semipro team in Hoboken, New Jersey. We hear one fan speculate to three others whether Brown could be Jackson, noting how he has hit a double and two home runs in his previous three at bats. Seated nearby, Jackson's former White Sox teammate, George "Buck" Weaver (Cusack), overhears the fans' conversation and interrupts to tell them that he saw

FIG. 6 Joe Jackson (D. B. Sweeney) about to hit a triple for Hoboken after his expulsion from MLB in *Eight Men Out* (1988).

Jackson play—"He was the best, the best. Run, throw, hit"—adding, "That's not him. Those fellas are all gone now." Sayles then shows us Jackson bat, and on the first pitch he lines a long drive into the right center field alley that pounds off the wall. In a dramatic tracking shot, Sweeney as Jackson rounds first and second at full speed and coasts easily into third base before the throw. Although Sayles explained that Sweeney, like John Cusack and Charlie Sheen, was cast as part of a deal with producers to add the box office draw of these three young film stars in return for funding for the project, the director admits that he was happy with the actor's performance as Jackson. Sayles notes that Sweeney "played him with a sense of joy in the field and a feeling of worry and caution off it." The joy in playing is foregrounded in this shot of the triple as well in an earlier composition with a similar tracking movement of the camera showing Jackson hitting another triple earlier in the film to establish his hitting ability in 1919 while still with the White Sox. Besides recalling his satisfaction with Sweeney's acting, Sayles also complimented him for his ability to look like a professional ballplayer in this description of the first triple during the game in Chicago: "I needed DB [Sweeney] to hit a real triple, with us starting on a dolly behind the plate and tracking to meet him sliding into third base, the ball and outfielders always in view, and he hit a perfect one in the gap within about ten minutes of shooting. Left-handed, which is not his natural swinging side."[19]

Along with the formal similarity and realism they offer using an actor with the ability to look like a professional ballplayer, the two shots of Jackson's triples also ask the viewer both to admire his skill and to feel outrage at how such an exceptional performer is under-rewarded, first by the Sox owner Comiskey, and in the last scene by the low pay in semipro ball. Ironically, one of the fans at the Hoboken game in the second scene doubts the idea that Brown is Jackson by commenting. "These guys make peanuts. Those guys made a fortune off those games [in the 1919 World Series]." By concluding his film with this shot emphasizing Jackson's undercompensated excellence, Sayles adds emotional power to this historical re-creation in support of his interpretation of the economic forces that disadvantaged the White Sox players caught up in the fix.

However, despite his success in making *Eight Men Out* a historical film, Sayles paid a price at the box office for telling a story in which, as Daniel Nathan puts it, "there are no heroes and a variety of villains."[20] *Eight Men Out* made the least money of the baseball films (*Bull Durham, Field of Dreams*, and *Major League*) released at the end of the 1980s. The latter three big-budget movies all opened in more than 1,000 theaters: *Major League* and *Bull Durham* earned $49 and $50 million, respectively. *Field of Dreams* did even better, pulling in $64 million. By contrast, Sayles film opened in only 349 theaters and made considerably less, just $5.6 million.[21] As much as the historical complexity of *Eight Men Out* may offer the viewer an informed story of what happened in the 1919 World Series as well as an example of how the economics of the sport worked to the disadvantage of even the best players for much of the game's first century, Sayles failed to give audiences the kind of empowered masculinity expected in baseball films.

The Game That Ruth Built

Prior to Babe Ruth home runs were a rarity in baseball. The dominant offensive strategy in the game instead was "small ball," a style best defined by New York Giants manager John McGraw that emphasized bunts, stolen bases, and the hit-and-run. Although Joe Jackson led the American League in triples in his last season (1920), he hit only fifty-four home runs in his thirteen-year career. After his arrival in New York that same season, Ruth made power hitting the most popular aspect of the game, leading the league in home runs ten of his fifteen years playing with the Yankees. In his time playing in New York (1920–1934) the Babe's offensive production helped the Yankees became the dominant team in baseball, winning seven American League pennants and four World Series titles during Ruth's tenure there. Most histories of the sport credit Ruth's spectacular power hitting with distracting fans from the negative publicity that resulted from the 1919 fix of the World Series. With Ruth the Yankees home attendance more than tripled to well over a million paying spectators in 1920—the first time any team had sold that many tickets—and stayed above a million for eight of the next ten years until the Depression pushed revenue down.[22] Initially the Yankees had played in the Polo Grounds, which were owned by the New York Giants, but in 1923 they opened Yankee Stadium, baseball's biggest ballpark that sportswriter Fred Lieb named "the house that Ruth built."[23]

A contributing factor in Ruth's enormous popularity was that he came from such modest origins. Labeled "incorrigible," he was sent by his father to the St. Mary's School for Boys in Baltimore at age seven, but by nineteen he was playing professional baseball. Biographer Leigh Montville has called Ruth "the patron saint of American possibility."[24] Ruth also fit into the cultural diversity of New York as a city filled with immigrants. Robert Creamer attributes Ruth's nickname, the Bambino, to how "New York's polyglot immigrants, and their children, found themselves strangely excited by Ruth and baseball."[25] Ben Rader describes Ruth and the Yankees as a reflection of New York, and urban America more broadly, with its "ethnic and religious heterogeneity."[26] Both Ruth and Lou Gehrig, the Yankees' second best player in the 1920s and 1930s, had spoken German as boys, and through the 1940s the team would field stars from German and Italian immigrant families like Ruth, Gehrig, Mark Koenig, Tony Lazzeri, Frankie Crosetti, and Joe DiMaggio.[27] By contrast, Rader notes that the dominant team in the National League from 1926 to 1946, the St. Louis Cardinals, winning nine pennants during that time, represented the nostalgic, nativist tendency in baseball. The Cardinals symbolized what Rader calls "Protestant homogeneity," associated with the small town and farm life, using "old-stock, country boys——Dizzy Dean, Pepper Martin, and Ripper Collins."[28]

In 1947 Allied Artists hired Ruth biographer Bon Considine to write the screenplay for a film about the life and career of the slugger. Now twelve years past his retirement, Ruth's health had gone into rapid decline and he had been diagnosed with nasopharyngeal cancer. Allied therefore put the movie on a fast track to get it done before his death. Ruth was promised that he could act as a technical advisor and have script approval, but he was so ill during production that most of the film was already shot by spring 1948 when he was finally able to spend a day on the set working on batting technique with the actor who played him, William Bendix. Even though he was very weak, Ruth attended the New York premiere of *The Babe Ruth Story* in July 1948, although Creamer reports that he felt so uncomfortable that he left to return to the hospital before the end of the screening.[29]

Part of Ruth's discomfort may have come from how the movie presents him as talented on the field and generous to his fans, but also a sap in his lack of awareness of his value to the Yankees. *New York Times* critic Bosley Crowther wrote about the film that "it is hard to accept the presentation of a … noble spirited buffoon which William Bendix gives in this picture."[30] The movie makes a weak attempt to establish its historical legitimacy by opening with footage of the Baseball Hall of Fame in Cooperstown accompanied by a voice-over informing us that Ruth was "the most famous and colorful athlete in the game's history" whose "astounding hitting" distracted fans from the Black Sox scandal. Yet whatever its filmmakers' intentions to celebrate Ruth in the last days of his life, *The Babe Ruth Story* falls short of an accurate biography. Neither Bendix nor the other actors in the action scenes are plausible as professional athletes—Crowther called the baseball in the film "studio action which is patently phony and absurd," and with the exception of one scene showing Ruth hitting his sixtieth home run in 1927 (a record for a season that would stand until 1961), none of the games were filmed in Yankee Stadium or other major league parks.[31]

The Babe Ruth Story also dispenses with historical accuracy when it comes to the slugger's infamous off-the-field partying. We see some of the drinking but none of his extramarital affairs. Ruth's first wife, Helen Woodford, is never mentioned, probably because Ruth, while still married to Helen, had begun seeing Claire Hodgson (played in the film by Claire Trevor), who would become his second wife. Rather than an informed account of Ruth's life and career, what *The Babe Ruth Story* offers instead is lots of lowbrow humor, mostly at the title character's expense. After Ruth meets Claire and wants to express his feelings, he reads to sportswriter Phil Conrad (Sam Levene) the first line of a letter he has written to her: "You know I love you, so why don't you marry me and put a stop to it." When Conrad offers to revise the letter for Ruth, the latter responds: "Brother Matthias (the head of St Mary's School for Boys where Ruth grew up) always said I murdered the English language."

Oddly enough, what is most historically accurate in the Ruth biopic is how the film portrays him, despite all his success on the field and the revenue he generated for the Yankees and organized baseball, as mistreated by ownership. In the scenes in which Ruth discusses salary, the film emphasizes his lack of intelligence as if to explain why he accepts such bad deals. When first approached by the owner of the Baltimore club, Jack Dunn (William Frawley), at age nineteen and offered $600 per year to play for the Orioles, Ruth responds enthusiastically: "There ain't that much money in the whole world." Six years later after establishing himself as a star in Boston, Ruth's contract is sold to the Yankees for $100,000 and a $300,000 line of credit for Red Sox owner Harry Frazee. In his first meeting with Yankees owner Jacob Ruppert (Matt Briggs), the latter announces to Ruth that "the Red Sox paid you ten thousand last season. Twenty thousand is what we wish to pay you." Ruth quickly accepts the offer by responding: "You have your wish. Throw in a cold beer and it's a deal."

Although much more than most players at the time made, twenty thousand dollars was a relatively small salary considering the large sale price the Yankees had paid for his contract and dramatic increase in revenue he would bring the club. Biographer Jane Leavy comments that "by 1923 Ruth was a box-office sensation, an indispensable cog in the economic powerhouse the Yankees were becoming."[32] A passing shot in the opening scene of *The Babe Ruth Story* shows a plaque at the Hall of Fame that describes him as "the biggest drawing card in the history of baseball." Consulting records of Yankee revenues from ticket sales and concessions, economist Michael Haupert reports that by Ruth's last year with the Yankees, 1934, the club had made $1.25 million on the $100,000 it had paid Frazee for his contract.[33] Leavy correctly points out that Ruth's income from his Yankee salary, endorsements, and appearances "was an astonishment of riches compared with the earnings of the men he played with and against and all those who came before him." Nonetheless, Haupert concludes that "compared to what the Yankees made off him," Ruth was paid "chump change."[34]

Near the end of the Ruth biopic, we get a third affirmation of the rights of ownership at the player's expense. In 1935, after fifteen years with the Yankees, an aging Ruth is let go to the lowly Boston Braves, whose owner Emil Fuchs had bought his contract from New York to boost attendance. To get him to come to Boston Fuchs had promised Ruth a front-office position and a chance to manage the team the following year. Unfortunately, Ruth at age forty-one can no longer perform on the field consistently, so Fuchs releases him, and the front-office job and offer to lead the team disappear. *The Babe Ruth Story* shows this disappointing moment for Ruth, but when a young Boston player tells him "You should sue!" for breach of contract, Ruth responds, "Sue baseball? No kid, that would be like suing the church."

In all three of these encounters with ownership, Ruth's initial signing with Baltimore, his first contract with the Yankees, and his termination by Boston, the film's representation of the terms and treatment of Ruth are generally accurate. Yet, while the real Ruth fought hard in salary negotiations to get paid more of what he earned for clubs, the movie uses its dim-witted version of him to justify a willing acceptance of the reserve clause and the unfair control it allowed major league owners to have over players until the 1970s.[35] Former Yankees pitcher turned author Jim Bouton summed up how such manipulation had characterized baseball's first century when he stated: "The owners exploited the players from the advent of the reserve clause . . . until . . . free agency . . . , nearly a hundred years."[36] In *The Babe Ruth Story* the title character's acceptance of ownership limiting how much he, as the biggest star in the game, was paid endorses that history of economic control.

Such a comic portrayal of the Yankees superstar in 1948 to defend the interests of ownership might be explained as a Cold War reaction to fear of communism and its radical ideas about worker rights. A brief scene toward the end of the film seems to allude to such ideological preoccupations when the Babe's sportswriter friend, Phil Conrad, sits in a bar watching a television newscast in which the announcer refers to "communist control" of an unnamed country just before reading the story of Ruth's cancer diagnosis. Made more than four decades later, a second Ruth biopic, *The Babe* (1992), stars John Goodman, who like William Bendix in the earlier film plays Ruth as ignorant, inarticulate, and governed by his impulses and addictions. Released just two years after a federal arbitrator ruled in 1990 that MLB owners had colluded to suppress free agent salaries, resulting in a $280 million settlement paid by the teams to the players union, and during a tense period of labor conflict that would culminate in a strike and the cancellation of the 1994 World Series, *The Babe*, like *The Babe Ruth Story*, presents a caricature of its subject to affirm the sport's economic status quo.[37] Although *The Babe* concludes with two scenes that side with players by

vilifying owners, one showing an imperious and ungrateful Colonel Rup-
pert (Bernard Kates) calling Ruth an "overgrown child" and a subsequent
sequence in which Braves owner Emile Fuchs (Steve King) describes the
slugger as "a circus act" who "draws a crowd," the film sadly accepts such
mistreatment and finishes with the Babe hitting a home run and walking
off to an orchestral score reminiscent of the music in the final scene of *The
Natural*. Like that film, the ending of *The Babe* responds to management
mistreatment of a star player by endorsing the idea that self-reliant heroism
is the only possible remedy.

Newspapers, Radio, and Television: Representing Baseball

Not only did the Yankees make big profits off Ruth, the rapidly growing
newspaper business also created a symbiotic relationship with the Babe that
drove up circulation while building his stardom. Readership of American
newspapers grew 25 percent from thirty-two million in 1920, the year Ruth
arrived in New York, to forty million by 1929.[38]

Ruth was particularly good for the new tabloid press that started in New
York with publisher Joe Patterson's launch of the *Daily News* in 1919. According to Ruth biographer Jane Leavy, "Patterson's cheeky tab[loid] . . .
completely reinvented the way news was covered in the city, giving . . . prominence to sports, especially baseball."[39] The shift made by the *Daily News*
"from word to image and information to entertainment" made Ruth the
perfect story, and just two days after Boston sold his contract to the Yankees
in January 1920, the slugger made his debut on the back page of the tabloid
that had become "a front page for sports."[40]

Just as the later movies about him showed the Babe as apparently oblivi-
ous of the profits the owners were making from his stardom, likewise the
sports editor of the *Daily News*, Marshall Hunt, commented that he doubted
Ruth "was ever aware of how concerted publisher Patterson's strategy was
in using him to build circulation."[41] Leavy disagrees, pointing out that Ruth
"understood the injustice of ownership" and chose Christy Walsh as his agent
"to represent and protect his interests."[42] Whether Ruth was aware of the
money newspapers made off him or not, by 1927 the *Daily News* had reached
circulation of almost a million, just short of three times that of the *New York
Times*.[43] Paul Gallico succeeded Hunt as sports editor at the tabloid and
joined other prominent New York sportswriters, such as Ring Lardner and

Damon Runyon, as "the highest paid men in the newsroom" who "dined out daily on Babe Ruth."[44] In describing the writing of such star sportswriters from the 1920s, Ben Rader characterizes their stories about athletes as using "powerful, often onomatopoetic verbs, colorful figures of speech and alliterative nicknames," such as the Sultan of Swat for Ruth, or all three names of a player, as when the Babe became George Herman Ruth, "conferring upon them a kind of tongue-in-cheek grandeur."[45]

Both to promote Ruth's stardom and to shield him from the potential bad publicity generated by his flamboyant lifestyle, his agent Christy Walsh set up a syndicate of sportswriters to produce ghostwritten stories favorable to the slugger. Such writing, which the syndicate did also for other stars from baseball, college football, and boxing, offered fans what Patterson called "the best thoughts of the best athletic minds in the best manner."[46] Established in March 1921, the Christy Walsh Syndicate quickly began churning out copy that offered "bright, shiny words with little mettle that generated lots of cold, hard cash for author, subject and the syndicate man, casting a gauzy glow over the putative authors while offering readers the illusion of being in the know."[47] When Walsh closed down the syndicate in 1937 he estimated that he had paid thirty-seven ghostwriters to produce 5,641 newspaper pages, writing about which Gallico later commented that he was astonished at "how much of the hogwash was taken as gospel."[48]

In 1920, just before Walsh launched his public relations machine to promote Ruth, the Babe appeared in *Headin' Home*, a film written by *Washington Times* sportswriter Arthur "Bugs" Baer, who had coined the famous alliterative nickname for the slugger, the Sultan of Swat. Released at the end of his first season with the Yankees, *Headin' Home* created a wholesome, and highly fictionalized, image for Ruth by presenting him as a young ballplayer from a small town called Haverlock who loves playing ball and whittles his own bats, has a job delivering ice, and lives with his mom, his kid sister, and her dog. Babe gets thrown off the local team for hitting a ball through the church window but tries to redeem himself by protecting a local woman, Mildred (Ruth Taylor), from a predatory drifter. Babe leaves Haverlock and finds stardom as a ballplayer before returning two years later to pay for the broken window, marry Mildred, and hit a homer for the hometown fans.

Seven years later, under Walsh's management, Ruth appeared in another film, *Babe Comes Home* (1927), that again constructs a wholesome image for him as a generous family man. *Babe Comes Home* was a bigger Hollywood production than *Headin' Home*, costarring Anna W. Nilsson as Babe's girlfriend, Vernie, and directed by Ted Wilde, who the following year would make *Speedy* with Harold Lloyd in which Ruth made a cameo appearance as himself. By 1927 Walsh had built Ruth's stardom to a national level and was able to get the Babe a $25,000 paycheck for doing *Babe Comes Home*.[49] In the second film he is a ballplayer named Babe Duggan, who has the fault of loving chewing tobacco even though his girl finds it a disgusting habit, but he eventually agrees to give up the stuff when he "realizes that it was Vernie's love that helped him succeed."[50] Just as the staff of ghostwriters in Walsh's syndicate held Ruth up as a model for growing boys, both *Headin' Home* and *Babe Comes Home* sold fans a wholesome image of the Yankee star.

Like newspaper circulation, the U.S. audience for radio also grew rapidly in the 1920s, and its coverage of sports was a big reason why. Historian Warren Susman describes radio, movies, tabloid newspapers, and magazines as what he calls the "new ways of knowing" that after World War I eclipsed books and the printed word as the central sources from which Americans sought information about their world.[51] Baseball fans, who previously had only been able to attend a game in person or read a newspaper account of the contest, could now hear games on the radio or see their heroes in moving pictures, newsreels, and dramatic tabloid photos.

Commercial radio coverage of baseball debuted in 1920 with KDKA in Pittsburgh broadcasting a Pirates and Phillies game live from Forbes Field. In the fall WJZ in Newark offered a play-by-play re-creation of the World Series transmitted to the radio announcer by a telephone call from the park.[52] By 1922 radio manufacturer RCA-Westinghouse along with WJZ broadcast the first two games of that year's World Series from the Polo Grounds, with sportswriter Grantland Rice describing the play. Even fans who didn't own a radio could hear the broadcast over loud speakers outside of radio stores.[53] Transmission over telegraph lines by AT&T the following year improved the sound quality of the World Series broadcasts, and a professional singer, Graham McNamee, was hired to announce them. Comfortable behind a microphone, McNamee "understood the rudiments of pace, style and performing for an audience, even one he could not see." He remained the radio voice of the World Series for the rest of the 1920s, later explaining that he saw his job as to make the listener "feel that he or she . . . is there with you . . . watching the movements of the game."[54] Rader states that, like the star sportswriters, announcers like McNamee, "while remaining loyal to the basic facts," looked to "add drama by resorting to hyperbole." Because fans listening to the radio coverage of games, like newspaper readers, weren't at the games, both sportswriters and announcers "were freed to take liberties with the content," writes Rader.[55]

The popularity of McNamee's World Series broadcasts prompted some teams to begin radio broadcasts of regular season games. In 1924 both Chicago teams put all their games on radio. Cubs owner William Wrigley in particular thought radio increased fan interest in his team.[56] Some owners, however, feared that radio was giving their product away and wondered why fans would pay to come to the park if they could hear games for free. The *Sporting News* supported this view, arguing that the in-person experience was superior to listening to radio broadcasts with the statement that "baseball is more an inspiration to the brain through the eyes than it is by the ear."[57]

Contrary to the skepticism of some owners, attendance increased in the 1920s in those cities where teams had their games on the radio. Although Wrigley's example with the Cubs was not generally followed, after his team's World Series contests against the Yankees were announced by McNamee in 1926, Cardinals owner Sam Breedon allowed the club's games to be broadcast on KMOX in St. Louis. While from 1934 to 1938 the New York teams stopped radio broadcasts, St. Louis continued game coverage through the 1930s on several stations: KMOX as well as KWK and WIL.[58] Media scholars James R. Walker and Robert V. Bellamy report that, after the Cubs, the Cardinals were the team that most embraced radio as a marketing tool to attract fans.[59] They add that although rights payments were limited at first, "radio and later television developed new Cardinal fans and stimulated attendance."[60] Redbirds broadcasts were initially sponsored by, and the team later owned by, brewers. Therefore, not coincidentally, "broadcasts [of Cardinals games] succeeded in selling two products, both of which could be enjoyed at home as well as at the park: baseball and beer."[61] By the 1940s the Cardinals had 120 stations in their radio network spread over nine states.[62]

The influence of newspaper and radio coverage of baseball on fans conception of the sport beginning in the 1920s and increasing during the next two decades is evident in the 1942 Lou Gehrig biopic *The Pride of the Yankees*. Although studio head Samuel Goldwyn was more interested in making a film about a national hero during wartime and focused the story on the romance between the Yankee star and his wife Ellie, the main character's notoriety had come from his achievements on the baseball field, so there was no way to avoid scenes about the sport. To make its portrayal of baseball plausible to fans and also to define Gehrig's as a courageous but self-effacing figure, the Goldwyn film draws on the conventions of sports writing and radio coverage to contrast him with Ruth, whom the movie offers as a hedonistic hero more appropriate for simpler times. The first draft of the script for the film was written by longtime New York sportswriter Paul Gallico, who had published a biography of Gehrig. Although Goldwyn brought in veteran screenwriters Jo Swerling and Herman J. Mankewicz to move the focus of *The Pride of the Yankees* toward patriotic heroism and romance, in the opening credits Ellie Gehrig is thanked for her "assistance" in making the movie and Christy Walsh, who had been Gehrig's agent as well as Ruth's, for arranging the cooperation of the Yankees. In fact, Walsh had a much bigger role in making the Gehrig biopic than such an acknowledgment implied. He later wrote that the contract Ellie Gehrig signed giving Goldwyn the rights to make a movie about her late husband granted him as her agent "approval or disapproval of all references to Lou in the film."[63]

Despite his disinterest in baseball, Goldwyn seemed to have understood that to give the film an aura of realism and attract fans of the national pastime he would need to include the voices of the sportswriters, whose interpretations of the game and its stars had for decades exerted a big influence. In addition to choosing Gallico for the first draft of the script, Goldwyn hired Damon Runyon, who was working as a writer and producer for RKO after starting his career covering baseball for the Hearst newspapers, to author the patriotic statement that opens the film pronouncing it the "story of a hero" who "faced death with that same valor and fortitude . . . displayed by thousands of young Americans on far-flung fields of battle." Moreover, Walsh's influence as a sports agent and former head of a syndicate of sportswriters famous for building the public images of star athletes is clear in how *The Pride of the Yankees* tells Gehrig's story. Richard Sandomir suggests that "Walsh's ghostwriting work might have led him to suggest the addition to the film of a pair of feuding sportswriters to represent the baseball press that traveled by train and dined with players and shared in the joint spoils of ghostwriting. Sam Blake [Walter Brennan] . . . Gehrig's fictional pal, . . . [and] Hank Hanneman (Dan Duryea) [who] took Ruth's side."[64]

A series of scenes midway through the movie include the sportswriter characters prominently to portray Gehrig as self-effacing but an inspirational hero while Ruth pursues a public image intended to grow his popularity and earnings in support of a hedonistic lifestyle. Soon after Gehrig joins the Yankees as a rookie, we see several New York players in a card game on the train when Ruth arrives wearing a sporty new panama hat. His teammates rib him about his sartorial flair, and once the Babe gets dealt into the game, the new hat falls victim to a practical joke as it is surreptitiously passed around and several players take a bite out of its brim. When Ruth angrily discovers the prank the hat is in Gehrig's hands. The scene then cuts to Blake and Hanneman observing the hijinks and the latter comments sarcastically on how Gehrig getting caught with the hat demonstrates his lack of sophistication and star potential: "The chump of all time. Falls for a gag like that. . . . He's a boob with a batting eye. He wakes up, hits the ball, reads the funny papers and goes to bed. That's personality, a real hero." But consistent with the biopic's interest in presenting Gehrig as modest and self-sacrificing during wartime, Blake responds that Lou is the right kind of hero with "no front page scandals . . . a guy who does his job and nothing else."

Gehrig's lack of concern with self-promotion and stardom is emphasized in the subsequent scene when he, Ruth, and other Yankee players visit a sick boy Billy (Gene Collins) in the hospital on the day of a World Series game. Surrounded by cameras, the Babe promises Billy that he'll hit him a home run and even guarantees that it will go over the wall in center field. After the Babe ducks out with the press in tow, Hanneman promises that the photo just taken of Ruth with Billy will be on "page one of every rag from coast to coast." Gehrig is the last one left in the room with Billy and with no press watching has a sincere talk with the boy in which he agrees to hit two homers in the game that afternoon if Billy promises he'll "get up out of this bed and go home." With all the other reporters and cameramen gone following Ruth, the only witness to this more genuine act of inspirational heroism is Blake, eavesdropping from the hallway.

The following scene presents the aforementioned World Series game from Sportsman's Park in St. Louis. Ruth follows through on his word and in the first inning hits the homer to center field he promised Billy. Yet as much as the film acknowledges the home run hitting prowess that got Ruth so much attention in newspapers and on radio, its larger concern is with affirming Gehrig's more genuine embodiment of heroism as he belts two home runs in the game. Hanneman had bet Blake thirty dollars that Gehrig wouldn't be able to hit both homers and the latter excitedly celebrates as the second drive goes over the wall. Sandomir makes clear the film's hagiographic and patriotic goals when he explains that the World Series game in St. Louis as the movie shows it never happened.[65] Gehrig did hit two homers in a World Series game against the Cardinals in 1928 but without having promised the long balls to a sick boy, and Ruth's promise to hit a homer to center occurred in the 1932 World Series against the Cubs.

Regardless of such liberties with baseball history, *The Pride of the Yankees* employs the sportswriters to position us to root for Gehrig to outdo the Babe, and its representation of radio coverage of the game supported by newsreel footage adds an aura of realism in support of its interpretation of the two men's character. The scene of the St. Louis game opens with the announcer (played by NBC play-by-play man Bill Stern) using the kind of hyperbole that Rader ascribed to baseball on the radio in its early years, telling us that "this is a World Series that will make history, go down in history, be history." We see the ensuing game through a combination of shots of action done for the film combined with inserts of newsreel footage from real contests, views of Stern calling the play by play, Blake and Hanneman at their typewriters in the press box, and reactions from the crowd in the stadium and from radio listeners. Just before Ruth's first-inning homer, we see Hanneman leave the press box to hand Stern a message that he relays to the radio audience explaining about "the IOU from the Sultan of Swat to a little crippled kid." After Babe homers, Blake in turn brings Stern a message about Gehrig's promise of two long balls, and the radio announcer uses even more colorful language to build the drama of the competition between the two Yankee stars, explaining that "this is a batting duel between the two kings of clout." Gehrig hits the second homer later in the game, prompting Stern to load on more exaggerated praise by stating that "from now on they're going to have to spell Gehrig in capital letters." Yet, as much as *The Pride of the Yankees* ensures a realistic representation of the game by reaffirming the kind of star-making hyperbole that baseball fans were used to from sportswriters and radio announcers, consistent with its characterization of Gehrig as a true hero less concerned with his own fame and more with how he inspired a sick boy, the movie shows what it considers the real meaning of Lou's impressive power hitting by cutting away to Jimmy in his hospital bed beaming in happiness as he listens to the broadcast of the game.

Just as MLB owners initially were reluctant to accept radio broadcasts of games out of fear that they would compete with fan interest in buying a ticket and attending in person, similarly they viewed televised baseball as potentially cutting into box office revenue.[66] As he had been with radio, Cubs owner William Wrigley was the main exception, viewing the new medium as a good way to market his team and grow the fan base.[67] The nascent television industry, launched in the years after World War II, was eager to have the rights to show baseball to attract the sport's sizeable audience. Walker and Bellamy go so far as to state that "baseball helped to create television."[68] They emphasize that over time the new medium created a profitable synergy similar to what the sport had built previously with newspapers and radio.[69]

The first telecasts of MLB contests provided viewers only a limited view of the games because of the small number of cameras used and the difficulty therefore of showing the large space of a baseball field. Walker and Bellamy describe 1949 telecasts as using just two or three cameras, one following the action from behind home plate and the other(s) from along the first and/or third baselines. Wide-angle lenses were soon added to provide a better view of the entire infield, along with telephoto lenses to show the outfield, and, in the next decade, the number of cameras employed increased and other new technologies were adopted to improve the viewing experience.[70] By 1953 it had become standard to use four cameras: two behind home and one along both the first and third baselines.[71] By the 1960s, Harry Coyle, director of the NBC production unit doing baseball telecasts, had added color, instant replay, and a camera beyond the center field wall using a telephoto lens to show both the pitcher and the hitter in the same shot.[72] As Walker and Bellamy put it, with such innovations 1960s coverage of MLB on "television offered a perspective not available to the naked eye. . . . TV was better than being there [at the ballpark]."[73]

As the quality of broadcasts improved, TV audiences grew along with the rights payments that sponsors like Gillette and later the networks paid MLB. In 1956, with Gillette spending $2.7 million on advertising and promotion, the audience for the World Series grew to 100 million viewers, more than 60 percent of the U.S. population at the time.[74] The following year NBC and CBS paid baseball $9.3 million for the television rights.[75] NBC had long been the main network offering baseball telecasts, showing the World Series from 1947 to 1976, but as CBS and ABC also began to bid for the rights the sums paid to MLB rose significantly.[76] The fees that networks paid had reached $92 million for the 1975–1979 contract, $185 million for 1980–1983, and $1.2 billion for 1983–1989 deal, money the owners needed as free agency drove up their labor costs.[77]

As baseball on television increasingly moved to cable in the 1990s, revenue from ESPN and Fox added further to the money paid to teams. Even as audiences got smaller in a media environment in which viewers had increased options, with two lines of revenue, subscriber fees and advertising, cable networks could afford higher rights costs. Moreover, for ESPN baseball was an essential part of validating its claim to be *the* sports network with year-round coverage, and Fox wanted sports to brand itself as the equal of ABC, NBC, and CBS, to promote its other programming, and to reach young male viewers.[78]

Overall, television has been both good and bad for baseball. On the one hand, it has brought lots of revenue to owners and made it possible to pay higher player salaries, yet the unequal distribution of television money has exacerbated the problem of big-market teams having much more payroll than small-market franchises, resulting in a lack of competitive balance on the field. Such lack of parity not only hurts fan interest but also reflects how MLB owners have been unwilling to collaborate in the same way that owners of NFL teams have to maximize the value of working together among themselves and with their media partners.[79]

Yet regardless of the pros and cons of television for the business of baseball, the telecasts themselves have seen progress to a better—if more expensive—experience for fans. Since the first regularly scheduled telecasts in the late 1940s, the technology used to show baseball on television has steadily brought viewers closer to the action. Telephoto lenses provided fans closer views of players on the field, and the increase in the number of cameras gave them more and different vantage points from which to view the action.[80] Walker and Bellamy write that "the developmental pattern for television cameras since the inception of televised baseball has been to produce images that are clearer, closer, and more focused on specific events."[81] This improvement of the cameras used to show baseball on television progressed steadily from the 1960s to the 1980s, and in the 1990s the addition of high-definition imagery provided a dramatic boost in quality.[82] From the initial two or three, the number of cameras increased to a standard of six or seven in the 1960s and as many as twenty-eight by the 2006 World Series.[83] The center field shot that became the most used in telecasts by the 1960s emphasized the individualized nature of baseball competition. About the view from the center field camera, Walker and Bellamy comment that "the shot's ubiquity is tied to the rhythms of the game. Much of the game takes place between pitcher and batter."[84]

Such steadily improving access to the action and its focus on player against player competition made television's style of baseball coverage a perfect fit for the emphasis on individual heroism in Hollywood movies about the sport. While baseball films in the television era still relied on diegetic announcers to narrate the action scenes, by bringing viewers the closer views of players typical in telecasts of games, Hollywood movies could reinforce the focus of their stories on main characters and how their agency determined outcomes.

The 1989 film *Major League* exemplifies such use of a television visual style. The movie tells the story of a group of misfit Cleveland Indians players who raise their game to thwart the plan of the team's owner Rachel Phelps (Margaret Whitton) to lose as much as possible and push down attendance below 800,000 for the season, allowing her to break a stadium lease and move the team to Miami. Yet the success of the team, as they start winning and challenge the Yankees for the Eastern Division crown, rests primarily on the leadership of veteran catcher Jake Taylor (Tom Berenger) and the pitching of Ricky Vaughn (Charlie Sheen).

Three-quarters of the way through the season, Cleveland has a mediocre record of 60 wins and 61 losses, but when manager Lou Brown (James Gammon) informs the team of the owner's plan, Jake inspires his teammates by announcing: "Well, I guess there's only one thing left to do . . . win the whole fucking thing." As the Indians begin a winning streak, the film employs the pattern of TV baseball coverage with two shots of Vaughn on the mound, followed each time by center field shots of the batter he is opposing striking out. Jake's contribution to the winning streak is also shown by a center field shot of him hitting a long home run.

Major League again uses a television visual style in the climactic one-game playoff against the Yankees to solidify the heroic roles of Vaughn and Taylor. With the game tied at two and the bases loaded in the top of the ninth, manager Brown summons Vaughn to pitch. The entire crowd sings his signature song, "Wild Thing," as Ricky strides in from the bullpen. We then see a series of shots of Vaughn on the mound followed by center field shots of the Yankees slugger he faces, Haywood (Pete Vuckovich), striking out on three pitches. The only variation on the typical TV style of camerawork is the addition in this sequence of shots from the center field camera focusing on Jake behind the plate with the hitter not fully shown, to emphasize the catcher's role in calling the right pitches and guiding Vaughn through the at bat. A more typical combination of medium shots of Jake up to bat, the

FIG. 7 Ricky "Wild Thing" Vaughn (Charlie Sheen) shown pitching in a center field shot in *Major League* (1989).

Yankee pitcher and views from center field are used in the bottom of the ninth as we see Taylor lay down a surprise bunt to bring in the winning run.

In their history of baseball on television Walker and Bellamy mention *Major League* and how the Cleveland television announcer who narrates the game scenes (played by real Milwaukee Brewers play-by-play man Bob Uecker) is named Harry Doyle, a clear reference to Harry Coyle, the director of the NBC television unit who brought so many innovations to the network's coverage of MLB.[85] This reference to Coyle could be viewed as an indication that director David Ward, and perhaps others involved in making *Major League*, were aware of the television style of showing baseball that they used so effectively to make heroes of Jake Taylor and Ricky Vaughn.

Curt Flood and Free Agency

While the movie version of Babe Ruth didn't want to sue baseball, all-star outfielder Curt Flood did just that in 1969. Flood's choice to sacrifice his own career to stand up for the right of ballplayers to play for the team that makes them the best offer is chronicled in the 2011 HBO documentary *The Curious Case of Curt Flood*. Bill Nichols has written that documentaries "differ from various genres of fiction [film]. . . . They are made with different assumptions about purpose."[86] Certainly *The Curious Case of Curt Flood* supports Nichols's point by offering a very different perspective on the negotiating rights of major league ballplayers than in the two Babe Ruth biopics. While *The Babe Ruth Story* portrays its subject as ignorant and undisciplined so as to justify the right of major league owners to control him and the 1992 remake concludes by showing Ruth's mistreatment but offers no remedy except individual resolve, the Flood documentary instead fulfills the mandate that Nichols says documentaries accept to "speak directly about the historical world . . . tell us what leads up to actual events or real changes, be they the experiences of an individual or an entire society. Documentaries tell us how things change and who produces these changes."[87] Ezra Edelman's HBO documentary about Flood uses such a larger historical context to explain the factors that influenced the life and career of Curt Flood and the personal price he paid to challenge the reserve clause and open up the possibility of free agency for players in Major League Baseball.

Flood had a lot to lose when he decided to sue. In his fifteen-year career he had been an all-star three times, won seven consecutive gold gloves from 1963 to 1969 for his outstanding defensive play in center field for the Cardinals, and had been a member of three pennant-winning teams, two of which won World Series titles. However, in October 1969 Flood was traded to the Phillies. He refused to go to Philadelphia, instead consulting his personal lawyer about his options and then contacting the head of the Major League Baseball Players Association, Marvin Miller. Edelman's documentary presents how, in December 1969, Flood wrote a letter to baseball commissioner Bowie Kuhn summing up his motivation for suing: "After twelve years in the major leagues, I do not feel I am a piece of property to be bought and sold irrespective of my wishes."

At the time of Flood's suit every major league ballplayer signed a contract that included Paragraph 10 (a), specifying that he could play only with the team with which he first signed, unless that team traded or released him. Prior to Flood, two players had challenged this reserve clause, only to run up against the fact that the courts on several occasions had ruled baseball exempt from antitrust laws. Players union head Miller referred to the irrationality of such rulings when he commented that "the courts were saying 'Yes, you're an American and have the right to seek employment anywhere you like, but this right does not apply to baseball players.'"[88]

As part of its emphasis on evidence-based historical representation, Nichols describes an "expository mode" used by documentary, which "emphasizes verbal commentary and an argumentative logic."[89] On several occasions in *The Curious Case of Curt Flood* interviewees make powerful statements that communicate the validity and importance of his case against baseball. To explain the inhuman treatment the reserve clause facilitated, Flood's former Cardinal teammate, Bob Gibson, states that "you were their [the owners'] property. They could do anything they wanted with you," and another former teammate, Tim McCarver, adds: "You were traded just like cattle or pigs or hogs or anything." Such comparisons of players to property and animals have particular power coming from Gibson, a Hall of Fame pitcher, and McCarver, who after twenty years as a player went on to a second career as a TV commentator for CBS, ABC, and Fox Sports, during which he covered twenty-four World Series.

Besides how it presents Gibson's and McCarver's forceful statements about the inhumanity of the reserve clause, the HBO documentary also includes the recollections of players union head Miller regarding how his initial conversation with Flood over the possibility of an antitrust suit against baseball showed the player's willingness to sacrifice his own economic security to make compensation for players fairer. Miller explains that he told Flood, "If the million to one shot comes home and you win it [the suit], you're never going to collect any damages." Miller remembers that he then twice answered yes when Flood asked, "If we won, would it benefit all the other players? . . . And the players to come?" Flood then concluded: "That's good enough for me."

As its title makes clear, *The Curious Case of Curt Flood* is a documentary about an individual whose experience was distinctive and had an impact worth explaining. However, as part of demonstrating the importance that Flood's suit against baseball would have on the sport, the film also shows how his awareness of injustice and the need to respond to it were impacted by the racial discrimination he faced as an African American. Growing up in Oakland, Flood had limited exposure to segregation but encountered it directly when he signed a contract with the Cincinnati Reds in 1956 and was sent for spring training to Tampa, Florida. Remembering how Black players had to live in different hotels and even had to dress in a separate part of the ballpark from their White teammates, Flood states in the documentary that "I felt like a N-word." One factor in Flood's unwillingness to go to Philadelphia when he was traded in 1969 was the reputation of Phillies fans for racist behavior. Dick Allen, the African American player Flood was traded for, wore a plastic batting helmet when playing in the field in Philadelphia as protection from batteries, fruit, and garbage thrown at him from the stands.[90]

As a young player Flood's reaction to his experience of racism was to become involved in the civil rights movement. In 1962 Jackie Robinson invited him to participate in an NAACP event in Mississippi hosted by Medgar Evers. Flood's wife Judy Pace Flood comments in the HBO documentary that "Jackie Robinson was his superman . . . he was his hero," and family friend Bill Patterson notes that Curt "emulated him [Robinson] by wearing his number." We see footage of Flood alongside Robinson and speaking at the 1962 event, promising to be involved in the NAACP's efforts and stating that "I'm really sincere about our civil rights." Players union official Dick Moss in the film states that Flood "regarded it [his suit against baseball] not so much as an antitrust case, which is what it was technically. He regarded it as a civil rights case and that is what it really was." In a television interview included in the Edelman documentary, Flood states: "As a Black man, I'm probably more sensitive to the rights of other people because I have been denied those rights." In another interview journalist Richard Reeves links Flood's sacrifice to the larger cause of civil rights: "The people who stand up . . . buy the rest of us a little freedom."

Even though he was represented by former justice Arthur Goldberg, Flood lost his case in the U.S. Supreme Court. The judgment fit with the well-established partiality of the courts toward Major League Baseball as an almost sacred American institution. Justice Lewis Powell, who was reported to be sympathetic to Flood's cause, recused himself because he held stock in Anheuser-Busch, the brewery owned by Augie Busch who also owned the St. Louis Cardinals. Chief Justice Warren Burger switched his vote from Flood's side to baseball's at the eleventh hour and the antitrust challenge lost 5-3-1. In an acknowledgment of MLB's favored judicial status, the Supreme Court in its decision stated that Flood should have the right to be a free agent, but the owners' long-established antitrust exemption could be removed only by an act of Congress. Free agency, the court ruled, "should be attained through collective bargaining."[91]

The disappointment of his loss in the Supreme Court took a heavy toll on Flood personally. No one in baseball would hire him; he fell into depression and began drinking and smoking heavily. In the early 1970s Flood left the United States to live for several years in Europe, where economic problems and guilt he felt from being separated from his children compounded his depression. The documentary shows the dysfunction that Flood experienced at length in order to underscore the price he paid to open the way of greater opportunity for other players.

Regardless of Flood's personal sacrifice, the Supreme Court's suggestion that collective bargaining respond to the need for free agency for major league players is exactly what happened. After the owners locked out players in 1973, a settlement was reached that included the establishment of impartial arbitration in matters of salary. Such an arbitrator in 1976 ruled that two players, pitchers Andy Messersmith and Dave McNally, who had played the 1975 season without written contracts, were therefore no longer bound by the reserve clause. This circumvention of the reserve clause in Messersmith's and McNally's cases opened up the possibility of free agency more broadly. Biographer Brad Snyder in the HBO documentary makes clear Flood's contribution to this victory when he comments that his "lawsuit changed the climate of public opinion about free agency. It raised the awareness that the system [wasn't] fair." Ironically, Flood, like Ruth, weakened his body with years of too much drinking and smoking, and the two men both died from throat cancer in their fifties. Near the end of the documentary we hear Reverend Jesse Jackson describe Flood at his funeral with words that, with the name changed, could be used for Ruth as well: "Baseball didn't change Curt Flood. Curt Flood changed baseball."

After Curt Flood sued baseball and the players won the right to free agency, the average MLB salary increased from $51,501 in 1976 to approximately $3.3 million by 2014.[92] However, while owners' revenues continue to rise, players' salaries have decreased in recent years with less club interest in free agents. Journalist Rob Neyer points out that with the average career at less than six years, many players don't make it to the seventh year of major league service, when they become eligible for free agency.[93] In a comment that resembles Tim McCarver's comparison in *The Curious Case of Curt Flood* of players to livestock under the reserve clause, Neyer concludes: "It's not until their seventh year as major leaguers that most players are able to choose their employers. Before that, they can still be traded like cattle or pigs or hogs."[94]

The Sabermetric Gospel

The 2011 film *Moneyball* was based on Michael Lewis's 2003 best-selling book of the same title. With Brad Pitt starring as Oakland A's general manager Billy Beane and Jonah Hill as his statistician assistant Peter Brand, the film was nominated for six Academy Awards, including best actor and best picture, and it has earned $110 million.[95] Yet in addition to *Moneyball*'s critical and commercial success, statistician Benjamin Baumer and economist Andrew Zimbalist point out that, like the book it was based on, the movie helped spread "the sabermetric gospel," the idea that new digitally supported empirical ways of analyzing baseball productivity offer a better understanding of the game. The term "sabermetric" comes from the acronym SABR, which refers to the Society for American Baseball Research, an organization of statisticians, researchers, and fans, founded in 1971. Baumer and Zimbalist explain the interest in MLB for such new metrics when they write that the "explosion in player compensation naturally led front offices to seek more information on the best ways to evaluate and to exploit player talent."[96] Besides the interest of ownership in maximizing the efficiency of their investment in players, Baumer and Zimbalist also point to how digital technologies have been essential in "both the gathering and processing of [player] statistics." They conclude that both the book and the movie "tell a good story with some underlying validity and . . . reinforced . . . the momentum [toward sabermetric analysis] . . . already in play."[97]

The main insight that the film *Moneyball* emphasizes is the importance of on-base percentage (OBP) as an underappreciated statistic, the value of walks in particular, and how, according to Baumer and Zimbalist, "by focusing on OBP, the A's could identify undervalued players and assemble a winning team on the cheap."[98] However, despite this insight, the movie follows the conventions of Hollywood storytelling in ways that oversimply Oakland's use of sabermetrics in general and during the 2002 season that *Moneyball* focuses on in particular. By emphasizing Beane's and Brand's use of OBP to give greater value to several previously underappreciated players, *Moneyball* ignores the important contributions of established A's stars such as infielders Miguel Tejada and Eric Chávez and pitchers Barry Zito, Tim Hudson, and Mark Mulder. Both Tejada and Chávez hit more than thirty home runs and drove in over a hundred runs in 2002, Tejada was selected as AL MVP, Zito won the Cy Young Award as the league's best pitcher that year, and he, Hudson, and Mulder together had an average WAR of almost 6.[99] WAR refers to an important statistic in the sabermetric system, wins above replacement, which is a way of measuring a player in relation to a substitute whose production is the performance average. According to Fan-Graphs, a website known for its detailed supply of baseball statistics and analysis, a WAR of 5 to 6 classifies a player as a superstar.[100]

Another distortion that Baumer and Zimbalist point to is the exaggerated conflict the film shows between Beane and Brand, as they promote sabermetric analysis of players, and the team's staff of veteran scouts who favored a more traditional method of on-field evaluation. The emphasis on this workplace conflict was the main reason why the real-life inspiration for the Brand character, A's assistant general manager Paul DePodesta, declined to allow his name to be used in the film. DePodesta explained: "I think it's overblown [in the movie]. . . . Surely there were spirited debates at different times internally, but they were always very respectful, with everybody largely on the same page. . . . Some of the metrics we came up with were things that were born out of conversations we had with longtime scouts."[101] Besides exaggerating the conflict between Beane, Brand, and the veteran scouts, the film also shows the analytic methods as new to the A's in 2002, as if their addition made a dramatic difference in bringing about Oakland's successful season. In fact, DePodesta came from the Cleveland Indians four years earlier, in 1998, and the implementation of sabermetric ideas to improve the A's was a much more gradual process.

Both these choices, making the film primarily about Beane and Brand while excluding the star players and emphasizing how the two executives prevailed in the conflict over performance evaluation, exemplify the Hollywood tendency to foreground one or two main characters as the heroes of a story, whose agency in overcoming opposition results in an affirmative outcome. Such a narrative structure in *Moneyball* fits what John Sayles calls the "simplification" of most commercial historical filmmaking, incorporating "things that weren't literally true" of the specific time or events being shown, but that "were true of that general . . . period . . . true to the larger picture."[102] Robert Rosenstone describes the concern that many historians have about the kind of Hollywood film like *Moneyball* that "tends to compress the past into a closed world by telling a single, linear story with essentially a single interpretation . . . denies historical alternatives, does away with complexities of motivation or causation, and banishes all subtlety from the world of history."[103]

Moneyball presents such simplification and singularity of interpretation by condensing the impact of Beane's and DePodesta's success with a sabermetric mode of analysis over a four-year period (1998–2002) into the 2002 season, viewed as a way for the small-market A's, with a limited budget, to compete with the big-market teams. When the film begins, three of those wealthier clubs, the Yankees, Red Sox, and Cardinals, have just signed away the A's three best players, Jeremy Giambi, Johnny Damon, and Jason Isringhausen, to big free agent deals. Baumer and Zimbalist refer to this agenda of celebrating sabermetrics as leveling the playing field for teams regardless of revenue when they write about *Moneyball*: "It is a David and Goliath story, and Billy Beane together with moneyball slay the giant."[104] Casting a big star like Brad Pitt in the David-like role of Beane is another typical Hollywood practice to gain audience belief in, and identification with, *Moneyball*'s story about the power of sabermetrics to enable underdog teams like the A's to succeed.

While the main characters in *Moneyball* are general manager Beane and his assistant Peter Brand rather than the players, the film still uses the television style that individualizes on-the-field performance not so much to focus on its heroism but instead to show such play as validating the sabermetric analysis adopted by the A's front office. In *Moneyball* this TV style of showing the baseball action brings realism and therefore a rhetorical force to support the movie's argument about the game-changing value of such interpretation of statistical data. One example is the climactic game when the A's team built by Beane and Brand is poised to set an American League record by winning its twentieth game in a row. The A's blow an 11-0 lead against the Kansas City Royals, but Scott Hatteberg (actor Chris Pratt in the film), one of the players whose career was revived by the new methods of valuation Beane and Brand had implemented, hits a home run to win the game. *Moneyball* shows Hatteberg's at bat in typical TV style. It begins with a shot of him at the plate from the third base camera, then we see the pitcher and a center field view of the pitch. Hatteberg, demonstrating the good eye that give him a high on-base percentage valued by sabermetrics, takes the first pitch inside for ball one. We again see the pitcher and then the third base camera shot of Hatteberg before a cut to the center field view as the next pitch arrives and he swings, driving the ball high into the upper deck beyond the right field wall. The film exaggerates the closeness of the composition on Hatteberg as he hits the ball, but then, as if eager to remind us that the heroism we have just seen really happened, it inserts actual TV footage of the home run shown from a center field camera in a more conventional extreme long shot as well as a closer view from the telecast showing him arriving at the plate mobbed by his teammates.

Despite such an affirmative feel-good narrative, *Moneyball* concludes with a scene showing Boston Red Sox billionaire owner John Henry (Arliss Howard) trying to hire Beane away from the A's. What this ending implies is that Beane's and Bart's sabermetric innovation would soon be adopted by other teams, in particular those big-market clubs that had been spending the most on free agents. As Baumer and Zimbalist point out: "While it is true that small market teams that effectively practice sabermetrics have a chance to make up some of the lost ground from their revenue inferiority, large market teams also have the ability to practice sabermetrics."[105] In fact, in the time since Lewis's book was published both small- and big-market teams have adopted sabermetrics to help them spend on talent as efficiently and effectively as possible.

The increasing adoption of new forms of statistical analysis throughout Major League Baseball has not only neutralized the ability of small-market teams like the A's to overcome their "revenue inferiority" and compete with the richer clubs but also supported the push of baseball owners as a whole to roll back the salary gains of players resulting from free agency. Baumer and Zimbalist link the focus in baseball front offices on analytic forms of player evaluation to an "explosion in player compensation [since the advent of free agency in the mid-1970s]."[106] In other words, teams' desire to control labor costs has been one of the main motivating factors in the adoption of sabermetrics throughout the sport. Besides how such analytics, and the addition of digital technology more broadly, can help develop younger, less expensive players and also identify undervalued talent with the ability to contribute productively on the field, teams also want to quantify a player's performance as well as possible to support their assertions of his value, or lack thereof, come contract negotiation time. Tyler Drenon cautions against the trend toward teams privatizing all of their analytics because "they are also limiting player agents and the Major League Baseball Players Association (MLBPA) from being able to perform due diligence on behalf of players." "If they [teams] control data, they control evaluation," concludes Drenon.[107]

Until the pandemic in 2020 revenues in MLB had steadily increased for almost two decades, reaching an all-time high of $10.5 billion in 2019.[108] Well more than half of that revenue has come from media rights payments and sponsorships. Team value has also continued to rise, increasing by 400 percent in the last decade to an average of $1.85 billion in 2020.[109] Yet despite such good financial balance sheets for baseball owners, CBS Sports reporter Mike Axisa wrote that, even before the 2020 downturn, "teams simply are not spending on free agents like they once did."[110] Sabermetric champion Brian Kenny from MLB Network described the recent decline in free agent deals when he was quoted in the *New York Post* in 2019 as saying that "a lot of teams pulling back has kept bidding down."[111] So while the average MLB salary had reached over $4 million per year in 2019, this figure was skewed by the earnings of a few superstar players, and in fact 65 percent of players were paid less than $1 million.[112] Teams with the means to sign free agents are finding that it is less expensive to trade for established players, and an increasing number of lower revenue clubs present themselves as "rebuilding" and therefore not spending on top talent to win right away. Sabermetric analysis increasingly shows that younger players in the first six years of the major league careers before they qualify for free agency not only are cheaper but also score higher on some of the most trusted metrics like WAR. Axisa describes this strategy: "Rebuilds are cool. Everyone falls for the ostensible promise of a better future."[113] Underlying such an approach is the economic reality that getting better may not always be more profitable for most MLB teams. With the steady growth in media revenue and team value, along with revenue sharing whereby richer clubs pass on some of their income to small-market teams, Axisa explains that owners have begun to realize profits don't necessarily require a winning team. Because of the lower player costs involved "owners have discovered it can be more profitable to field a 70-win team than an 88-win team that has a shot at October," he states.[114]

Outspoken pitcher Trevor Bauer has commented that part of the problem for older players in baseball is their resistance to using the new statistics and technology to analyze and improve their performance on the field. In their book *The MVP Machine: How Baseball's New Nonconformists Are Using Data to Build Better Players* Ben Lindbergh and Travis Sawchik describe Bauer's use of a new Edgertronic camera that "shows with perfect clarity how his right arm moves and his fingers impart spin to the ball," allowing him to analyze and improve his pitching form.[115] While the adoption of digital technology and careful analysis of the data it collects offers players an opportunity to improve performance on the field, the downside of sabermetrics for their compensation is how it also being used to undermine what Michael Baumann calls "the set of norms" on which "the economic structure of baseball has rested" since the dissolution of the reserve clause in 1975.[116] From the end of the reserve clause until recently, "players would have little autonomy and be paid relatively little at the start of their careers but more talented and experienced players would be rewarded for their performance later on," Baumann explains.[117] Now teams can use analytics to squeeze players at both ends of their careers. In addition to the decline in free agent deals for MLB players with at least six years of service, after his third year, when a player is eligible for outside arbitration, teams can also employ data to go to the mat on not increasing salary. Just as the rewarding of successful veteran players is no longer a given, this approach to younger players is a marked departure from how "for years it was generally accepted that it was undesirable for a team to let arbitration eligible players actually go to a hearing over salary since a hearing would force the team to bad-mouth a player; the morale costs outweighed the potential financial gain from holding a hard line."[118]

Certainly a few big stars are still getting multiyear free agent deals or extensions for tens of millions of dollars per season. Yet the large amounts of money paid to players like Gerrit Cole, Mike Trout, Anthony Rendon, Mookie Betts, and Bryce Harper is less an endorsement of free agency as a central part of building winning teams than a way to hype a few exceptional megastars needed to make MLB on television and online must-see media. After all, revenue from those rights deals is the sport's central revenue stream. The high profile of elite free agents is also important to companies that want to associate their products with Major League Baseball. For example, besides his $30 million in salary, Bryce Harper in 2019 earned another $6.5 million from companies like Under Armour, Rawlings, Sony, and Gatorade, and his Phillies jersey was one of the top sellers.[119] Yet the "middle class" of major league players who have established themselves in their first six years but aren't one of the handful of elite superstars are not faring so well. Agent Mark Pieper, who has represented several of the highest paid players in MLB, comments that "players that are valuable but are maybe more replaceable are getting hurt the worst in free agency. It is a complete destruction of the middle class of players."[120]

The two Ruth biopics ask us to laugh along with the Babe while the home runs and wild lifestyle lasted but ignore how owners took advantage of his dysfunction to make big profits off his stardom. By contrast, Edelman's documentary tells the sad but significant story of Curt Flood's self-sacrifice to help bring about free agency. And while *Moneyball* wants to celebrate the use of sabermetrics to give the small-market team a chance, it also champions a system of analysis that is now being used by MLB owners to maximize their profits and suppress player salaries. In sum, all four of these films raise questions about how much the history of baseball has really delivered on its celebrated creed that players' hard work and achievement lead to the American dream.

Underpaid Dreamers

If the Ruth films, the Flood documentary, and *Moneyball* tell different parts of the long history of owner suppression of player compensation, life in the minor leagues offers an even sadder story. An organized arrangement of minor league teams has existed since 1903, and their economic relationship as a "farm system" providing players to major league clubs was established in the 1930s.[121] Many of the players in the minors today make less than fifteen thousand dollars per year.[122] Jared Wyllys in *Forbes* bluntly sums up the reality of low pay in the minors: "The major league ballclubs pay their [the minor league players'] salaries, and for a long time, they've paid them abysmally."[123] Some minor leaguers offset such low pay with the big bonuses they received to sign, but most do not, and there have been efforts in recent years to organize farm system players to gain a living wage from major league clubs. While, as Wyllys points out, low pay for minor leaguers is a longstanding practice, collective bargaining on behalf of minor leaguers doesn't seem promising to produce better pay and working conditions, partly because of the pervasive attitude among major league players that if you can't handle the pain of the minors you don't deserve to make it to the majors. Former minor league pitcher Dirk Hayhurst points out that the major league players association "routinely bargains away the rights of minor leaguers and amateurs even though minor leaguers and amateurs have no say about representation on or power over the MLBPA's negotiating table."[124] Big league clubs as recently as 2018 lobbied Congress and President Trump to pass the Save America's Pastime Act to exempt MLB from paying federal minimum wage and adhering to overtime laws. Tom Goldman reports that "MLB reportedly paid millions lobbying for the act, which formalized what has been status quo—no overtime pay; no pay during spring training and the off-season."[125] Despite such a long-standing practice of low pay in the minors and big leaguers' resistance to sharing the pie, Wyllys reports that MLB may be beginning to realize that paying minor league players a better salary could be good for business.

Because currently they are paid only during the season, one of the biggest challenges for minor league players is finding the time to develop their baseball skills in the off-season when they have to work other jobs to pay the bills. Minor league pitcher Jonathan Perrin argues that teams offering year-round pay would be "an investment in your prospects, . . . to eventually create a better big league product."[126] Goldman notes that if each team paid its roughly 200 minor leaguers $2,000 per month year round, that $24,000 per player would cost the big club $4.8 million, or "a little more than the average salary of one major league player."[127]

Tony Okun's 2010 documentary *Time in the Minors* focuses on two minor league players, Tony Schrager and John Drennen, and how the limited resources as well as the competitive pressures of the minor leagues made their experience very difficult. Both Schrager and Drennen were exceptional in that they were high draft picks who got substantial bonuses. Drennen in fact was a first-round pick out of high school and received $1 million to sign with the Cleveland Indians in 2005. So, even though there is mention in Okun's documentary of the low monthly pay—Schrager recalls he started in 1998 at $850 per month with the Chicago Cubs, most of which went to pay for room and board, and Drennen starts out in the Indians system at $1,175 per month seven years later, the emphasis in the film is on the many challenges young players face as they try to make it to the major leagues. In addition to playing 140 games over the course of a six-month season, well more than double the number of games played in high school or college, the Okun documentary tells of the constant need for player training and long hours spent in travel. We see numerous scenes of both players in the gym and taking extra practice, on tiring bus rides, some as long as sixteen hours, and the resulting injuries as they push their bodies to a degree they have not in the past: both players in *Time in the Minors* get hurt during the two seasons shown in the film.

Yet regardless of the increased workload, exhaustion, and injuries, there is constant pressure to be successful on the field. Schrager notes: "You have to perform to get the opportunity [to move up]. . . . You have to constantly prove yourself." Both players know the daunting statistic that of the fifteen hundred players drafted every year by big league clubs, only 10 percent will ever play in the majors. Tony's father, Harley Schrager, concludes at the end of *Time in the Minors*, "It is a cruel, tough business," and this proves true for these two players, both of whom played nine years in the minors and never made it to the majors. As if to dismiss the difficult conditions that both Schrager and Drennen face, the documentary presents a utopian comment from sports psychologist Kenneth Ravizza: "What does the umpire say before the game? 'Play ball!' which doesn't mean work ball or stress ball but rather to play with the innocence of a child . . . who is totally absorbed with his toys. And if you can have that connection . . . you'll be doing pretty good."

Such urging to simply enjoy the privilege of playing ball at such a high level constitutes the response that Hayhurst notes is common when the problems of low pay and grinding work conditions in the minor leagues are brought up. Here he summarizes that response, as it dismisses the economic disadvantages of life in the minors: "You have baseball, the dream, the game, the joy, the crack of the bat and the roar of the crowd. You fly over all in a fantasy land where money has no value."[128] Yet Hayhurst also points out that such a utopian view of the privilege of playing ignores the exploitation that structures the minors as part of the business of professional baseball: "But minor league baseball is not a fantasy, it's a profession. A cruel one that justifies its cruelty by offering a golden carrot so valuable and coveted that young men will put their blinders on and drudge after it until they get their teeth on it or get put down trying."[129]

Even more than Okun's film, another documentary, *The Battered Bastards of Baseball* (2014), emphasizes the sheer pleasure of playing the game as the best response to the economic deprivations of minor league baseball. *The Battered Bastards of Baseball* focuses on the Portland Mavericks, an independent team set up in Oregon in 1972 by Hollywood character actor Bing Russell, father of Kurt Russell, who himself played part of the four years he spent in the minor leagues with the Mavericks before starting his movie career. The team is a collection of mostly older players who have been let go by other teams, and only one, pitcher Jim Bouton, is able to make it to the majors. Nonetheless, *The Battered Bastards of Baseball*, directed by Bing Russell's grandsons Chapman and Maclain Way, shows the players as determined to have a great time playing the game they love, and with nothing to lose, they compete well against the other teams made up of younger players whom major league teams have invested in with the expectation that some will become big league stars. Interviews with players from the Mavericks emphasize how their experience was more about enjoying baseball and helping the fans of Portland share in their fun and less about making money by developing player product for Major League Baseball, the goal for most affiliated minor league teams. While drinking in a number of scenes contributes to the fun and socializing of the Mavericks, it doesn't lead to the destructive or antisocial behavior shown in the films about Ruth and Curt Flood, where alcohol was used to escape the emotional scars, pressure, and disappointment of their lives and careers.

Yet the homosocial pleasure of baseball as an escape from the economic exploitation of the minor leagues comes apart at the seams in the IFC TV comedy series *Brockmire* (2017–2020). Although it is really less about baseball and more about its title character, announcer Jim Brockmire (Hank Azaria), and his struggle with his inner demons traced to an abusive father and a failed marriage, *Brockmire* foregrounds sex, drugs, and alcohol as a response to the disadvantage and alienation of life in the minor leagues. Ten years after he was fired as a television announcer for a major league team, Brockmire surfaces as the public address voice of the Morristown Frackers, an independent minor league team in an economically depressed postindustrial town in Pennsylvania. Brockmire drinks to excess, encourages the Frackers fans to do the same, and soothes his pain by having lots of sex with team owner Jules Jones (Amanda Peet). He even identifies the sport itself as a kind of distraction from the disadvantage that is pervasive in Morristown, telling the fans during the game that they are "victims of the unbridled capitalism that made a lie out of the American dream." "Baseball," Brockmire continues, "is just a diversion that keeps us from pondering our own personal hells."

Time in the Minors, The Battered Bastards of Baseball, and *Brockmire* all show the low pay, difficult working conditions, and limited opportunity that make life in minor league baseball so difficult. The two documentaries emphasize the determination of players, despite such disadvantages, to enjoy the game itself; however, if MLB can return to its past levels of profitability, maybe owners will also decide to improve pay and working conditions for minor league players. Such an increase in support would hopefully be recognized in major league front offices as fitting into the current focus on using empirical evidence to better understand how to make on-field performance higher, and therefore as part of a more effective, and equitable, business plan.

3

Screening Who Gets
to Play

● ● ● ● ● ● ● ● ● ● ● ● ● ● ● ● ● ● ●

On April 15, 1997, Major League Baseball celebrated the fiftieth anniversary of Jackie Robinson breaking the color barrier in 1947. As a sign of just how important his story has become, since 2004 MLB has acknowledged Robinson every year by having players, coaches, and managers wear his number 42 during games played on April 15. In 2020, with baseball shut down by COVID-19, the celebration went on TV and online with Jackie Robinson–related programming running all day on MLB Network, MLB.com, and MLB's YouTube, Facebook, and Twitter sites.

By contrast, the NFL and NBA, both professional sports leagues with a majority of African American players, make no special effort to mark their history of racial integration during the same period after World War II. Baseball, however, has a greater need to point out this milestone of Black inclusion because it has been losing its appeal to African Americans. As much as Robinson's opportunity to play for the Dodgers was about selling MLB to Black fans and helping Brooklyn put a stronger team on the field, his presence also enabled baseball to get closer to embodying the promise of opportunity for all that it had always claimed to represent and that made it America's national game. Mitchell Nathanson writes that, from its origins in the nineteenth century, the "creed" of the sport has been "offering baseball as a way to acculturate into mainstream American life."[1] Unfortunately, Nathanson qualifies that promise by stating that "of course, . . . the baseball creed was little more than a cultural fiction (there has always been a substantial disparity between the ideology of the game and its realities)."[2] That it took more than a decade after Robinson joined the Dodgers for every MLB teams to hire at least one Black player and that no African American managed until Frank Robinson took over the Cleveland Indians in 1975 showed that baseball was more intent on limiting than facilitating Black access.

Now almost seventy-five years after Robinson joined the Brooklyn Dodgers White men retain firm control of organized baseball. Even as MLB globalizes with the addition of more Latino and Asian players, in 2021 Whites still make up 62 percent of big league rosters, and more importantly they own and run the teams. Only 7.6 percent of players are African American, and with just a few exceptions, majority owners, presidents of baseball operations, general managers, and field managers are White.[3] Media representation of the sport also reflects this lack of diversity. Television coverage of baseball still features primarily White announcers and commentators describing and analyzing the action with just a few non-Whites and women mixed in to create the impression of inclusion. Movies about baseball follow the same racial and gender patterns: nostalgic films like *The Natural*, *Bull Durham*, and *Field of Dreams* define the genre, and even a more recent movie like *Moneyball* celebrates White male characters using new methods of statistical analysis to revolutionize evaluation of player performance. By contrast, the two highest earning baseball films are *A League of Their Own*, about women in professional baseball, and the Robinson biopic *42*. One explanation for the additional revenue they generated could be that such exceptional films appealed to more women and non-White viewers not used to seeing themselves as the main characters in films about the sport.

But while its remembrance of Robinson may be therefore more about flattering Whites for their acceptance of racial difference than the actual diversity of MLB, as a business the big leagues have to be concerned with the marketing implications of their decline in African American participation. Former commissioner Bud Selig on Jackie Robinson Day in 2011 acknowledged the problem by stating that "somewhere we lost a generation or two of African Americans," and in response to the declining number of Black players MLB has initiated programs to recruit more young African Americans to play the game.[4] In 1989 the Reviving Baseball in Inner Cities

(RBI) Program was established to promote the participation of kids ages five to eighteen, boys in baseball and girls in softball. In 2006 a second program, the Urban Youth Academies, opened in Compton, California, followed by others in Cincinnati, Dallas, Houston, Kansas City, New Orleans, Philadelphia, and Washington, D.C. Thousands of young people have participated in both programs, and from the Youth Academies about 150 players have been drafted and a dozen have made it to the major leagues.[5]

The protests in 2020 prompted by the killing of George Floyd and other African Americans by police have presented MLB with an important opportunity to define itself as less White. On Opening Day 2020, MLB showed its support for the Black Lives Matter movement by stamping BLM on the pitcher's mound of the first two games of the season in Washington and Los Angeles, shown nationally on ESPN. Players wore Black Lives Matter batting practice shirts before those two games as well as patches reading "Black Lives Matter" and "United for Change" on their uniforms. Prior to the playing of the National Anthem for the opening contests, the four teams playing, the Yankees and Nationals, Dodgers and Giants, held a two-hundred-yard-long black cloth joining them while they knelt for sixty seconds. During this ceremony a recording made by actor Morgan Freeman was played in which he read a statement describing the participants "as equals, all with the same goal—to level the playing field, to change the injustices. Equality is not just a word. It is our right."[6]

While it took MLB nine days to release a public statement after George Floyd's death, making it the slowest of the four major North American professional sports leagues to react, by contrast the actions on Opening Day 2020 were driven more by players. Veteran African American outfielder Andrew McCutchen led players in developing the idea for the cloth and moment of unity, and a larger group of 150 current and former Black major leaguers, known as the Players Alliance, produced a video that was also played during the opening games. Despite its initial hesitance, MLB has been receptive to the players' public gestures, and a new web page on MLB .com was set up with readings about, and to foster conversation focused on, social justice.[7]

Time will tell whether MLB can sustain such movement toward supporting racial diversity and the issues of social justice that accompany it. Beyond whatever personal convictions about racial equality that may drive the efforts to increase opportunities for Black players and respond to the protests for structural change in American society, MLB is also motivated by an awareness that the perception of racial diversity increases its appeal to younger fans. As Hua Hsu points out, the changing demographics of American society whereby the majority of the population under the age of eighteen will soon be non-White will have a big impact on the culture as well as on the tastes of consumers.[8] Yet concern about diversity for economic reasons in baseball is not a recent development. It goes back to the time of Jackie Robinson's arrival. A big part of his acceptance by White owners was due to how he attracted new paying customers.[9] Robinson's comment at the time that racial attitudes changed "because I would help fill their wallets" sums up that fact.[10]

To understand how Major League Baseball actively worked to exclude diversity from its world prior to the arrival of Jackie Robinson, it's useful to consider the story of Ty Cobb, a player who emphatically represented the sport's privileging of White masculinity. Cobb played twenty-four seasons in Major League Baseball (1905–1928), twenty-two of them with the Detroit Tigers. He won twelve batting titles and set the record for the highest lifetime batting average (.366). Ben Rader notes that Cobb, in addition to such exceptional hitting, was an extraordinary baserunner: "He tried to take an extra base at every opportunity," writes Rader, and he led the league in steals six times.[11] Yet Cobb's aggressiveness on the bases also frequently led to conflict with opposing players. He was ready to spike any fielder who tried to tag him out, and that often led to arguments and fights. As Rader puts it, for Cobb baseball wasn't a game but "was a form of warfare."[12]

Cobb's life off the field was also marked by aggressive, violent behavior. He exchanged taunts with fans and on one occasion jumped into the stands to beat a disabled man who had heckled him. He got embroiled in several altercations, at times involving firearms. Originally from Georgia, Cobb had strong biases against Blacks, Jews, and Roman Catholics that he expressed openly and frequently. Several of his violent assaults were directed against African Americans, including on at least two occasions Black women.[13]

Historian Steve Tripp notes that despite all of the conflict and controversy associated with Cobb, he was such a skilled and charismatic player that many fans came to the ballpark to see him play. Even if they disliked his aggressiveness and violence, many fans, according to Tripp, were "deeply appreciative of his skills as a player and fascinated by the daring that he brought to the game."[14] Tripp reads such fan fascination with Cobb within the larger context of a rapidly changing American society during the time he played. Like him or not, Cobb symbolized to fans what Tripp calls "raw manhood . . . a masculine ideal that emphasized independence, assertiveness, decisiveness and physicality" that the modern world they lived in no longer accepted.[15] Rather than such bold self-assertion, "the modern city and corporation encouraged compatibility, cooperation and compromise," writes Tripp.[16] During his career as a player Cobb proved that the ballpark was one of the few places left where such traditional aggressive masculinity could still be demonstrated. Tripp notes that the hostile reaction of many fans, taunting and even at times engaging in direct physical confrontation with Cobb, showed how at games they "acted out their manhood in ways that they themselves would probably not have found acceptable beyond the gates of the ballpark."[17]

Such assertion of an old-fashioned idea of masculinity was not just about nostalgic ideas of gender. It also reflected anxiety regarding how the changes in modern society challenged the privilege of White men. Cobb's performance of strong, even violent masculinity was a response to the question that Tripp states many White male fans faced: "How could America's favored sons hold their own against the swarming hordes of immigrants and the growing assertiveness of women at home?"[18] As evidence of how Cobb's violent assertion of masculinity was a response to such larger social pressures, Tripp gives a detailed account of his infamous beating of a disabled fan in the stands at a game with New York, which includes the important point that what most provoked his anger was how the man insulted him with the accusation of being mixed race.[19] Add to Tripp's question about responding to the challenge of immigrants and women the influx of African Americans to northern cities after World War I to escape Jim Crow and to find better jobs and it sums up the threat to which White male fans saw Cobb as presenting a forceful response.

The 1994 biopic *Cobb*, starring Tommy Lee Jones in the title role, presents the retired star with all his defects but also as a response to anxieties about strong masculinity that make 1961, when the story takes place, as well as the time when the film was released, appear like Tripp's description of the society when Cobb played. As a former pro ballplayer and maker of other baseball films, writer and director Ron Shelton has credibility presenting such an unvarnished portrayal of Cobb's anger, hatred, and violence complicated by his excellence on the field. The story takes place in the last few weeks of Cobb's life when he hires a sportswriter, Al Stump (Robert Wuhl), to author his autobiography. While the retired star's incessant insults, excessive drinking, and threats of violence shock and repulse Stump, the sportswriter is also fascinated by Cobb and sympathetic to his sad state, marked by ex-wives and a daughter who won't talk to him and declining health at age seventy-five.

Stump's fascination with Cobb also exemplifies Tripp's description of the fans who went to the ballpark to see his assertion of White masculinity. Stump suffers from self-doubt because of his wife's request for a divorce, and the longer he spends time with Cobb, the more he begins adopting his uncompromising assertions of "strength." Near the end of the film the sportswriter accompanies Cobb to his hometown of Royston, Georgia, where a man arrives at their hotel to serve Stump with the divorce papers. Stump responds as the ex-ballplayer has to many perceived affronts throughout the movie, swearing at and insulting the man, threating him, and even firing Cobb's pistol above his head. Cobb dies as Stump is finishing the autobiography, and when he returns to his sportswriter friends in California and they ask him what Cobb was like, he responds: "A prince and a great man has fallen." In voice-over as the film ends Stump explains his lie as motivated by the fact that "I needed him [Cobb] to be a hero."

Ultimately the extreme pathology of the title character makes *Cobb* less of an affirmation of the priority of White masculinity that fans saw the ballplayer as offering during his twenty-four-year career, that Stump needed during his short time with the retired star, or that was offered by the nostalgic baseball films of the decade prior to the film's release such as *The Natural, Field of Dreams, Major League*, or even Shelton's own *Bull Durham*. Instead *Cobb* presents a picture of a toxic masculinity that prevents its subject from coexisting peacefully with others and offsets the idea that only White men can define a heroic model for American society as a whole.

Seeing such filmic representation of Cobb's ideas of his racial supremacy and considering Tripp's analysis of how White fans, even if repelled by his violence, were drawn to the defense he asserted of that privilege helps us understand what Robinson faced as he entered MLB in 1947, how he represented an exception not only to baseball's racial norms but also to the dominance of stories about Whites up to that time in movies about the sport. Four films about this exceptional figure, *The Jackie Robinson Story* (1950), *42* (2013), the sixth inning of Ken Burns's documentary *Baseball* (1994), and Burns's follow-up in 2016 *Jackie Robinson*, exemplify Robert Rosenstone's notion that movies about history respond to the time when they are made, here in regard to both ideas about race and the importance of access to opportunity and cultural diversity in American society, as well as the economic pressures on baseball to increase its fan base and grow revenues.[20]

When initially proposed during his first year with the Dodgers, the idea of a biopic about Robinson showed Hollywood's reluctance to change its pattern of representing African Americans only in subordinate roles. Lawrence Taylor had written a script about Robinson in 1947 soon after he came to the major leagues but was unable to find funding from Hollywood studios unless the focus was shifted from a Black as the lead to "show a white man teaching Robinson to be a great ball player."[21] By 1950, however, Robinson had won the NL MVP award the previous year and his popularity had also been boosted by a much-publicized appearance before Congress rebuking Paul Robeson's comment that African Americans would not fight in a war against the Soviet Union.[22] That popularity prompted the Eagle-Lion Studio to put up $300,000 to make a low-budget film titled *The Jackie Robinson Story*. Dodgers president Branch Rickey, who had signed Robinson and brought him to the major leagues despite resistance from some club owners, media, and fans, insisted on having Taylor's script rewritten by his assistant, Arthur Mann, whose involvement ensured that the film would focus on Robinson's achievements, conclude with his testimony before the House Un-American Activities Committee, and emphasize the meaning of his experience as a "triumph of democracy."[23]

Playing himself in the 1950 film, Robinson portrays the values of hard work, discipline, deferral of gratification, and self-reliance to overcome White resistance to Black opportunity. When they first meet, Rickey (Minor Watson) tells Robinson: "I want a player with guts enough not to fight back." After a graphic description of the racist abuse that he will face, Robinson assures Rickey that he can turn the other cheek. The racism that we subsequently see directed at Robinson in the movie occurs through hostile comments and attempts at intimidation from individual fans or opposing players, implying the appropriateness of his disciplined, self-reliant restraint.

Yet despite how Rickey controlled the movie to present an interpretation acceptable to Whites through individualizing the Black player's experience, Robinson's performance in the title role at several points counters this dehistoricizing tendency by invoking an African American cultural aesthetic. Sometimes called "tricky baseball" for its emphasis on unsettling and deceiving opponents, examples of this approach occur in the action scenes in which Robinson uses an aggressive, improvisational style of play perfected during his time in the Negro Leagues before signing with the Dodgers. Ben Rader describes the Negro Leagues as "more opportunistic, improvisational and daring than white ball. . . . Nothing summed up the uniqueness of black baseball more than its sheer speed . . . combined with the bunt, the hit and run play, [and] the stolen base."[24] However, although *The Jackie Robinson Story* shows the effectiveness of this tricky style, it never credits Black baseball as its source. In fact, the film does more to discredit the Negro Leagues than celebrate them by showing Robinson's frustration during his year with the Kansas City Monarchs because of low pay, long bus rides, and the inability of the Black players to get service in Whites-only restaurants.

While *The Jackie Robinson Story* reaffirms Cold War–era belief in capitalist self-reliance with only a subtext of cultural difference in the action scenes, Ken Burns's film *Baseball* foregrounds the more mainstream influence of multiculturalism at the time it was made. Writing in 1993, Henry Louis Gates defined multiculturalism as "the representation . . . of cultural identities . . . cultural diversity," and he quotes John Brenkman, who justifies its importance by claiming that democracy "requires citizens who are fluent enough in one another's vocabularies and histories to share the forums of political deliberation and decision on an equal footing."[25]

Within this climate of greater cultural pluralism that Gates describes, the following year Ken Burns released his eighteen-and-a-half-hour, nine-part documentary about the history of baseball that by the filmmaker's own admission emphasized race as a central theme.[26] In the interviews that form the backbone of the Robinson segment, Burns was influenced by multiculturalism to include several African Americans: former Negro League players Buck O'Neil, Sammie Haynes, and Riley Stewart, cultural critic Gerald Early, tennis champion and historian of Black sports history Arthur Ashe, former MLB player Curt Flood, and Jackie Robinson's wife Rachel. Most of the Blacks whom Burns talks with either testify to Robinson's strong character as an individual or describe how he understood his role representing his race and was viewed by others as an ambassador for African Americans. Buck O'Neil tells the story, which would be dramatized later in the feature film *42*, of Robinson demonstrating the courage to tell a White gas station attendant that the Kansas City Monarchs team would not buy the fuel for their bus at his service station if they couldn't use the bathroom. Rachel Robinson describes the personal traits that prompted Branch Rickey to choose Jackie to be the first Black player: his assertiveness, religious conviction, and determination to handle what she calls the "scath-ing experience . . . without . . . giving up." She later adds that there were days in which the abuse made Robinson discouraged, frustrated, and angry, but he never talked about giving up. He was determined to succeed, Rachel Robinson states, because he saw "a higher goal . . . the mission."

The 2013 biopic *42* clearly aims to appeal to younger and more multicul-tural fans by characterizing Robinson with an assertive masculinity and sex appeal drawn from hip-hop culture. MLB supported the film's production and marketing because of its interest in selling baseball to the same audi-ence. By contrast, Ken Burns's four-hour 2016 PBS film, like his 1994 film about baseball, sticks with more traditional documentary conventions that emphasize in-depth historical information and an inspirational interpreta-tion of Robinson's success as evidence of his intelligence, athletic ability, and courage. The first half of Burns's later film tells the story of Robinson's life from his family's move out of Georgia soon after he was born to Southern California, and his youth there in Pasadena up through his first historic sea-son with the Dodgers. The entire documentary puts great emphasis on Robinson's intelligence and fortitude, but the latter part of the film fore-grounds these qualifies less in regard to how they enabled his own achieve-ments in the face of challenges he confronted on the baseball field and more in how, especially after he retired from baseball in 1957, Robinson used his abilities to fight for the rights of all African Americans.

Burns previews the direction that the second part of the 2016 film will take by referring to Robinson, with Keith David's voice-over narration early in the documentary, as an "uncompromising crusader." By contrast, as the story moves toward his historic debut with the Dodgers, it makes clear that for Branch Rickey Robinson was less a civil rights leader and more a "lone pioneer" who would prove the viability of Black players in the major leagues and pave the way for a gradual and limited addition of more African Amer-icans like Roy Campanella, who came to the Dodgers in 1948, and Don Newcombe, who was promoted to Brooklyn in 1949. As Burns makes clear, Rickey was interested not in empowering Blacks as a group to access greater opportunity for success but rather in controlling the integration of baseball for his own benefit and that of the other club owners. As Mitchell Nathan-son writes, "Rickey's actions . . . had the effect of taking the integration effort out of the hands of those who were the victims of segregation and placing it instead into the hands of the very people who had practiced segregation for decades."[27]

Burns in *Jackie Robinson* goes beyond the focus of the 1994 documentary and the two Hollywood biopics on Robinson's baseball career to show his later work on behalf of civil rights. Yet Burns's second documentary also includes lots of footage of Robinson hitting and running the bases, showing the "tricky" ball that former Negro Leagues star Buck O'Neil describes as the fast-paced, aggressive Black style of play "that Jackie took . . . to the major leagues." Not only does Burns show how Robinson's emphasis on getting on base through bunting and on stealing and taking extra bases proved effective in helping the Dodgers win, but the documentary also clearly establishes the popularity of this up-tempo, risk-taking type of play with fans. African American sportswriter Wendell Smith glibly summed up the economic impact of Robinson's appeal when he wrote: "Jackie's nimble, Jackie's quick, Jackie's making the turnstiles click." While we learn that in 1947 Rickey paid Robinson just $5,000, the league minimum, we also learn that the Dodgers set the record that season for the highest attendance since Ebbets Field opened in 1913. Robinson helped increase attendance for other teams in the National League as well. When he made his debut in Chicago in 1947, Robinson played before the largest paying crowd (47,572) to date at Wrigley Field. Despite the boost in revenue that he brought, Peter Dreier notes that in his career with the Dodgers Robinson's salary "never exceeded $42,000—less than several white stars—even though he was undoubtedly the sport's biggest drawing card."[28]

Early in the second half of Burns's 2016 film the focus shifts to Robinson's more political orientation when sportswriter Howard Bryant comments that being allowed to play in the majors was not enough and that he began to focus on pushing to get Black players the right to stay in the same hotels with their White teammates and to exert greater control over how the media portrayed them. Rachel Robinson comments that turning the other cheek to the racist abuse and proving on the field that he belonged in the majors had made him a "good boy," but that as Jackie became more vocal about the need for change he was described by some Whites as "uppity." At this point in the Burns documentary, David's narration adds that the 1950 biopic solidified the conservative, compliant image of Robinson as deferential to Whites rather than documented the shift toward a more political stance that he took beginning in his third season.

A big part of the confrontational Jackie Robinson was his work on behalf of civil rights for African Americans, especially after he retired from the Dodgers in 1957. Rachel in the 2016 Burns film comments that Jackie viewed baseball as just "a bridge to the civil rights movement," a way that he had gained recognition that allowed him to be active on behalf of the needs of all Blacks. As one example of Robinson's involvement, Burns's film shows us that in 1962 Dr. King invited Jackie to travel to Albany, Georgia, to support several hundred African Americans who had been jailed for protesting and trying to register to vote.

However, as the civil rights movement in the 1960s became increasingly militant, Robinson grew frustrated by how he was perceived as too moderate in his views on race in American society. While in the late 1940s and 1950s he had symbolized strong Black masculinity, by the late 1960s other figures from the sports world such as Muhammad Ali and Jim Brown portrayed a more aggressive, militant identity that had greater appeal, especially to younger Blacks who saw little improvement of their rights and opportunities in American society. Yet, as Howard Bryant points out in the Burns documentary, until Robinson died from a heart attack at age fifty-three in October 1972, he continued his efforts on behalf of Black Americans. Just nine days before his death he had thrown out the first pitch at a World Series game and spoken briefly to the crowd about how he would be more proud when there was a Black manager in Major League Baseball.

While the 1950 and 2013 biopics about Robinson focus primarily on his life as a ballplayer and emphasize his collaboration with Rickey as a kind of "White savior" who allowed him the opportunity to break the color line, the 1996 HBO film *Soul of the Game*, like Burns's 2016 documentary, presents Robinson both on the field and as a member of the Black community, exemplified in the former film by the Negro Leagues, where he was playing when he signed with the Dodgers. Historian Rob Ruck notes that by the 1920s the major league owners had succeeded in eliminating all competition and, using the reserve clause, had established control over their "all-white labor force."[29] The only exception to this monopoly in professional baseball was the Negro Leagues, which offered the same level of top baseball talent, but because they were made up of African American players not allowed in the major leagues and most of their customers were Black, they were not viewed by MLB owners as directly competitive. For the Black community, however, the Negro Leagues had enormous importance. As Ruck puts it: "They helped knit Black America together, giving African Americans teams and heroes of their own."[30] Supported by the increased Black populations of eastern and midwestern cities resulting from the migration starting in the 1910s of African Americans from the South in pursuit of work and greater freedom, the Negro League teams fielded stars such as Smokey Joe Williams, Oscar Charleston, Satchel Paige, Cool Papa Bell, and Josh Gibson, who beat the White major leaguers in 61 percent of the 445 games they played each other in head-to-head competition between 1886—when Blacks were banned from playing on teams with Whites—and 1948.[31]

Veteran African American film and TV director Kevin Rodney Sullivan made *Soul of the Game* as less a biopic about Robinson's success and more an ensemble story showing how his chance with the Dodgers came because he fit into Rickey's plans to improve the team and increase profits, and how this move was viewed resentfully by top Negro League stars who weren't given the same opportunity. By including in the film representation of the contrast between Rickey's public statements about breaking the color line and his actions to bring Robinson to the Dodgers, along with the frustration of Satchel Paige and Josh Gibson that they were passed over, *Soul of the Game* makes clear that Robinson's promotion was not about opening up opportunity for Black players as a whole.

Sullivan's film demonstrates that Rickey's selection of Robinson as the "right" player to break the color line showed that the Dodgers' executive was less interested in creating more room for Blacks in baseball than in controlling integration to give Brooklyn a competitive edge at the lowest possible cost. Except for the advantage it gave the Dodgers on the field, Rickey's interest in adding a Black player was what Nathanson calls a "conundrum," entirely inconsistent with his values and politics throughout his life. An archconservative, who opposed any kind of radicalism and was angered by the role of the communist newspaper *The Daily Worker* and the Black press in pushing for the integration of baseball, Rickey after his retirement in 1964 supported Barry Goldwater for president "rather than . . . civil rights advocate Lyndon Johnson."[32] In 1950 Rickey left the Dodgers to go work for the Pittsburgh Pirates, where he brought in no Black players for four years. Instead, while at Pittsburgh, Rickey focused his efforts on finding the best players for the lowest price in Latin America. Nathanson sums up Rickey's time in Pittsburgh as consistent with his work as a baseball executive as a whole when he states: "Just as he had with his farm system in St. Louis and with his plundering of the Negro Leagues in Brooklyn, Rickey attempted to corner a relatively cheap market and reap the benefits."[33] Nathanson acknowledges that he may have been "a sharp baseball man with an eye on the bottom line," but insists that Rickey was not a civil rights pioneer or in any way interested in issues of social justice.[34]

In contrast to how it makes clear Rickey's focus on gaining an advantage on the field at the lowest price, *Soul of the Game* does an outstanding job, using strong performances by Delroy Lindo as Paige and Mykelti Williamson as Gibson, of showing the culture and style of the Negro Leagues that made it so appealing and such an important source of identity for African Americans. Yet besides how *Soul of the Game* showcases the popularity of the Negro Leagues, we also see the tragedy of Gibson's failing health—he died in 1947 at age thirty-five from a stroke caused by a brain tumor—and Paige's frustration created by his unwillingness to compromise his expectations of fair compensation. While Robinson signed for the five-thousand-dollar MLB minimum, Paige makes clear to Rickey (Edward Herrmann), in the one scene in which the two men talk face-to-face, that in the Negro Leagues he receives 15 percent of the gate.

Besides how Sullivan's film emphasizes the culture of the Negro Leagues and the contributions of Paige and Gibson as much as the story of Rickey and Robinson's integration of MLB, the movie also shows the gap between how the Dodgers executive portrayed his motives publicly and his actions behind the scenes. *The Soul of the Game* depicts Rickey during the process leading up to his signing of Robinson apparently unconcerned about the challenges, and costs, it would create because adding the young African American player would put him on the right side of history. Yet we also see Rickey acting to get top Black talent without compensating Negro League owners. The first scene in which Rickey presents his plan as about taking the moral high ground rather than profit occurs when he encounters baseball commissioner Happy Chandler (Jerry Hardin) on the street in New York. Chandler, a former U.S. senator from Kentucky, was open to the integration of baseball in contrast to his predecessor, judge Kenesaw Mountain Landis, who had opposed it for decades. However, in their conversation in this scene, Chandler urges Rickey to wait on bringing in a Black player because of potential problems. Chandler tells Rickey that other baseball owners are "extremely nervous" about rumors that the Dodgers are planning to sign a Black player. The commissioner points to "practical problems" it could create, such as "race riots in the stands" and the logistical issues of Jim Crow barriers in Florida during spring training and how "the big hotels and restaurants" won't accommodate Blacks. Chandler mentions that President Truman is planning to integrate the military. "Why should you go first [with integration] before the U.S. Army?" asks the commissioner. Frustrated by their conversation, Chandler gets in his car and leaves.

Just after this talk with Chandler, Rickey continues to represent his interest in Robinson as ethical rather than motivated by money. When he learns that New York mayor Fiorello La Guardia is pushing for economic sanctions against the New York teams if they don't hire Black players, Rickey rushes to his office and tells scout Pete Harmon (Richard Riehle) that they have to sign Robinson quickly because "I will not be denied our place in history." That Rickey here seems to be motivated most of all by how he will be viewed as a visionary leader moving baseball in a progressive direction by giving a Black player the opportunity to play in the major leagues fits with what Nathanson calls the most popular, canonical story of how he signed Robinson to break the color line. Nathanson sums up this version of events as an action that foreshadowed the great milestones of the civil rights movement such as the *Brown v. Board of Education* Supreme Court ruling almost nine years later. In this interpretation, according to Nathanson, "Together, Rickey and Robinson, through the medium of baseball, joined hands to provide one of America's transformative moments. There is no purer moment of baseball as America than the one described in this story."[35]

However, *Soul of the Game* also portrays Rickey the businessman in a different light, one less complimentary of his interest in the moral high ground and place in history as a twentieth-century Abraham Lincoln. In marked contrast to his self-effacing exchange with Chandler, in another scene Rickey is approached by Kansas City Monarchs owner J. L. Wilkinson (R. Lee Ermey) while scouting Black players at the 1945 Negro Leagues all-star game at Comiskey Park in Chicago. Rickey acknowledges that he is "interested in some of your players," but when Wilkinson states that he would expect compensation, the Dodgers executive denies the validity of any contractual relationship between Negro League players and their teams. "Your league was created to hide the profits of racketeers and hustlers. I will not traffic with such a league" Rickey proclaims. In response Wilkinson asks incredulously: "You're stealing our assets and we're the racketeers?" This view of Rickey as willing to play on his advantage as a successful businessman to avoid compensating Negro League owners shows the Dodger executive as clearly more interested in profit than racial justice.

Kevin Rodney Sullivan's care in *Soul of the Game* to show the high level of play and style of the Negro Leagues, as well as how the teams were successful entertainment businesses, was in part a reaction to another film about Black baseball made two decades earlier, *The Bingo Long Traveling All-Stars & Motor Kings* (1976). If *Soul of the Game* is serious in tone and concerned with an accurate historical representation of the Negro Leagues and Robinson's transition to MLB, *The Bingo Long Traveling All-Stars & Motor Kings* by contrast is a comedy focused on entertaining as much as informing viewers about Black professional baseball before integration. The star power of Billy Dee Williams, fresh off roles opposite Diana Ross in *Lady Sings the Blues* (1972) and *Mahogany* (1975), the skilled acting and screen presence of James Earl Jones, along with Richard Pryor's comedic brilliance all contribute to the movie's appeal. Because he was more concerned with comedy and entertainment, director John Badham took liberties with the historical record. Paul Petrovic states that Badham "positions *Bingo Long* as a comedy, and one that references the historical past only then to embellish it."[36] Despite its historical distortions and omissions, *Bingo Long* still presents some aspects of Black baseball accurately, if somewhat altered to fit the movie's dramatic conflicts and comic exaggerations.

One historical element of *Bingo Long* comes from how its title character played by Williams and Jones's Leon Carter invoke Paige and Gibson, the biggest stars in the Negro Leagues at the time the story is set. Another character in the film, the hard-hitting and speedy young center fielder Esquire (Tony Burton), who at the film's conclusion is signed to a contract to play on a White team, seems to combine traits of both Jackie Robinson and Willie Mays, although the movie's historical laxity appears in how 1939, when the story takes place, was long before both those players integrated the major leagues. After they learn of Esquire's signing, Carter points out to Bingo the historical irony that although they have struggled to get the fair pay that their outstanding skills merit, the new opportunity for a few Black players will mean the end of the Negro Leagues. "Ain't no Black folks gonna pay to see us play now they can see kids like Esquire playing with the White boys. . . . This the end of Negro ball." Rader explained that indeed "racial integration spelled disaster for the black leagues. The Negro National League dissolved after the 1948 season and the Negro American League fielded only four teams in 1953 before expiring in 1960."[37]

Comedy and history are combined in *Bingo Long* through the Richard Pryor character of all-star right fielder Charles Snow, who has a plan to pretend to be Latino to gain access to White baseball. As historian Adrian Burgos points out, "Until the Dodgers signed Robinson, transnational actors who exploited racial understanding to open up organized baseball to Latinos were typically driven by management's desire to secure new sources of labor without disrupting the color line."[38] In other words, some Latino (and also Native American) players were allowed to play in White professional baseball well before 1947 as long as they weren't too dark skinned. Snow tries both these impersonations, spending most of the film pretending to be Carlos Nevada and then returning after an injury in the film's conclusion with a Mohawk haircut and claiming to be Chief Takahoma.

The story's central premise, that skilled Black players are underpaid and can go on the road to make more money playing in games they arrange rather than for greedy Negro League owners, reflects the pro-labor attitudes in baseball during the mid-1970s. It is true that Black Negro Leagues players made on average only one-quarter what White ballplayers were paid, and because most Black-owned teams didn't have big ballparks in major population centers, they would often barnstorm.[39] However, when the Jones character shares the ideas of Black self-empowerment from W. E. B. Du Bois with Bingo and tells him to "seize the means of production" by setting up his own itinerant team, it seems as much a statement of the countercultural ideas still circulating in the 1970s as a revolutionary mindset among Black players in the 1930s. The push for the end of the reserve clause that succeeded in 1975, the year before the film was released and led by an African American player Curt Flood, also informs the film's pro-labor attitudes.

The racist hostility the all-stars encounter when they go on the road and play White teams creates the need for them to revert to clowning to lessen such resentment of their skill on the baseball field, change the anger of White spectators to laughter, and unfortunately affirm their racist stereotypes about Blacks. For those scenes, Badham drew on the comedic routines of the Indianapolis Clowns Negro League team. MLB.com describes the Clowns as "the Negro Leagues version of the Harlem Globetrotters."[40] Petrovic insightfully points out that the appeal of such clowning by Bingo and his team "diminished not so much the players . . . who act on their recognition of the fans preconceptions, but rather the [White] crowd itself."[41] Yet Petrovic also notes that making such "threat of racial violence . . . farcical . . . amusing and comical," rather than take a position of condemnation, shows that Badham was "too concerned with securing a profitable production to make an ideological stand."[42]

Besides making light of the economic injustice and violence of racism, *Bingo Long* also favors comedic entertainment over acknowledging the larger importance of the Negro Leagues for Black America. As is often the case in baseball films, the actors (with the exception of former MLB star Leon Durham, who plays first baseman Sam Popper) show none of the athletic skills on the field that made the Negro Leagues the equal of all-White MLB, but what is also problematic is the movie's use of the Black team owners as greedy dramatic antagonists for the self-empowering players. While Negro Leagues owners certainly underpaid players just as White owners in MLB did, this villainous characterization distorts the larger role Black teams played in the 1930s to offer what Rob Ruck calls "an arena affirming [African American] business competence and athletic artistry."[43] As Ruck notes, the dominant team in the 1930s, the Pittsburgh Crawfords, owned by numbers king Gus Greenlee, not only featured some of the best Black players in the game such as Oscar Charleston, Cool Papa Bell, and Josh Gibson, and won nine consecutive Negro National League pennants from 1937 to 1945, they also presented Black professional baseball as "a highly visible institution with an aura of accomplishment that fostered a positive sense of an emerging black America."[44] Especially during the Great Depression era when *Bingo Long* is set, Ruck notes that Negro League owners "contributed to its [the Black community's] welfare by funding soup kitchens and political campaigns, and employed thousands, including baseball players, in its underground economy."[45] The excellence on the field, the teams' success as entertainment businesses, as well as the willingness of Greenlee and other Negro League owners to fund Black businesses and support social services showed how "black baseball offered the community the chance to build greater unity and a strong identity."[46]

While Ken Burns tried to use Robinson's story to headline a multicultural idea of baseball as the sport symbolic of America's diverse identity, and *42* sought to appeal to young people for whom Blackness is cool, watching these films is similar to how audiences must have seen the 1950 biopic, *Bingo Long* in the 1970s, or *Soul of the Game* two decades later: all these movies tell well-intentioned stories about responding to racism in an American society that neither was nor is now postracial or in which the "racial transcendence" that Hsu sees as the central goal of contemporary youth culture has been achieved. As David Levering Lewis points out, Barack Obama's presidency concluded with voting rights rolled back and widespread problems with race in the criminal justice system. Lewis stated accurately in 2013 that "when this decade ends it will have confirmed the relevance of Du Bois's grim prophecy about America's everlasting racism."[47] MLB continues to limit the participation of African Americans, no longer because of the gentleman's agreement between the owners that kept them out before Robinson but now using a nostalgic culture that discourages Black participation.

Yet, at the same time, those who run MLB seem to understand that baseball needs more of the flair and style of African American culture to appeal to younger fans. This combination of control and need is how *Souls of the Game* shows the motivations behind Rickey's decision to sign a Black player, and for that reason the film appears more relevant today than *Bingo Long* or the four movies that celebrate Robinson's individual strengths.

As discouraging as such lack of progress may be, Derrick Bell has advocated for the value of stories as a way to help bridge the gap between different viewpoints in discussions on race, because he writes that "people . . . will often suspend their beliefs . . . and then compare their views . . . with those expressed in the story."[48] Of course, the effectiveness of stories to create dialogue on race depends on the stories themselves and who is telling them. Catherine Squires critiques the idea that America is a "post racial" society when she writes that in narratives about race there "is a surplus of individualistic approaches and ahistorical frameworks, at the same time that there remains a deficit of representations of a post-racial society authored by people of color."[49] In other words, the utopian nature of these four film portrayals of Robinson's experience in baseball, their tendency to focus on his personal strength and determination, is typical of how the complexity of race in America is avoided, and they exemplify the type of story circulated in the media about Black people but usually not told by African Americans. Major League Baseball certainly wants to endorse such a limited portrayal of Robinson to create the impression that he solved its problem of racial exclusion, when in fact he did not, and to appeal now to young fans who are attracted to images of cultural diversity. While the positive traits that the two biopics and two documentaries about Robinson assign to him, courage, intelligence, self-discipline, a commitment to excellence, and a willingness to speak out about racial injustice, could have a transformative impact on the racial biases of viewers, such qualities by themselves haven't ensured equal opportunity in MLB and won't affirm the rights of Black citizens in American society more broadly.

No League of Their Own

As much as the history of African American participation in MLB has been about White control and restriction, access for women to professional baseball has been even more limited. Jennifer Ring makes a strong case for how part of the justification for keeping women out of baseball has required denying the history of their involvement in the game. She traces the origins of this omission to nineteenth-century characterizations of baseball that viewed the game as defining normative masculinity. Ring explains that as early as the 1890s "baseball's masculine exclusivity was institutionalized when the game was declared *our national pastime* . . . and associated with American militarism and global expansionism."[50] In 1911, former Chicago White Sox player, manager, owner, and sporting goods entrepreneur Albert Spalding summed up this idea that baseball teaches military masculinity with the emphatic statement that "Baseball is war!" Ring views these words as asserting that the sport Spalding "loves is the equivalent of history's ultimate descriptor of masculinity," adding that his statement was an attempt to link baseball to the "military prowess and the global spread of American power at the end of the 19th century."[51] In 1887 Spalding had led an international tour of American professional ballplayers with stops in Hawaii, Australia, Ceylon, and Egypt to, in his words, "spread baseball as a 'civilizing' American influence on 'little Brown men.'"[52] Twenty years later a commission established by Spalding released a report on the origins of the game that posited the now debunked idea that baseball was invented in Cooperstown, New York, in 1839 by a U.S. Army general, Abner Doubleday. That Doubleday was a cadet at West Point in 1839 who would have been unable to be in Cooperstown and that he denied any involvement with baseball both support Ring's assertion that the Spalding report was "pure fiction," but nonetheless it was used to support the idea of baseball as defining a military masculinity.[53]

The subsequent development of softball by twentieth-century educators as an alternative for girls and women helped baseball hang on to its masculinist identity.[54] Little League baseball was limited to boys until the National Organization of Women (NOW) filed a lawsuit on behalf of Maria Pepe, a twelve-year-old from Hoboken, New Jersey, that allowed girls to play beginning in 1974.[55] In addition to how Ring documents that the history of baseball has sought to only include boys and men, she also notes that film representations of the game have generally excluded girls and women.[56] Three movies about girls' and women's baseball, *Blue Skies Again* (1983), *A League of Their Own*, and *I Throw Like a Girl* (2014) demonstrate their ability on the field, yet also the ideas and actions that have limited their access to the game.

Blue Skies Again imagines the story of a woman trying to play professional baseball. That Paula Fradkin (Robyn Barto) gets a tryout with the fictional Denver Devils at their Florida spring training complex rather than with a real MLB franchise says a great deal about big league baseball's disinterest in supporting the film's premise of giving women a chance to play. The Devils' manager (Kenneth McMillan) thinks enough of Paula's skills to let her play in a spring training game, and in her one at bat, she takes advantage of the opportunity by doubling to drive in the tying run. Besides showing a woman as strong, resilient, and able to play with men, the film's feminist message is also supported by Mimi Rodgers as Liz West, an agent representing Paula who doesn't back down from male outrage at the idea of her client playing for the Devils and also understands how to flatter and persuade the men so that they give her a chance to play.

By showing Paula's ability to compete with men, what *Blue Skies Again* reveals is how the exclusion of women from professional baseball is not about a lack of ability but rather male insistence on keeping them out. After her successful performance in the spring training game, Paula is given no further chance to continue playing because the other players oppose it and most of all because Devils owner Sandy Mendenhal (Harry Hamlin) won't allow her on the team. Similarly, in probably the best-known film about women playing professional baseball, *A League of Their Own*, their excellence at the game gets subordinated to decisions made by male owners about how and for how long they can play.

Considering baseball's origins as an affirmation of military masculinity, it's fitting that *A League of Their Own* represents a time when women got an opportunity to play as professionals because men were away at war. Director Penny Marshall shows how the women's professional baseball league validated its existence as another example of how women did important jobs at home while men were away fighting World War II. Marshall, who started her career as an actress in television comedy, starring in the sitcom *Laverne and Shirley* (1975–83) before going on to become the first woman to direct a feature film that earned more than $100 million (*Big* in 1988), effectively uses humor to soften the challenge the AAGPBL offered to gender norms when the league was running and when the film came out in 1992. Such humor is part of how *A League of Their Own* balances dominant ideas of femininity with the players' impressive demonstrations of their skill on the baseball field. One example is the scene I described in chapter 1 of the Geena Davis character Dottie making a spectacular catch while showing off her legs in the skirts the women had to wear while playing. The shock of the male coach played by Tom Hanks and the male reporter and photographer who record the flashy play creates humor that conceals how in fact Dottie is performing femininity in order to conceal that she is also demonstrating a level of skill playing baseball that many men might find threatening.

Yet while Cahn notes that the AAGPBL shown in *A League of their Own* offered a great opportunity for White women to play professional baseball, it didn't allow African Americans. Much like MLB before Jackie Robinson, a few light-skinned Latinas were accepted but no Blacks. Because of a shortage of skilled players in 1951 the league discussed allowing Black women but decided against it because they were viewed as not fitting in with the standard of femininity so important to the AAGPBL. According to Cahn, this idealized "image [of femininity was] rooted in white middle-class beliefs about beauty and respectability" that "tended to exclude or deprecate black women, making black athletes almost by definition less likely to meet league standards."[57]

Marshall's film generally avoids the issue of race, except for one brief scene. Historian Amira Rose Davis describes this exclusion in *A League of Their Own*, making clear that "Their" in the movie's title refers only to White women: "In a scene lasting twenty-one seconds, a ball rolls away from the Rockford Peaches practice to the feet of a black woman. When Geena Davis, portraying the Peaches' star catcher, calls for the ball, the black woman steps into a hard throw . . . offers a nod and a sardonic smile as if to say, 'I can play too,' before walking away. A league of their own, indeed."[58] Samantha Sheppard notes the irony of how such a brief scene so effectively critiques the exclusion based on race that was practiced in the AAGPBL:

> This moment is significant to understanding Black women's incommensurability within sports film. . . . This scene could have easily been tossed out of the film by Marshall, having no narrative function necessary for telling this feminist tale of women's neglected sports history. . . . Its deliberate inclusion, then, is telling and far-reaching in its impact, despite its brevity, in part because of how it scripts the Black female sporting body into the mise-en-scène of white women's athletic empowerment as a diegetic critique of the league's racial apartheid.[59]

In contrast to the brief allusion to Black women's exclusion from the AAGPBL in *A League of Their Own*, in 2014 Spike Lee made a documentary telling the story of a young Black woman who plays baseball. *I Throw Like a Girl* focuses on Mo'ne Davis, who that year became the first female

FIG. 8 Spike Lee compares Mo'ne Davis to another famous Philadelphia sports hero in *I Throw Like a Girl* (2014).

player to win and throw a shutout in the Little League World Series for her Taney Dragons team from South Philadelphia. After her success at the Little League World Series, Davis went on to become a national media star: trending on Twitter, named by *Time* magazine as one of the twenty-five most influential teens in 2014, and awarded Sportskid of the Year by *Sports Illustrated*.

In Lee's film, sponsored by Chevrolet, he presents Mo'ne as an American hero. Lee interviews her first coach, Steve Bandura, who tells us about how quickly she learned to play baseball. We meet her parents, Lakeisha and Mark, and siblings who clearly love, support and are proud of Mo'ne. Mo'ne demonstrates her modesty when she credits her coach, teammates and God for her success and explains that she tries not to take sports competition too seriously because she "wants to keep it fun." Lee even includes interviews with kids who have played with Mo'ne and their parents who compliment her for her friendliness, modesty, and work ethic to improve her skills.

Yet, despite the family and community support that Lee shows for Mo'ne, he also wants to make sure we understand how notable her success has been.

Sports Illustrated writer Albert Chen, who wrote a cover story about Mo'ne, points out how in one week she went from "a complete unknown" to a "national sensation." Chen also makes the important comment that Mo'ne has been recognized not because she is African American or a girl, but because of how good she is: "You can talk about race, you can talk about gender, but the bottom line is the story of Mo'ne Davis is about a pitcher just absolutely blowing away . . . hitters," states Chen. Lee reaffirms this point in the film's last scene, as we see Mo'ne run up the steps of the Philadelphia Art Museum in an allusion to the famous training session from *Rocky* (1976), another movie about a Philadelphia sports hero. On the voice-over track accompanying this last scene, Mo'ne states: "I throw 70 mph. That's throwing like a girl."

In his last comment in *I Throw Like a Girl*, Coach Bandura asserts that "Mo'ne can do whatever she wants." Yet, despite her extraordinary ability on the baseball field, as she got older barriers were put up that blocked the realization of her dreams. After all the notoriety of her Little League success, recognition by the national media, and a film by Spike Lee, Mo'ne went on to the prestigious Springside Chestnut Hill Academy for high school, where she played soccer, basketball, and softball, but not baseball, even though she commented that "in baseball, I'm more comfortable. I feel like I'm in control. I feel very confident." However, as a pitcher on her high school baseball team with boys, Mo'ne didn't even get a chance. She quit, explaining that "I wasn't pitching" and that the coach couldn't give her an explanation that satisfied her. She explained: "If I'm just going to be sitting there . . . I might as well . . . try softball."[60]

Davis's experience exemplifies Jennifer Ring's observation about the price girls pay who play on teams where almost all their teammates are boys. Ring notes that generally speaking "the only girl on teams where boys are taken more seriously and assumed to have greater playing ability . . . paid a psychological price in confidence and sacrificed playing time."[61] That describes exactly what happened to Mo'ne Davis when she tried to play baseball at Springside Chestnut Hill Academy. While Davis may have enjoyed softball, she made clear she would have preferred to play baseball, an illustration of Ring's point that softball is not an acceptable alternative for girls and women who want to play baseball instead.[62]

It seems patently unfair for a young person with as much talent for baseball as Davis demonstrated when she played in the Little League World Series to not be allowed to develop that ability. This denial of the opportunity to play baseball for Mo'ne Davis is another example of how the exclusion of young women, often after they complete Little League, makes the sport less than the national pastime. As Ring states, "When girls and women can choose to play baseball from Little League to the Major Leagues, the United States truly will possess a 'national pastime.'"[63]

The experience of television analyst Jessica Mendoza offers another poignant example of how baseball is still resistant to women's participation. In 2014 Mendoza, who had worked for ESPN since 2007 covering softball and as a sideline reporter for college football, joined the network's Baseball Tonight program, analyzing MLB games. The following August she became the first female commentator for Sunday Night Baseball, ESPN's flagship MLB game broadcast, and by spring 2016 Mendoza had joined the broadcast team for Sunday games full time. A former All American softball player at Stanford from 1999 to 2002, Mendoza was a member of the gold-medal-winning U.S. team during the 2004 Olympics. Writing in the *Atlantic* in September 2016, Betsy Morais quoted Mendoza describing her opportunity to do the ESPN MLB telecast: "You can't say 'This is not a big deal,' because it is. Not just for me, but for my entire gender. If you screw this up, Jess, the door is gonna close."[64] Former tennis champion and activist for women athletes Billie Jean King seconded Mendoza's acknowledgment of the importance of her hiring to do Sunday Night Baseball by stating "She's not doing this just for her. . . . She's doing this for others."[65]

In an October 2018 YouTube video feature produced by Katie Couric Media and *People* magazine, Mendoza responded to criticism on social media of her performance as an analyst. One hostile tweet quoted in the video states that "ESPN needs to put this Jessica Mendoza thing to rest, men analyze baseball, not women, go back to softball." The video cites Mendoza's response in which she asks viewers to focus on her analysis and not the fact that it is presented by a woman—"I want you to hear me instead of simply writing me off because I'm a woman" she states. Mendoza's previous work for ESPN on softball had never been questioned, and her sideline work with college football only asked her to do interviews with coaches and players and not analyze their play. Guy Harrison, in his writing on women's experience working in sports media, reports on research showing that male announcers were rated as exhibiting higher levels of authoritativeness, by both male and female respondents. Harrison also notes findings that explain the criticism necessitating that Mendoza defend her work on ESPN coverage of baseball because "women reporters were evaluated more favorably when they contributed to coverage of women's sports but less favorably for men's sports."[66]

Regardless of such negative assumptions about women's inability to commentate on men's sports, hiring Mendoza to cover baseball fit with ESPN's increased emphasis on targeting female viewers. While historically advertisers have regarded sports TV as aimed at male fans, ESPN had begun to focus on attracting women viewers both in response to subscriber loss as a result of "a shift from traditional TV viewing to online consumption" as well as to respond to advertiser concern about how "it's getting more difficult to reach women through general primetime programming." Nielsen figures showed women doing more "out of home" viewing than men, and head of ad sales for ESPN, Ed Erhardt, is quoted in the *Wall Street Journal* as saying that "if we took top programs that delivered females 18–49, historically you would have found a very large percentage of primetime programming." However, by 2017, Erhardt continued, "about 75% of those programs are sports now," which he labeled a "drastic shift" in recent years regarding "where females are available at mass scale."[67] With a $5.6 billion contract with MLB to televise baseball, ESPN had a big investment in accessing the growing female audience and using Mendoza seemed a strategic move to help achieve that.

However, Mendoza's role diversifying the personnel for ESPN coverage of baseball to appeal to female viewers was complicated when she was hired in the spring of 2019—in addition to her TV work—by the New York Mets to act as an advisor to general manager Brodie Van Wagenen. Her job with the Mets led to the perception of possible conflict of interest, prompting the Los Angeles Dodgers to block Mendoza from entering their clubhouse as a media member before games broadcast by ESPN in the 2019 season. Mendoza compounded the criticism she received about conflict of interest when she disparaged former Houston Astros pitcher Mike Fiers for revealing that his team stole signs during their World Series title run in 2017. Mendoza later backtracked on her criticism of Fiers, but because recently retired player and the Mets new manager Carlos Beltran was also implicated in the sign stealing scandal, the damage had already been done. At the time of Mendoza's comments, Beltran, who was the only player mentioned in MLB's sign-stealing report, was still manager of the Mets. He was dismissed shortly thereafter without ever managing a game for New York.

As fallout from how her comments about Fiers created a conflict of interest between her allegiance to the Mets and her journalistic responsibility to ESPN, Mendoza later resigned from her role as an advisor to the New York general manager and was dropped from the broadcast team for *Sunday Night Baseball*. Regardless of how her work for the Mets may have compromised her objectivity to comment on the cheating scandal, the negative response to Mendoza revealed a continued gendered double standard in baseball and its media coverage. Mendoza's partner on the Sunday Night Baseball telecasts, Alex Rodriguez, had worked for the New York Yankees while also doing the ESPN telecasts, and another prominent TV baseball analyst, Pedro Martinez, also criticized Fiers's admission of the sign stealing, even though he worked for the Boston Red Sox, a second ballclub tangled in the scandal. Nonetheless, Rodriguez remains on the Sunday Night Baseball team, and no change was made in Martinez's assignment as an analyst for coverage of MLB on TBS and MLB Network. Apparently realizing the unfairness of removing her when male commentators with similar conflicts of interest got a second chance, or perhaps because they really need to draw female viewers, ESPN has brought Mendoza back to baseball telecasts.

4

The Glocalized Game

• • • • • • • • • • • • • • • • • • • •

Manfred Steger states that "'globalization' emerged as *the* buzzword of the 1990s" because it summed up the increasing interconnection across borders throughout the world facilitated by new information and communications technology and "the global integration of markets."[1] Yet such transnational intersection of markets was not new. American multinational corporations since the nineteenth century have done business around the world, but writing in the last decade of the twentieth century, Walter LaFeber notes that their practices had recently changed in several significant ways, including the shift of production overseas to reduce costs and a greater focus on selling culture, knowledge, and communication instead of the previous emphasis on natural resources and industrial products.[2]

Baseball in recent decades has followed this globalizing tendency in some regards but not entirely. Most of MLB's business is still done in North America, and the majority of what it sells, the players and the games they compete in, continues to be developed and take place here. However, since the 1990s MLB has also followed the globalizing trend of investing abroad to reduce player costs and to create new markets by supporting international play. MLB has also set up an international division to sell its properties globally, using events, marketing partnerships, and media—for example, its games are telecast in 189 countries. MLB views this international division as helping "to grow its position as the leader in the international market-place" for the sport.[3]

In response to what Barrie Axford has called "a regrettable tendency to treat culture—usually particular cultures—as the victims of globalization . . . often subsumed under the rubric of westernization," sociologist Roland Robertson in 1992 coined the term "glocalization."[4] As Axford's comment makes clear, globalization has increasingly been understood as a linking of the world's various cultures and economies, "resulting in a homogenization and standardization," what Steger calls "spreading the logic of capitalism and Western values by eradicating local traditions and national cultures."[5] By contrast, Robertson's idea of glocalization allows for the continued possibility of what he terms "indigenization" or "particularization of the universal."[6] Glocalization asserts the possibility for a coexistence between cultural homogenization and heterogenization, universalism and particularism together in a globalized world.

Robertson's qualification of the sameness of globalization with the particularity of glocalization works well to understand baseball in an international context. Although the sport is often celebrated as the national pastime of the United States, it is also played in many other parts of the world. Anthropologist William Kelly notes that even as baseball was becoming "explicitly 'nationalized' as the American pastime in the 1860s," it was also "simultaneously moving abroad—to Cuba in the same decade, to other parts of the Caribbean soon after, . . . and to Japan . . . in the early 1870s."[7] Yet even as baseball took root and became popular internationally, the business of the game, as played by professional athletes for paying fans and in the media, has remained dominated by the North American organization of MLB. The World Baseball Classic (WBC), set up in 2006 after baseball was removed from the Olympic Games and modeled on the World Cup soccer tournament, involves twenty national teams playing for the title of world champion of baseball. The United States has not been the dominant team on the field, winning just ten of the twenty games the American national team has played in the first four tournaments and only one title. Nonetheless, MLB has retained organizational and financial control over the WBC since its inception, prompting Kelly to write that "the WBC [has been] organized by the US Major League Baseball (MLB) and the MLB Players Association, which reserved for themselves a major share of the proceeds."[8]

Besides such control of international competition, MLB, with its billions in revenue and $4 million average player salary, continues to be the number-one destination for the best players from all over the world.[9] Kelly sums up the hegemony of MLB in regard to top talent: "The MLB team baseball academies in the Dominican Republic have become critical channels for recruiting young and inexpensive prospects, the machinations in enticing Cuban players to defect and sign with MLB clubs, and the extensive scouting efforts in Japan and other East Asian countries have resulted in the increasingly multi-ethnic composition of MLB teams. The effect is to draw the best players to the U.S. rather than to nurture elite level completion elsewhere."[10] Early in Ken Burns's 2010 documentary *The Tenth Inning*, the narration acknowledges that, starting in the 1990s, "Latin and Asian players would transform the game, just as waves of immigrants continued to enrich the country that created it." By characterizing players from Latin America and Asia who have come to play professionally in the United States as like immigrants bringing new life to baseball, Burns highlights the cultural renewal created by the globalization of MLB player development, but without noting the concentration of revenue in the hands of MLB ownership that results from the internationalization of its rosters.

Alan Klein describes how, since the 1980s, MLB has "vigorously cultivated the business opportunities in foreign markets," moving "abroad primarily to find talent . . . to globalize the game."[11] Yet the motive for the pursuit of talent outside of the United States, Canada, and Puerto Rico, where the amateur draft mandates set bonus and salary money depending on when a player is selected, comes primarily from one of the same incentives that drives economic globalization in general: the pursuit of reduced labor costs. Historian Adrian Burgos has stated that MLB is currently interested in players from the Dominican Republic, Venezuela, and Cuba (the three main Latin American countries for producing top talent) for the same reason they long have been: "It's about getting good talent as cheaply as possible."[12] As reduced trade barriers and improved travel and communications technologies have facilitated economic globalization, the result has been increased competition between workers in developing and developed countries that has driven down wages in the latter.[13] Those same transportation and communication technologies have also changed sports, not only facilitating the evaluation and movement of players internationally to reduce labor costs, but also enabling teams to "incorporate market segments available through regionalized TV, radio, newspapers, magazines . . . advertising, and the Internet. Local markets could be saturated and distant markets could be accessed."[14] That telecommunications company Altice Dominicana since 2009 has shown many MLB contests on television in the Dominican Republic and that MLB games in which Japanese stars play "draw huge television audiences in Japan" both exemplify such global media outreach.[15] Moreover, media saturation in Latin America and Asia has been an important stimulus to MLB's player development system, helping to create the dream of reaching professional baseball in North America for young men in those parts of the world.

In direct response to the rapid growth in player salaries since the establishment of free agency in 1976, MLB began to focus on finding less expensive player talent in Latin America. In the five years after free agency began the average MLB salary more than tripled, and as Ezequiel Lihosit points out "the number of Latin American players in Major League Baseball . . . increased dramatically from 1980 to 2015."[16] Latinos made up 11 percent of MLB players in 1980, 27 percent by 2015.[17] In 2020 the Dominican Republic alone produced 110 of the 291 MLB players born outside the United States.[18] Scholars like Samuel Regalado and Alan Klein, who have both written extensively about baseball in Latin America, characterize this development of a pipeline of new baseball talent from the Dominican Republic to North America as a kind of neocolonialist business practice.[19] To the degree MLB relies on Latin American players, Lihosit describes it as "similar to other global companies in that it produces entertainment with cheap overseas labor and sells it at full retail in the United States."[20]

The poverty of the Dominican Republic gives MLB a huge negotiating advantage in regard to their business relationships in general on the island and with young players in particular. Rob Ruck estimates that the thirty MLB teams pump $125 million each year into the Dominican economy in what they spend on their development academies, another $200 million through the bonuses they pay to all the players they sign, and then there is "whatever comes home from the estimated $400 million paid to Dominican major leaguers."[21] While that money is an important part of the Dominican economy, the savings that such investment creates from not having to develop U.S. talent are indicated by how in 2019 MLB teams incurred only one-fifth of the cost for international players of what they paid to those born in this country.[22]

MLB maintains a position of leverage even in their acquisition of players from the highly developed professional leagues in Japan. Because salaries in Japan average about one-fifth of those paid in MLB, the top professional league there, Nippon Professional Baseball (NPB), has insisted on a posting fee system whereby MLB teams compensate Japanese clubs when their players are recruited away to play in North America.[23] But according to Major League Baseball's collective-bargaining agreement, an incoming international player under the age of twenty-five can sign only for the league minimum salary. A recent example of how this arrangement benefits MLB owners is that of the young Japanese star Shohei Ohtani, who left the Hokkaido Nippon-Ham Fighters to sign with the Los Angeles Angels in December 2017. As Ohtani was viewed as a future superstar because of his ability to both hit and pitch at a very high level, the Angels were willing to pay his former team a $20 million transfer fee for the rights to sign him, and they paid him a $2 million bonus equal to what he was making per season in Japan, yet under the MLB rules Ohtani's salary for his initial three-year deal was limited to the league minimum, which at the time he signed was $545,000.[24] With only nine Japanese players in MLB in 2021, recruitment from NPB is much more selective than from Latin America, in large part because the players who come from Japan are established stars whom MLB teams use to create immediate fan interest and revenue and not the en masse development of young talent from Latin America motivated by long-term cost savings. Nonetheless, as Ohtani shows, because of the limits on what younger international players can be paid, Japanese stars can contribute to the trend of acquiring international talent at reduced cost.

Moreover, the biggest star to ever to come from Japan, Ichiro Suzuki, shows how bringing players from NPB also fulfills another promise of economic globalization: growing new markets. When Ichiro came to Seattle in 2000, the Mariners were owned by Nintendo president Hiroshi Yamauchi, who had faced the perception that his investment in MLB was just another "attempt on the part of the Japanese to 'buy up' more of Americans' national heritage."[25] Ichiro, who had already been a seven-time batting champion in NPB, had immediate and lasting success in American baseball and contributed significantly to increased fan interest in the Mariners both here and in Japan. Alan Klein notes the irony that Yamauchi was initially a "victim of MLB prejudice," toward Japanese investment, but by signing Suzuki he was seen as "helping MLB look progressive and globally active."[26] Yet while Ichiro's presence may have seemed to represent a progressive move toward cultural diversity, in fact his signing was determined primarily by the cost of his services on the baseball field and the increased fan interest and profitability he generated. In this sense Yamauchi followed the same logic on controlling labor costs through international signings that the other MLB owners had established since the advent of free agency. When Suzuki signed with Seattle he cost the Mariners a $13 million posting fee, a $5 million bonus and a $14 million three-year contract, for a total outlay of roughly $32 million, an average expense of about $10.66 million per season. That year eighteen MLB players, only five of them born outside the United States, cost more than Ichiro.[27] Suzuki dominated MLB in his first season, winning the batting title and Rookie of the Year and MVP awards; the Mariners' attendance jumped by over 7,000 per game, and the team generated "the third-highest local media revenue in baseball," behind only the Mets and Yankees, proving what a bargain signing Ichiro had been for Yamauchi.[28] Such revenue increases after the arrival of Suzuki confirmed the wisdom of Seattle's plan that Burns describes in his *Tenth Inning* documentary addendum as "hoping [Ichiro] would attract a large following among Asian Americans living in the Pacific Northwest." In addition to such a big jump in local and regional revenue, the Mariners and MLB also benefitted from the interest that Suzuki's success generated in Japan. Burns recalls that hundreds of print media and television reporters came from Japan "to send back news of [Ichiro's] every move to a nation eager for any information about their hero."

Yet as much as MLB continues to dominate the international business of baseball and its recruitment of players from outside of North America is driven by a business model aimed at reducing labor costs, nonetheless baseball cultures in other parts of the world differ in some regards, and Robertson's concept of glocalization helps describe such coexistent sameness and difference. Kelly supports the relevance of glocalization to describe international baseball, stating that the term "captures the sense that local appropriation is seldom simply assimilating and imitating. Rather, it is generally a process of . . . appropriating the foreign objects and practices by recontextualizing them into local . . . meaning and value."[29]

After the United States, Japan has the longest and most established history of professional baseball, the largest fan base, and the most extensive media coverage.[30] Since the mid-twentieth century baseball has been Japan's national game, but while Japanese baseball may look like the sport in the United States, in fact it is different enough to offer an example of a global sport with significant local variations. Although Americans favor the power game of superstar players, Japanese baseball by contrast tends to be "team-spirited, cautious, self sacrificing, [and] deeply deferential," with a mindset like that of the samurai ethos, seeing the sport as similar to a martial art to be perfected and executed with precision.[31] Americans as a result have often viewed Japanese baseball as too serious and pedagogical and not allowing enough room for individual excellence. Former MLB slugger Reggie Smith, who spent two seasons with Tokyo's Yomiuri Giants in the 1980s, commented during his time playing in Japan that "this isn't baseball—it only looks like it."[32] Yet despite such criticism, Kelly notes that the Japanese see their version of baseball as "vindicated by the considerable success it [has] enjoyed on the field."[33] One measure of that success is how the Japanese national team won the first two WBC titles, in 2006 and 2009, has been in the championship round in every tournament, leads all countries in WBC games won, and took the gold medal when baseball returned to the Olympics in 2021.

The 1992 Hollywood film *Mr. Baseball* illustrates the contrast between the American and Japanese versions of baseball. Tom Selleck stars in the film as Jack Elliot, an aging slugger for the Yankees whose drinking, late hours, and bad knee have prompted New York to release him. The only professional team interested in Elliot's services is the Chunichi Dragons in the NPB Central League. Klein comments that there are two kinds of Western players or *gaijin* who go to Japan: those simply trying to stay in professional baseball and "an occasional major leaguer (invariably past his prime)." Jack exemplifies the latter, and from the time he arrives in the Dragons' home city of Nagoya his ego creates conflict with his new team. Klein calls the emphasis on conditioning and long hours of practice in Japanese baseball "legendary," but for Jack such hard work is just a major annoyance.[34] As they run wind sprints at practice, Jack grumbles to another American on the Dragons, Max "Hammer" Dubois (Dennis Haysbert): "This is crazy Max. We're not athletes. We're baseball players." Jack also violates Japanese expectations of total respect for his manager Uchiyama (Ken Takakura) by disregarding the older man's critique of his swing. The Dragons have high expectations about marketing the American slugger to their fan base and bring in Uchiyama's daughter, advertising executive Hiroko (Aya Takanashi), to manage Jack's image with the media and fans. However, Jack frustrates her efforts: showing little interest in doing the ads for products Hiroko places him in and losing his temper and getting into fights on the field. Used to being the star and focusing only on his own success, Jack demonstrates a total lack of what is referred to in Japanese baseball as *wa*, or group harmony.[35] He's a perfect example of the trouble many American players have faced when trying to make the transition to playing in Japan, about which Klein comments "under the lens of intense media scrutiny, and disoriented by cultural difference, most of these players perform poorly."[36]

However, *Mr. Baseball* combines its well-informed story about the differences between U.S. and Japanese baseball with the conventions of romantic comedy. So as an attraction develops between Jack and Hiroko, she is able to persuade the American player that he needs to understand and "accept" baseball culture in Japan. Working with his interpreter Yoji (Toshi Shioya) Jack prepares an apology speech he gives in Japanese to his alienated teammates and he also accepts a plan to work with Uchiyama on his conditioning. As a result of such compromise and acceptance Jack plays better and the Dragons start winning. At an important moment in the climactic game in which Chunichi clinches the Central League pennant, Uchiyama gives the sign to swing away, but Jack instead choses to adhere to the Japanese custom of sacrificing individual performance for the good of the team and bunts to bring home the winning runs, despite how that choice cost him an opportunity to impress a Dodgers executive who had come to Japan to look at him to fill a need Los Angeles has for a first baseman.

In November 1990, less than a year prior to the start of production on *Mr. Baseball*, the Japanese electronics conglomerate Matsushita bought MCA, owner of Universal, the studio where the film was made. After the change in ownership, rewrites were done on the script for *Mr. Baseball*, shifting it from a broad comedy about the cultural clash between an American star player and his Japanese team to a story more about the former's acceptance of *wa*. Yet despite such revisions to improve the appeal of the film in the Japanese market, *Mr. Baseball* still dealt critically with the challenges faced by Western players in Japan. One scene shows Jack having to accept what is clearly a bigger strike zone for him than for Japanese players and the other comes when he begins to hit well and opposing pitchers walk him rather than allow Elliot to break the NPB record set by Uchiyama when he was a player for home runs in consecutive games. Despite the script changes that created a greater balance between humor about the incongruity of American and Japanese baseball and the Selleck character adjusting to the ways of the latter, Thomas Pollack, chairman of Universal, denied any involvement from Japanese ownership in the rewrites. "There was absolutely no involvement by Matsushita," said Pollock. Yet the Universal chairman added: "But let's keep in mind that Japan is the second biggest movie market in the world. . . . We don't want to insult the Japanese or the Americans."[37]

As much as *Mr. Baseball* shows Jack learning to accept *wa* in a way that would appeal to the Japanese audience, the film's last scene seems to align also with Pollack's comment about the importance of portraying the resolution of the culture clash to suit viewers in both countries. As the film ends, Jack is back in the United States during spring training at the opening of the year after his season in Japan, and we see him in a Detroit Tigers uniform, while Hiroko watches from the stands taking work calls on her cell phone. Jack may have shown his ability to adjust to the different game and succeed while he was in Japan, but *Mr. Baseball* ends by endorsing the idea that success in Japanese baseball was just a way to demonstrate that he could still make it in MLB.

While *Mr. Baseball* juggles *wa* with Western ideas of individual stardom, the 2006 documentary *Kokoyakyu*, directed by Chinese American filmmaker Kenneth Eng, reinforces a more glocalized cultural meaning for baseball in Japan. Although global media representation of the sport and the success of top Japanese players in MLB have increased the influence of Western ideas of individual success and its financial rewards, high school baseball in Japan still functions less as a training ground for the select few who will make it into the professional game, as it often does in the United States, than as an activity to teach cultural values. Since 1915 Japanese high school baseball has culminated each August in a national tournament at Koshien Stadium in Osaka in which forty-nine schools from the more than four thousand with teams around the country are invited to compete for the national championship. *Kokoyakyu* shows the preparation and participation of two teams for the 2003 tournament: Tennoji, a public school with limited resources but a dedication to balancing athletic and academic excellence, and Chiben Academy, an elite private school with a reputation for success on the baseball field, having won three Koshien titles.

Eng has noted the emphasis in his film on the formative influence of Japanese high school baseball, commenting that *"Kokoyakyu* is a study about how baseball can be . . . used as an educational tool to teach kids values."[38] In preparation for its coverage of the Koshien tournament, the initial sections of the documentary present examples of Tennoji and Chiben players, coaches, family members and fans demonstrating the values that the game is meant to instill. In the film's first chapter on "heart," we see the parents of Daisuke, a Tennoji player, up at four fifteen so his mother can prepare her son's lunch for the day and his father drive him to baseball practice that begins at six. After watching the Tennoji players arriving at the field we meet their coach, Mr. Masa, who explains to us that "baseball develops heart," a statement of the emotional attachment the sport fosters. Tennoji team captain Takahiro expands on the concept of heart by telling us that Mr. Masa "dedicates himself to the baseball club." During a subsequent scene in which the eighteen young men who will represent Tennoji at Koshien are announced, we see a powerful example of Mr. Masa's emotional investment in his players when the last selected, a senior named Haruki, tells the group, "Even if I am on the bench I will give my loudest voice to raise the morale of the team." Mr. Masa then asks Haruki to stand again while he praises the young man's hard work and dedication to the team. As Haruki becomes overcome with emotion and begins to cry, Mr. Masa praises his player's effort to improve during the three years he has been on the team, and notes that "at first you could only talk about yourself," but that, in preparation for Koshien "you began to speak about what you could do for the team." "I was convinced then," Mr. Masa continues, "that I could trust you with the #18 [the last spot on the team]." As tears run down Haruki's cheeks, Mr. Masa makes direct reference to his emotion and praises it to the entire group: "Those are beautiful tears," he states. "I want you to shine more than another #18," he tells Haruki. Although young women from the two schools, along with mothers and female teachers, are shown only in supportive roles throughout *Kokoyakyu*, preparing meals and bringing water and tea to the players during practice, or in the cheering sections and as fans at the games, the movie's emphasis on the importance for the young men and their male coaches of modesty, generosity, and expression of feelings toward each other, such as in the Tennoji selection announcement scene, blurs the gender distinctions created by the more individualistic, emotionally guarded masculinity typical in media representations of baseball in the United States.

After we observe the strong bond between Mr. Masa and the players from Tennoji, the film turns to another value baseball teaches, "fighting spirit," and shifts to Chiben Academy in the city of Wakayama near Osaka, whose baseball team is led by Coach Takashima. While Mr. Masa had told us that playing baseball develops heart and feeling for the people you play with, Mr. Takashima, encouraged by his success as a three-time Koshien champion, emphasizes less the close relationships developed by the boys than the need for rigorous practice to develop physical strength and determination as the keys to winning games. "That's the baseball that came from America," Takashima explains. During the segment of *Kokoyakyu* titled "Dreams" we see a large bronze statue on the Chiben campus showing a baseball team celebrating with the English word VICTORY carved in capital letters across its top. In contrast to the modesty and gratitude for coaches, teammates and family communicated by the Tennoji players, the two Chiben players interviewed, Hayata and Ryohei, both emphasize their personal goal to play professionally. In his writing about high school baseball in Japan, Dan Gordon notes in recent years the "changing attitudes among Japanese youth toward self-expression" encouraged by the increasing popularity of American baseball. While Gordon comments that high school baseball in Japan "models itself after tradition," he also notes that Western professional sports by contrast emphasize individual success. Sports editor Yusuke Abe adds that the appeal of American baseball has increased in Japan as some of the top Japanese players have gone to MLB to play.[39] Takashima at Chiben Academy clearly maintains the authoritarian style of coaching traditional in Japanese baseball, both at the amateur and professional levels. Yet his focus on winning more than community fits the individual ambitions for professional success voiced by his two players and reinforced by the idea of stardom coming from Western professional sports.

Both teams initially play well at the tournament, but Chiben is eliminated in the second round and Tennoji loses their third game. Their reaction to defeat again contrasts the two coaches and the message they emphasize to their players. Following his team's 3-2 loss, Takashima explains that his players didn't hit well and didn't put out enough effort, yet then qualifies his focus on competitive performance with a more traditional Japanese acceptance of responsibility and self-sacrifice: "But in the end it's the coach's fault. He did his job badly," he states about himself. By contrast, Coach Masa continues to model to his players the value of support and connection. After his team's loss he tearfully tells his senior captain, Takahiro, how well he played, encouraging him to "have children and teach them baseball." The whole Tennoji team then gathers outside the stadium to thank each other, their fans and families. Each of the five Tennoji seniors addresses the group, and Haruki, who had been praised for his emotional commitment at the selection meeting, again expresses his bond to the group. After thanking the families and fans for cheering the team on, he concludes: "From now on, we seniors will retire and probably go our separate ways, but our hearts will always beat as one team."

Just as for the Japanese, baseball in Latin America negotiates a balance between the influence of globalization and the values of local tradition. Bernardo Ruiz's 2008 PBS documentary *Roberto Clemente*, made for public television's American Experience series, emphasizes the important role that the Puerto Rican superstar played in opening up Major League Baseball to Latino players. Ruiz shows Clemente, like Jackie Robinson, as a tremendous source of pride for his people, because of his accomplishments both on the field, but also off it for his work helping others. When Clemente came to the United States to play for the Pittsburgh Pirates in 1955 he faced a difficult initial period of adjustment. He had grown up poor in Puerto Rico, the youngest of seven children, yet even after demonstrating extraordinary ability and signing to come play in the United States. Clemente was surprised by the cultural disrespect and racist mistreatment he faced from Jim Crow laws in Florida during spring training and in Pittsburgh. The Ruiz film explains that Clemente had grown up watching players from the Negro Leagues in Puerto Rico where racial difference was less important than in the United States. Pittsburgh, however, was a fairly small, mostly White city, and Clemente was the only Latino on the team. Orlando Cepeda, another Puerto Rican player in the big leagues during the same period, explains in the documentary, "We [had] two strikes, being Black and being Latino." Actor Jimmy Smits' voice-over narration untangles the illogic of this perception when it notes that Clemente was regarded in Pittsburgh as Black and foreign even though African Americans didn't view him as one of them and by virtue of being born in Puerto Rico he was an American citizen.

Clemente's limited English skills when he first arrived were not only a barrier to communicating but the cause of a pattern of disrespectful treatment from the baseball media. Puerto Rican historian Adrian Burgos recounts an example of how a sportswriter mocked Clemente's English by attributing the following quote to him: "Me like hot weather, veree hot. I no run fast cold weather." Clemente reacted angrily to that insulting distortion of how he spoke: "I never talk like that. They just want to sell newspapers," he responded.[40] Close friend Luis Mayoral corroborated that Clemente was treated with disrespect by the U.S. media: "Su pronunciatión del inglés no era la correcta. Los periodistas se mofaban de él citandolo fonéticamente" (His pronunciation of English wasn't correct. The journalists would mock him, quoting him phonetically).[41] In the Ruiz film, writer Juan Gonzalez characterizes the disrespect that Clemente faced over the issue of language from the American sportswriters as part of "an attempt to deny the heritage of Latin ballplayers."

But again like Jackie Robinson, while Clemente had to put up with mistreatment grounded in race and cultural difference, he responded by transcending such bigotry both on and off the field. He played baseball in a way that not only made him one of the best players in baseball but also represented his Latino identity. George Will comments in the Ruiz documentary that Clemente "played hard all the time." Will insightfully adds that the intensity and energy with which Clemente competed represented not just the individual ambitions of one athlete but "the upward mobility of people who hitherto had been excluded." We see lots of footage that shows that intensity, with Clemente taking an extra base, sliding hard, running all-out to track down balls in the outfield, and making strong, accurate throws. In one regard Clemente's hard play was measured by his statistical productivity and awards: he hit .317 during his eighteen-year career, won four batting titles and twelve gold gloves for his defensive excellence, and holds the record for most assists by a right fielder with 260. But in another sense such impressive statistics and trophies don't encompass the attitude and style of Clemente's play that had meaning beyond his own individual accomplishment.

In the documentary Will calls Clemente's play "gorgeous to watch," and biographer David Maraniss, who was the senior consultant for Ruiz's film, writes that "he was an athlete whose style and beauty on the field of play could never be quantified adequately by statistics."[42] Clemente became known for one defensive play in particular in which he would run in to his left, field a batted ball, and quickly spin entirely around and make a strong, accurate throw to second or third. Ruiz shows us an example of Clemente making this signature play in the 1971 World Series against Baltimore. On the baseball field Clemente played with force, quickness, and confidence, but he also had a grace and beauty of movement that few players in the history of MLB have equaled.

While his productivity and flair won him many fans, Clemente still faced some resistance for how he represented a more expressive, flamboyant brand of baseball. In 1960 Clemente hit .314 and drove in 94 runs for the Pirates during the season, and after batting .310 in the World Series to help Pittsburgh defeat the New York Yankees, he was surprised by the overwhelming local fan reaction. Smits narrates how, as he left the Pirates clubhouse following the deciding seventh game, the Pittsburgh star heard a fan shout "There's Clemente!" and saw a crowd surge toward him. "It took him an hour to make his way through," Smits explains, and he describes Clemente's emotional response to this recognition: "After years of feeling himself an outsider, he had won them over. 'The fans of Pittsburgh,' [Clemente] said,

FIGS. 9 AND 10 Roberto Clemente catching a ball in right field and then spinning to make a throw, showing his grace as a ballplayer in the Bernardo Ruiz documentary *Roberto Clemente* (2008).

'had made it all worthwhile.'" Yet even with such fan recognition, still Clemente's dynamic and stylish play didn't appeal to everyone. Pitcher Jim Brosnan in a 1960 *Life Magazine* article criticized him for standing out too much, showing off, and displaying an arrogant attitude: "Look at *número uno* he seems to be saying," stated Brosnan.[43] The writers who voted for the National League Most Valuable Player in 1960 appeared to agree. Clemente finished a disappointing eighth in the balloting.

Even if the intensity and style of his game were too threatening to some, another way Clemente transcended attempts to limit and diminish him was as a leader as well as a great ballplayer. Ruiz's narration describes how by "the mid-1960s Clemente found himself engaged by events beyond the ballpark," adding, "He identified closely with the growing movement for civil rights." In the film Maraniss describes how Clemente admired the leadership of Dr. Martin Luther King Jr. and met with him when the civil rights leader visited Puerto Rico. As Maraniss puts it, Clemente "was interested in more than sports. He was very political." Pirate teammate Al Oliver in the Ruiz documentary suggests that perhaps Clemente's willingness to talk about issues that concerned him was part of what created miscommunication and distrust with the sports media. Clemente "would start talking about life," states Oliver, "and writers weren't ready for that." Close friend Luis Mayoral adds that "Roberto fue un pionero en crear conciencia sobre la igualdad y la enfermedad del racismo. . . . El hablaba y siempre dio a entender que estaba en contra de las injusticia" (Roberto was a pioneer in creating awareness of equality and the disease of racism. . . . He would talk and make it known that he was against injustice").[44]

Among his Pittsburgh teammates as well Clemente took on a greater leadership role. In 1971, at age thirty-seven, he led a well-integrated Pittsburgh team of Black, Latino, and White players to the World Series. All-star catcher Manny Sanguillén comments that "Era una familia de veramente. En eso momento, no habia nada de color" (It was a real family. At that time there was no color). With Clemente hitting .414 and winning the series MVP, Pittsburg went on to defeat the heavily favored Baltimore Orioles in seven games. Eight years later when the Pirates again beat Baltimore to win the 1979 World Series, Pittsburgh slugger Willie Stargell remembered: "I thought 1971 was Roberto Clemente's moment of glory. He had started something with his winning, driving attitude. Whatever contribution I've made has been merely an extension of what he started."[45]

Clemente's dedication to lead and help others went so far that he wound up giving his life for it. After the 1972 season he worked to send food and medicine to the victims of a devastating earthquake in Nicaragua, but died in December of that year when the DC-7 on which he was flying headed to Managua with a load of relief supplies crashed into the ocean soon after take-off from San Juan. Clemente's body was never found. Al Oliver, with a lump in his throat, tells us in the Ruiz documentary that Clemente's death "knocked me off my feet. We knew that we had lost our leader." After narrating the tragic events of his premature death, Ruiz ends his film with a statement about Clemente's selfless leadership from another close friend of the ballplayer, Osvaldo Gil, who says that "En la forma en que murió, por ir a ayudar a otras personas, eso lo iba a proyectar al mundo como un humanista" (The way in which he died, going to help other people, will define him to the world as a humanitarian).

Although he faced racism and criticism of his English skills and stylish play, Clemente responded throughout his career with what might be called a glocalized response. He showed fans in the United States that a Latino player could be one of the best in the major leagues with an intensity and flair that symbolized the aspirations and pride of the marginalized culture he came from, and he also endorsed the values of strong leadership that helped Pittsburgh win on the field but that Clemente saw equally as crucial in promoting community and combatting racism and poverty.

A quarter century after Clemente's tragic death the number of players with roots in Latin America had grown to more than one-quarter of big league rosters. The year 2008 saw the release of the film *Sugar*, about a young Dominican's struggle to make it to the major leagues that typifies the experience of many Latin American players. *Sugar* carefully shows the challenges that Dominican players, some of them signed as young as sixteen, face as they try to work their way up to that goal. The movie opens with its main character, Miguel "Sugar" Santos (Algenis Perez Soto), training at the Kansas City Royals' academy in Boca Chica, near Santo Domingo, his days full of hard work on the field and classroom time with his teammates learning English. The pressure on Miguel is also intense because of what his opportunity means to create a better life economically for his family. Early in the film his mother asks if he has been chosen to go to play in the United States, and when Miguel is later selected, he becomes one of only a select few (about 2 percent of the players in the academies) who get that opportunity.

Yet Miguel's assignment to a team in the minor leagues means moving to Bridgetown, Iowa, where the food is unfamiliar and everyone, except a few of his teammates, speaks only English and too quickly for him to understand. He pitches well at first, but an injury sidetracks Miguel and he leaves the team to go to New York, following a former teammate, Jorge, who had moved there to start a new life after being cut by the Royals. While most baseball films show the protagonist overcome the competitive challenges to find success on the field, *Sugar* instead ends with its title character finding a new life outside of baseball. Miguel doesn't become a star, but he finds a steady job in a diner in Queens and is able to send money back to his family. Relieved of the pressure of becoming a major leaguer, Miguel meets friends and colleagues who share his language and culture, and he can even continue to play ball, if only in an amateur league in a public park with Latino former professional players whose experience was much like his own.

Even when individual stardom doesn't materialize, as is the case for the majority of young Dominicans who spend most of their lives learning to play baseball and aspiring to be the next Pedro Martinez or Manny Ramirez, *Sugar* nonetheless makes what is an unsuccessful dream into a meaningful reality. The scenes at the end of *Sugar* showing Miguel working and playing in the park league games exemplify a more modest, but still important, type of success. It's not MLB stardom, but it is an immigrant experience that millions of people live in the United States.

Kokoyakyu, Roberto Clemente, and *Sugar* present examples of glocalization that distinguish the version of baseball they show from that offered by most media representation in North America. Ruiz's documentary tells how Clemente introduced the athleticism and style prominent in Latin American baseball to the major leagues. His story, like that of Miguel in *Sugar*, also communicates values central to the cultures they come from: the hard work and dedication required to be a professional, but also the responsibility that Latino players assume to help those from their community who are denied the chance they get. In the portrayal of Japanese high school baseball offered by *Kokoyakyu*, baseball is again just as much about responsibility to family and community as individual stardom.

Michael Real and Diana Beeson speculate that as baseball becomes more globalized, U.S. fans who have understood the game in nationalist terms, as America's pastime, will gain a broader cultural understanding from watching international stars: "As American sports fans' identity spreads to more internationally rooted ... superstars, the tendency toward isolation, insularity and exclusion of outsiders faces a direct psychological challenge."[46] In Burns's *Tenth Inning* documentary former ESPN executive Gary Hoenig acknowledges the contribution that international players have made to the game and its impact on fans: "That's the great thing about globalization. [Baseball] can go to an entirely different place and be recreated and regrown ... and come back and show you the game in a different way."

5

Fanball

• • • • • • • • • • • • • • • • • • • •

In his book *Textual Poachers*, cultural critic Henry Jenkins traces the origins of the term "fan" to late nineteenth-century journalistic writing about baseball "describing followers . . . at a time when the sport moved from a predominately participant activity to a spectator event."[1] Regardless of their claim to first exemplifying the term, followers of baseball were not able to avoid the negative stereotypes that Jenkins states have denigrated fans of all kinds of popular culture, such as that they "devote their lives to the cultivation of worthless knowledge" and are "social misfits. . . . unable to separate fantasy from reality."[2] While professional players, team management, and the media are quick to admit that organized baseball couldn't exist without the money that fans spend on the game, nonetheless there is a long history of portraying them in film and television as disillusioned, obsessed, silly, angry, and even dangerous. Consider the boy in *Eight Men Out* asking Joe Jackson to deny his involvement in the 1919 fix of the World Series; a young woman shown in the ESPN documentary *Fernando Nation* running onto the field to kiss Valenzuela when he suddenly became a star in 1981; Randy Quaid as Johnny the angry Cleveland fan in *Major League II* (1994); the venom directed at Steve Bartman by other Cubs fans when he took a foul ball away from Chicago outfielder Moses Alou in the 2003 NL playoffs in another ESPN documentary, *Catching Hell* (2011); fan resentment in response to the 1994–1995 strike recounted by Ken Burns in the *10th Inning* chapter of his PBS film; or Harriet Bird (Barbara Hershey) shooting Roy Hobbs (Robert Redford) in a hotel room in *The Natural*.

One of the most extreme of such negative representations of baseball fandom occurs in the 1996 Tony Scott film *The Fan*. Robert De Niro plays Gil Renard, a knife salesman whose work and family lives fall apart and who in response turns his obsession with San Francisco star center fielder Bobby Rayburn (Wesley Snipes) into murderous revenge. Director Scott is so intent on building the film around De Niro's past success playing angry, violent characters in roles such as *Taxi Driver* (1976), *Raging Bull* (1980), and *Cape Fear* (1991) that Renard's psychosis obscures the story's allusions to a pervasive discontent among baseball fans in the aftermath of the 1994 strike that led to the cancellation of the World Series. In a 1995 review of the Peter Abrahams novel that the film adapts, sports historian Warren Goldstein describes the book as having "a powerful undercurrent of disdain for the national pastime."[3]

Noah Cohan sees *The Fan* as a "cautionary tale" about how too much "sports obsession" leads to a "failed masculinity" because it renders men like Gil "economically impotent."[4] In the first half of the film we see how obsession with baseball distracts Renard from his work and contributes to him losing his job. Frustrated about paying too much for scalpers' tickets to attend the Giants' Opening Day game, Gil insults a store manager who doesn't want his product and arrives late and misses a meeting with a client. His increasingly angry and aggressive behavior, insulting his ex-wife when they discuss parenting, shoving her aside as he forces his way into her house, criticizing his son for his lack of confidence about Little League tryouts, threatening his wife's husband with a bat, and yelling insults at players and other fans at the Giants games all show us why his boss, Garrity (Dan Butler), lets Renard go, explaining that "people are scared of you Gil." His job in the company that his father founded gone and a restraining order in place to keep him away from his son, Renard snaps and becomes what Cohan calls "the crazed fan [who] resorts to violence to restore his masculine agency."[5]

For the remainder of *The Fan*, that agency is entirely defined for Renard by his obsession with Rayburn and the Giants. Having no hope to repair his own work and family lives, Gil becomes focused on the Giants slugger's early season slump under the pressure of living up to expectations created by the free agent deal that he signed in the off-season. After winning three MVP awards playing for the Atlanta Braves, Raynard accepted a $40 million contract offer from the Giants, but seems unnerved by the media and fan pressure to earn his big salary and the unwillingness of his San Francisco teammate Juan Primo (Benicio del Toro) to give him the uniform number eleven that Bobby believes had brought him luck in the past. Initially Gil is supportive of his favorite player, telling sports talk radio host Jewel (Ellen Barkin) that Rayburn is worth every penny of the $40 million: "He's worth twice that, three times that, yes sir." Yet when Rayburn continues to struggle and Gil hears him on the radio state that "he needs all the help he can get" to convince Primo to give up the number eleven, Renard tracks down the Latino player and brutally knifes him to death in a hotel sauna.

The tragedy of Primo's killing makes clear to Rayburn that his performance anxiety is trivial in comparison to his teammate's murder and he begins hitting. Yet Renard isn't satisfied with enjoying the increased productivity of his hero and team from afar and begins stalking the star player's beach house. When he sees Rayburn's son Sean (Brandon Hammond) struggling in the waves, Renard dives in to save the boy from drowning. Shaken by the incident and thankful for the stranger's help, Rayburn invites Gil into his home, but the men's subsequent conversation turns hostile. Gil seems to expect that Rayburn will thank him for removing Primo from the picture and getting back his lucky uniform number, but when instead the Giants player comments that die-hard fans are "losers" and "the only person you should play for is yourself," Renard becomes enraged. Sensing that Gil is dangerous, Rayburn calls it a night, but later finds that Sean is missing from his bed. Renard soon contacts Rayburn and insists that if he doesn't hit a home run in his next game and "dedicate it to Gil, a true fan," he will kill the boy. This threat sets up a nightmarish and chaotic conclusion in which the police shoot and kill Renard on the Giants' field and Sean is rescued from an old ballpark where he had been held captive, surrounded by memorabilia from Renard's fandom and childhood baseball glories.

Cohan interprets *The Fan* as about "the danger of fandom not merely as a delusion that emasculates and disempowers, but also as one that produces explicit violence and racism."[6] The fan obsession of the De Niro character certainly disempowers him, and his targeting first a Latino player, Primo, and then the African American star, Rayburn, for retribution supports Cohan's analysis of Renard's violence as an attempt to reassert his White privilege. Nevertheless, the psychosis of the Renard character is so extreme that viewer sympathy with his grievance on grounds of reverse gender, ethnic, or racial discrimination seems unlikely. Cohan argues that *The Fan* "allows its viewers little sympathy for its fan protagonist."[7] Yet a possible point of identification with Gil's problems occurs in the scenes showing his lost economic opportunity such as when Garrity criticizes his lack of enthusiasm for selling the company's outsourced knives that are of lesser quality than those his father made when he ran the business. Garrity tells Gil that he is out of touch with a contemporary world in which people "want cheap foreign product. When that fucks up, they want to replace it."

That exchange between Renard and his boss about a new globalized economy resonates with a feeling pervasive among disgruntled baseball fans at the time *The Fan* was released about how the greed of owner profits and the rapidly rising salaries of free agent players had debased their beloved game symbolic of the fair rewards available to all, not just a select few, in return for integrity and productivity. While the extreme violence perpetrated by the Gil Renard character in *The Fan* seems like little more than a failed attempt to build a film around the previous success De Niro had seen playing psychotic characters, the underlying causes of the character's economic impotence, the portrayal of Primo as a cultural other taking away opportunity from native-born players, and the movie's characterization of Rayburn as a selfish star in the age of free agency fit a broader fan discontent at the time it was made. Garrity's mention of "cheap foreign product" would resonate with some U.S. baseball fans who may have found it hard to identify with Latin American players like Primo who increasingly in the 1990s were being brought into MLB to give owners good production at a lower cost. And just prior to their tense exchange at the beach house when Gil confronts Rayburn about his lack of appreciation of the fans, Renard, pretending ignorance, asks the Giants star if he is Barry Bonds. In 1993 Bonds had signed a six year, $44 million free agent deal with San Francisco. Although the Giants' plan was to make the team more competitive, bring fans to the ballpark, and improve television ratings, Bruce Jenkins, a baseball writer for the *San Francisco Chronicle*, called Bonds "probably the most consistently bitter, arrogant and stand-offish player in the Giants' modern history." *New York Daily News* columnist Bill Madden agreed, writing that "Bonds merely makes it clear on a day-in, day-out basis he doesn't give a damn how the fans regard him."[8]

This harsh characterization of Barry Bonds is not fair to him, but the film nonetheless invokes the Giants slugger to villainize free agency. Burns in his

Tenth Inning film explains Bonds's disregard for negative views of him held by some fans and media as prompted by his resentment about how he saw his extraordinary talent as in fact undervalued for reasons of race and about how his father Bobby had been mistreated during his playing career from the late 1960s through the early 1980s. *The Fan*, however, is less interested in the factors that contributed to Barry Bonds's conflict with media and fans and instead uses him to refer to a pervasive discontent among fans, especially after the 1994–1995 strike, toward what they regarded as arrogant, overpaid players. While viewers hopefully don't identify with Renard's psychotic targeting of Latino and Black players for his murderous revenge, the Primo character and invocation of Bonds to characterize Raymond evoke a broader anger among fans about the business of baseball and how it increasingly reflected a global economy built on outsourced jobs and consolidation of wealth at the top.

Baseball's labor issues in 1994 and 1995 contributed to that fan anger. In an effort to roll back the players' salary gains resulting from free agency MLB owners in March 1994 proposed a payroll cap that would limit compensation. Players balked, starting a work stoppage in August of that year, and in September 1994 commissioner Budd Selig announced a cancelation of the remainder of the season, including the World Series.[9] Not only did the loss of the fall classic upset fans, but the following spring they were presented with the owners' threat to use replacement players. It wasn't until federal judge Sonia Sotomayor in March 1995 ordered both sides to resume play under the previous contract and negotiate a new deal that games started again. Unfortunately, the agreement that was reached the following fall added insult to injury for fans: its institution of revenue sharing and later a luxury tax on payroll created incentives for most teams to tank, not sign the best players and then get paid for losing by the handful of big-market teams that dominated the sport.[10]

Journalist Hannah Keyser has written about fan reaction to the 1994–1995 conflict between players and owners. She quotes Dave Anderson in the *New York Times*, who reported on fans' plans to boycott MLB games when they resumed. "People no longer cared about baseball," Anderson wrote, "and some might never care again." Average attendance at MLB games dropped from 31,000 per game in 1994 to just 25,000 in 1995. Based on her communication with a 29,000-member-strong Facebook group calling themselves "Baseball 1857 to 1993," Keyser reported a wide range of fan complaints regarding the direction of baseball, not just about the 1994–1995 suspension of play. Some in the group objected to the obsession with home runs hit by PED-fueled players, rule and strategy changes that slowed down and changed the sport, expensive tickets, and what Keyser calls "the shattered sense that the game was bigger than the business."[11]

Regardless of how they may be represented as obsessive, angry, and even violent, or how their emotional engagement and economic contributions are disregarded, baseball fans can still empower themselves through their knowledge of the sport. With its long history and extensive statistical record, baseball challenges fans to build their understanding of the game with research and study. In his history of baseball fandom, Fred Stein understates this tendency when he writes that "statistics have attracted the interest of baseball fans since the game's inception."[12] Ron Shelton, the director of the 1988 film *Bull Durham*, certainly qualifies as an informed baseball fan, although more through participatory experience than erudition. Shelton played minor league baseball in the Baltimore Orioles system for five seasons in the late 1960s and early 1970s, and as a result he distances himself from the scholarship of what he calls the "high minded authors fond of mythologizing America's pastime." "Most of those writers make me nuts," Shelton complains, "because they're not seeing the game I played."[13]

After working as a screenwriter, Shelton got his first chance to direct movies when he was able to sell Orion Pictures on the idea that his story about minor league baseball was one no other director knew more about. It also helped get the film funded that Kevin Costner, who had emerged as a bankable star after making *The Untouchables* and *No Way Out* in 1987, signed on for the lead role as Crash Davis, a veteran catcher for the Durham Bulls who is charged with mentoring a bonus baby pitcher, Ebby LaLoosh (Tim Robbins), with "a million dollar arm and a five cent head." Certainly one reason why *Sports Illustrated* has called *Bull Durham* the best sports film of all time is that it gives the audience an insider's view of professional baseball that only someone with Shelton's background could provide. Yet another part of the film's appeal comes from how it shows respect and affection for the experience of the fan. At the center of the movie's fan perspective is the Susan Sarandon character Annie Savoy, a college English instructor who spends her summers watching and analyzing the Bulls' play and sleeping with a player of her choice.

Bull Durham begins with Annie's voice-over rhapsodizing about her love for what she calls the "church of baseball" as we see a shrine to the game that she has set up in her Durham home. Annie immediately establishes her status as an informed fan who isn't reluctant to share her insights with the Bulls players she befriends. "Baseball is like sex," she proclaims as we watch Annie preparing to go to that night's Bulls game. "You just have to relax and concentrate," she concludes. As Annie leaves her Queen Anne house on a tree-lined street to walk to the ballpark, she adds: "There's a certain amount of life wisdom I give these boys. I can expand their minds." In the subsequent scene we see numerous shots of Annie and the other fans at the ballpark as LaLoosh makes his less than successful professional debut. Annie asserts her control over the meaning of the young pitcher's performance by sending him a note in the dugout explaining that his wildness is due to a failure to bend his back on his delivery to the plate.

In the film's first hour the focus is as much on Annie watching and commenting on Nuke and Crash's play as it is on the performances of two men themselves. Shelton gives us numerous shots of Annie, armed with her scorebook and binoculars and often accompanied by her friend Millie (Jenny Robertson), who with a speed gun records the velocity of Nuke's fastball, watching the men perform and offering suggestions for improvement. When Crash has a tough at bat in which he can't concentrate, we hear Annie encourage him to "just relax" and "take it easy," and when he strikes out she sends him a note of his own explaining that his swing is good but that he's pulling his hips out too early. As Annie and Crash talk the next day at a local batting cage she offers encouragement by informing him that she is aware he is just twenty short of setting the all-time record for home runs hit in the minor leagues. To boost his confidence she tells Ebby, "You need a nickname honey" and christens him Nuke. And when LaLoosh later continues to struggle with his control on the mound, Annie takes more drastic measures, counseling him "Don't think, just throw" and giving the young pitcher a garter belt to wear under his uniform, explaining that it will "help you see things differently . . . you've been pitching out of the wrong side of your brain." Only after Annie further advises Nuke to model his delivery on Fernando Valenzuela and rock and throw while looking upward to the heavens does the young pitcher find his form on the mound.

As Nuke begins pitching effectively and Crash hits home runs in pursuit of the record, the Bulls go on a win streak. This turn in a positive direction for the team starts in the last forty-five minutes of the film as the story moves in a more conventional direction, away from Annie's interpretation and more toward the men's accomplishments on the field. As if to acknowledge her role in guiding the narrative—as well as Nuke and Crash—up to this point in the film, a montage set to the John Fogarty classic "Center-field" begins the Bulls' winning streak, and we hear Annie's voice-over summarize that "everything fell into place.... The Durham Bulls began playing baseball with joy and verve and poetry." Shelton has been complimentary of all three leads in the film, calling Costner's performance "perfect" and Robbins "underrated ... he makes you really care about Nuke." However, the director reserved his strongest praise for Sarandon, describing her performance as "transcendent," perhaps a reference to how—at least for the first half of the film—her character rises above the convention of the supportive wife or girlfriend found in most sports movies to assert instead a much greater degree of interpretative control.

Besides how it gives in to the baseball movie tendency to reaffirm the centrality of White masculinity by focusing on the success of the ballplayers, *Bull Durham* is also ultimately guided by its hybrid genre mix of sports movie with romantic comedy. Once Nuke's success results in his promotion to the major league club, in its last act the movie shifts focus from Annie's fling with the young pitcher to a more meaningful romance with Crash. When in the film's final scene Crash tells Annie that he has decided to retire as a player and pursue an opening to manage, she tearfully tells him "You'd be great." But as she begins to explain why he would be a good manager, Costner's character cuts her off, informing Annie that he can hear her theories later but for now "I just wanna be." "I can do that too," answers the Sarandon character quietly. Even though the movie ends with Annie's voice-over, it is now not to present her view of things but just to quote a male commentary, that of poet Walt Whitman, about how "baseball ... will repair our losses and be a blessing to us."

Yet regardless of how Shelton qualifies his strong female lead with the demands of Hollywood genres and their celebration of the heterosexual couple and male accomplishment, *Bull Durham* is still an assertion of the value of fan knowledge and enjoyment. After his failed career as a ballplayer, Shelton has explained that until the success of this baseball film he could no longer watch the sport he had loved so much: "The movie kind of liberated me from what I view as my own failure.... [By making *Bull Durham*] I was able to enjoy the game again."[14] Certainly part of Shelton's liberation from the shortcomings of his own baseball career came from his creation of male players in *Bull Durham* who are more successful than he was. Yet his movie also succeeds because of both the unpretentious insider view of professional baseball that it offers and its acknowledgment of how insightful and enjoyable the experience of an informed fan can be.

Although its tone and conclusion are much more positive than *The Fan*, the 2005 romantic comedy *Fever Pitch* also focuses on a character whose masculinity is questioned because of his fandom. Yet for Ben Wrightman (Jimmy Fallon) his extensive knowledge of baseball complements his job as a high school math teacher, enabling him to understand and control his life. In his thirties, Ben may not have proven himself to be "'man' enough to have found a partner," but he clearly enjoys his teaching, in part because it leaves him the summers open to follow his beloved Boston Red Sox.[15] Ben's energy and good sense of humor endear him to his students, and in a scene in which we see him teaching the class is attentive and he shares a joke with them at the expense of a sourpuss principal who has popped in to chide Wrightman about his lenience. Baseball for Ben is also about humor and socializing, whether with his male buddies who talk about the game over drinks at the bar, on a trip to Florida for spring training, or most importantly using his coveted Red Sox season tickets to enjoy games with other diehard fans who for years—some for decades—sit in the same section at Fenway.

On a field trip with a group of his students to show them possible careers for a college math major, Ben meets Lindsey (Drew Barrymore), a successful investment analyst whose brains and hard work have put her on the fast track up the corporate ladder. The students enjoy learning about Lindsey's job, and after taking them back to school, Ben returns to her office to ask her out. The two begin dating, but typical of their "dumb white guy comedies" directors Peter and Bobby Farrelly poke fun at Ben's fan obsession, especially in a goofy interview on ESPN during the Florida trip when he tells network anchor Steve Levy that "the Red Sox, sex and breathing" are the three most important things in his life in that order. Besides how the obsession shown in the TV interview concerns her, Lindsey's yuppie friend adds to her reservations about Ben when she tells her during a gym workout that the problem with dating a school teacher is "they have a small . . . income." As Cohan points out about this joke, "The pregnant pause amplifies the double entendre, linking economic limitations to sexual inadequacy."[16]

Regardless of how such humor at the Fallon character's expense helps build the doubt about the relationship that rom-coms like *Fever Pitch* inevitably resolve, we see that Ben is not only happy with his life but also very much aware of why his combination of teaching math and baseball fandom work for him:

> BEN You know what's really great about baseball. You can't fake it. Anything else in life you don't have to be great in. . . . You can fool everyone for a while . . . not baseball. You can either hit a curve ball or you can't. That's the way it works. It's like math. It's orderly. Win or lose, it's fair. It all adds up. It's not as confusing or ambiguous as uh. . . .
>
> LINDSEY Life?

Like the poaching fans that Henry Jenkins celebrates for their ability to select from media texts what enables them to make meaning from their fandom, Ben here explains to Lindsey why teaching math and following baseball complement each other in his life. Regardless of his modest teacher's income and lack of career ambition, Lindsey seems persuaded by the qualities that Ben's equilibrium instills in him: he is attentive and considerate, he makes her laugh, and they have sexual chemistry. But her doubt about their relationship reemerges when they have an enjoyable evening at a friend's birthday party but afterward Ben complains about missing a particularly exciting Red Sox comeback win against the hated Yankees. What Ben's grouchiness makes clear to Lindsey is that as much as they get along well baseball is just as important to him as she is. This realization leads to a separation until Lindsey learns that Ben has reluctantly decided to sell his Sox season tickets. It's at that point that she appears to understand that baseball isn't the problem but rather part of what makes Ben attractive to her. In an absurdly comic reuniting of the couple scene typical of rom-com, Lindsey runs across the field at Fenway during a game to tell Ben not to give up the season tickets. She has decided that she can accept his fan obsession as part of the order and happiness of his life just as he accepts her workaholic schedule and ambition for what Cohan calls "traditional markers of family and career success."[17]

Cohen asserts that Ben overcomes his "deviance" and "gets the girl" as an example of Hollywood's default assumption that White men can always assert control when they really need it.[18] In fact, Ben doesn't change much in *Fever Pitch*. Rather he and Lindsey both realize they have to accept each other's choices. Certainly the anger and cynicism that fuel the disastrous violence of the Gil Renard character in *The Fan* make it an exception to most Hollywood baseball films in which a White male protagonist succeeds. By contrast, *Fever Pitch*, like *Bull Durham*, is a much better example of what Cohan calls "the relatability of sports fandom," how it can help make sense of and add enjoyment to living.[19]

Jenkins values fan culture not only because of the resistant readings of popular media that it enables but also for how it fosters community. "Fans assert their own right to form interpretations," Jenkins writes; they "raid mass culture, claiming its materials for their own use, reworking them as the basis for their own cultural creations and social interactions."[20] While Annie in *Bull Durham* and Ben in *Fever Pitch* to some extent connect with other fans as they offer the kind of oral pronouncements about baseball that make them what Jenkins calls "active producers and manipulators of meaning," another filmic representation of baseball fandom that puts greater emphasis on its communal character is the Cruz Angeles 2010 documentary *Fernando Nation*.[21]

Fernando Nation emphasizes the inspirational impact that Mexican lefthander Fernando Valenzuela's sudden stardom for the LA Dodgers in the 1980s had on Latinx fans. Although there were two million Latinx residents of Los Angeles County in 1980, many of them from or with family roots in Mexico, Valenzuela was the team's first Mexican star. Ironically, filmmaker Cruz Angeles begins his documentary about Valenzuela by showing how when the Dodgers decided to move to Los Angeles from Brooklyn in 1957 space was made for their new stadium in the Chavez Ravine area by removing its Mexican and Mexican American residents. Early in the film television producer Estela Lopez explains how the city claimed eminent domain to seize the land and J. Gerardo Lopez, former editor of the LA Spanish-language newspaper *La Opinion*, describes how "many" Chavez Ravine residents "were removed by force" as we see black-and-white footage of those evictions by police.

In his 2019 history of the Dodgers, Jason Turbow writes that Chavez Ravine in the late 1940s was home to about four thousand residents living in modest homes, without a unified sewage system or paved streets. Although the area is located just a mile northeast of downtown LA, its rugged hills at that time looked like a rural area with family orchards and gardens and animals grazing freely. However, in late 1949 a plan was proposed for the city to use federal money to build ten thousand units of public housing in Chavez Ravine. The plan included new schools, churches, a shopping center, and an auditorium for public events. Fearing the city of Los Angeles would claim eminent domain and take their land, some residents sold out and moved, but the development plan became a political football in the 1953 mayoral election when conservative candidate Norris Poulson "decried the socialist nature of subsidized housing."[22] After Poulson was elected, the development plan was scrapped, opening the way for the land to be sold to Walter O'Malley and the Dodgers when they moved west four years later.[23] *Fernando Nation* briefly summarizes this history of how LA politics took the land away from Latinx residents in Chavez Ravine, quoting writer Paul Rodriguez about the bad feeling that persisted toward the Dodgers after the stadium was completed in 1962: "Mexicans for the most part wouldn't go to the games. They had the stain of 'Remember Chavez Ravine.'"

Despite how Latinx residents had been pushed aside to clear the way for his new stadium, Dodgers owner O'Malley soon turned to the idea of finding a Mexican player who would appeal to them as Jackie Robinson had African Americans. The growing Latinx population in New York had prompted the Dodgers when they were still in Brooklyn to begin scouting in Latin America beginning in 1950. Dodgers general manager Al Campanis regretted losing Roberto Clemente, whom he had signed in 1954, but was later selected in the rookie draft by the Pirates when Brooklyn made the mistake of not adding him to its major league roster.[24] Although the Dodgers had signed several Mexican players previously, including Bobby Castillo, who taught Valenzuela how to throw what would become his signature screwball, it wasn't until 1979 that their scout Mike Brito signed the nineteen-year-old after seeing him perform in the Mexican League. The young pitcher became what we hear Jamie Jarrin, the Dodgers Spanish-language broadcaster, call in *Fernando Nation* "un Sandy Koufax Mexicano" to excite Latinos the way the Hall of Fame left-hander had made Jews into LA fans. Yet just as Cruz Angeles begins by telling the story of Chavez Ravine and the team's new stadium to communicate the irony of the anti-Latinx origins of the Dodgers franchise in a film about the team's Mexican star, likewise he shows the incongruity of how Valenzuela arrived in LA at a time when resistance to immigration was growing. In 1980, when Valenzuela first joined the Dodgers, Ronald Reagan was elected president, unemployment in the United States was high, and immigration raids targeting Mexicans were soon under way.

After establishing the larger social context of ethnicity and immigration for a better understanding of Valenzuela's story, the ESPN documentary then focuses on how the strong positive response to his successful pitching for the Dodgers was so pervasive—among Latinxs and with fans from other backgrounds as well—that it came to be referred to as Fernandomania. On Opening Day in 1981, Valenzuela's first full year playing in Los Angeles, he shut out the division champion Houston Astros and went on to go 8-0 with five shutouts to start the season. Valenzuela would win Rookie of the Year and the Cy Young Award as the best pitcher in the National League that year, and the Dodgers won the World Series from the Yankees. Valenzuela also boosted attendance dramatically, not only at Dodger Stadium but around the league. For his first start at Shea Stadium in New York, the crowd numbered 39,848, more than triple the 11,358 per game the Mets were averaging in 1981.[25]

Yet enthusiasm for Valenzuela was especially strong among Latinx fans in LA. The *Los Angeles Times* reported on "Valenzuela's ability to pull in as many as 10,000 extra Latino fans on the days he pitched at Dodger Stadium."[26] Besides the usual lineup of media people, historians, and former players explaining what happened and why, filmmaker Angeles foregrounds in his documentary the comments of numerous Latinx fans during the period of Fernandomania about what his success meant to them. One Latino watching a game with friends at a bar asserts that "if it wasn't for Valenzuela . . . the Dodgers wouldn't be up there." Another at a Dodger Stadium game states emphatically that "Valenzuela is great. I love him," and a third explains that "Nunca me pierdo un partido de beisball cuando pitcha Valenzuela" (I never miss a baseball game when Valenzuela pitches). Two Latina fans at Dodger Stadium state enthusiastically in the documentary, "We want Valenzuela to keep it up. . . . He is the greatest" and "I think everyone here has Fernando fever!" As if to describe the numerous shots of large numbers of Latino fans at Dodger games with Mexican flags, hand-painted signs exclaiming "Vive Fernando," and even a banner in Dodger colors stating "Esta es mi ciudad" (This is my city), one older fan reflects on Fernandomania by declaring, "El estadio . . . lo invadimos nosotros, los Latinos!" (The Latinos, we invaded the stadium!). By mixing comments from Latinx fans in both Spanish and English, Cruz Angeles supports Klein's comment that the Dodgers with Valenzuela were successful in attracting both Mexican and Mexican American fans. *LA Times* journalist Patrick McDonnell writes about Valenzuela that "not only did he attract Latinos and non-Latinos, his following transcended the broad cultural chasm between Mexican immigrants and U.S. born Mexican Americans."[27]

The enthusiastic statements presented in *Fernando Nation* offer examples of John Fiske's idea of the "enunciative productivity" that "accounts for

FIG. 11 Fernando Valenzuela and a young Latino fan in *Fernando Nation* (2010).

'much of the pleasure of fandom.'"[28] In the Angeles documentary we see and hear repeated examples of Latinx fans who state their emotional connection with and enjoyment of Valenzuela's success. They exemplify the kind of fans whom Jenkins describes as "articulating concerns which often go unvoiced within the dominant media."[29] But as marginalized as they had been previously, the ESPN documentary demonstrates that because of their response to Valenzuela, such fans became an important part of the team's following. Alan Klein quotes a Dodger executive, Kris Rone, who states that by the early 2000s the Dodgers had one million Latinx fans. As Klein puts it, "The Valenzuela windfall turned into part of the Dodgers economic infrastructure."[30]

Valenzuela pitched for the major league minimum salary ($32,500) in his first season. Yet even after all the revenue he brought to the Dodgers in 1981, Valenzuela had to hold out in the spring of his second year for twenty-six days to get a substantial raise. Angeles shows footage of an INS official, Omer Sewell, during the pitcher's holdout warning that "if he doesn't play for the Dodger organization, then ... we would have to ask him to return to his country." Valenzuela's lawyer and agent Dick Moss, who had negotiated baseball's first $1 million salary for pitcher Nolan Ryan with Houston in 1979, explains in the documentary that he eventually got the Dodgers to offer a one-year contract for $350,000. After Valenzuela won nineteen games in 1982 an outside arbitrator awarded him a $1 million contract for his third year. Dodger broadcaster Jarrin explained that the response of Latinx fans during Valenzuela's holdout was one of concern: They "feared that Fernando would sit out for the whole season. They feared losing him."[31]

To avoid viewing Valenzuela's importance only in how he demonstrated the economic viability of increased diversity in baseball, filmmaker Angeles traces not just the unfair treatment by the Dodgers in building their stadium but also the hostility toward Mexican immigrants at the time of his arrival in LA. In response to such anti-immigrant hostility, the focus on the reaction of the Latinx fans to Valenzuela in *Fernando Nation* emphasizes the emotional and motivational impact he would have on them. Labor leader and civil rights activist Dolores Huertes comments in the film that the pride that Valenzuela created for Latinxs "touched people. . . . what he was was also part of them." Writer Rodriguez states that his outstanding performance showed "a Mexican can be as good as anybody." McDonnell notes that Valenzuela's appeal was strongest among those Latinxs who had the least: "He lamented not having had a proper education. He carried himself with a certain humility and pride, striking just the right chord for his core constituency, the working-class Latino[s]."[32] Filmmaker Angeles reinforces this important appeal that Valenzuela had for working-class Latinx fans for whom his success was not just a leisure entertainment experience, an afternoon at the ballpark, or an evening on the couch in front of the TV. For those fans Fernando Valenzuela affirmed the possibility of their success. *Fernando Nation* ends with TV producer Lopez stating that "where so many Mexican families lost a dream [in Chavez Ravine], a Mexican [Valenzuela] came and placed a stake on a new dream."

Fantasy Baseball

Sports fans root for players and teams because they represent something to which those watching feel connected: a city, a school, a country, a family, an ethnic or racial group. But fans also enjoy sporting competition itself because those playing in it deserve attention and admiration. Players play well and therefore embody values of merit and achievement, the preparation and effort that made their good performance possible. Clearly both these forms of appeal are at work for the fans shown in *Bull Durham, Fever*

Pitch, and *Fernando Nation*. Annie and Ben root for players on teams that represent their cities and because of their success on the field. Moreover, for Ben such merit affirms his belief in a world that is orderly like a math equation. For Annie that well-deserved success has come about in part because of her insightful analysis and mentoring. The numerous Latinx fans given a voice in *Fernando Nation* root for Valenzuela because he represents their ethnic group but also because he affirms their hope that rewards for achievement are available to them as well. By contrast, the fundamental dysfunction of the Gil Renard character in *The Fan* occurs because the idea of merit has not been affirmed in his life. Renard looks to baseball for relief from his alienation and anger, telling his young son early in the film that "baseball is better than life, it's fair," but ultimately his loss of his job and family lead him into revenge and violence.

Fantasy sports fandom certainly includes such admiration of athletic achievement, but it also offers an enjoyment that is not just about watching what others do but also comes from what the fan has contributed. Fantasy sports empowers fans by giving them control over the assemblage and maintenance of the team in competition. Such control succeeds or fails in part based on the knowledge of the fan and for many contrasts with their real lives in which they may have a lesser degree of control. Of course knowledge counts for "real" sports fans as well, so that they can understand and discuss what happens and why in the competition they watch. Yet in fantasy sports that knowledge matters even more because it has been used to assemble the team that is competing.

The game of fantasy baseball, in which participants, "managers," select real MLB players to form teams and compete using those players' statistics, has a long history. One of the first versions to become popular and influence the growth of fantasy baseball was the Rotisserie League, developed by writer and editor Daniel Okrent in 1980. As a student at the University of Michigan in the 1970s Okrent had learned of an earlier incarnation of fantasy baseball called the National Baseball Seminar that his professor, Robert Sklar, had played in the 1960s with his colleague Bill Gamson. Okrent developed the rules for a more complex version of the game that he named Rotisserie Baseball in honor of La Rotisserie Francaise, a New York City restaurant where he and friends met to plan their fantasy league.[33]

Okrent's Rotisserie Baseball—like all fantasy leagues—simulated for its participants the control of team ownership and management. Sklar has commented that Okrent's intent in Rotisserie Baseball "was to make you a virtual GM," and Okrent has added that he set up the process for selecting players so each of the participants had to work within a budget and players' preestablished values as a "way of forcing people to allocate resources like a real owner." Okrent also carefully analyzed the six teams in the National League Eastern Division of MLB and came up with eight statistical categories for his game—average, home runs, RBI, steals, (pitcher) wins, saves, ERA, and WHIP—that he explains "tracked close to the actual standings." In other words, he chose the statistics to determine the outcomes of Rotisserie fantasy games that mattered most in real big league baseball.

Another aspect of the Rotisserie League that distinguished it from previous versions of fantasy baseball was that participants used future statistics rather than those the players had already put up. This also required that participants, like real MLB owners, general managers, and managers, predict the productivity of players. *USA Today* initially provided Rotisserie players with an important source of information on players, and as the popularity of fantasy baseball grew it helped the paper's circulation to such a degree that its parent company, Gannett, in April 1991 began publishing *Baseball Weekly*, devoted exclusively to compiling information about player performance. One month after starting publication *Baseball Weekly* had already reached a circulation of 250,000.[34]

The internet spurred the growth of fantasy baseball because it allowed managers to research players more easily and also gave them a platform for their games and facilitated their communication. As Okrent puts it, "When the Internet came around, there was an explosion."[35] During the 1990s participation in fantasy sports grew dramatically. Todd Nesbit and Kerry King-Adzima point out that the fantasy sports industry "would experience a rapid expansion in the mid-1990s with the proliferation of online, automated games."[36] The Fantasy Sports & Gaming Association reports that by 2019 there were 59.3 million people in the United States and Canada participating in fantasy sports, of whom 39 percent were doing baseball. Major media corporations such as Yahoo, CBS Sports, Fox Sports, and ESPN have all become "prominent providers of automated free-to-play fantasy leagues" that are monetized via advertising revenue.[37]

The internet has also made possible the development of daily fantasy competition, resulting in what Darren Heitner calls "the new generation of . . . well-funded gaming startups in daily fantasy sports [that] . . . . want you to bet on your favorite players or team through their app each night when you turn on your TV."[38] Supported by hundreds of millions in capital from major media companies and professional sports leagues like NBC, Comcast, Fox Sports, MLB, the NHL, the NBA, and the NFL, and with tens of millions of dollars spent on advertising, companies like FanDuel and DraftKings have turned fantasy sports into betting, but without the regulation most sports wagering faces. The Unlawful Internet Gambling Enforcement Act of 2006 regarded fantasy sports as games of skill, not chance, and therefore did not define them as gambling. The investment in daily fantasy from MLB in particular has been prompted by how it promises to "bring new ... fans, particularly younger fans to ... baseball."[39] Specifically, those who run MLB believe that daily fantasy sports "can leverage consumers' cravings for fantasy content into higher ratings" for games on TV and the internet.[40] To that point, Nesbit and King report a "35% increase in viewership of MLB games ... for fantasy sports participants," and Heitner sums up, "For a sport that is having trouble attracting a younger audience, it seems like a natural move for MLB to make."[41]

Besides the feeling of empowerment that control of a team offers, and in the case of daily play the financial incentive, fantasy baseball also attracts fans as a social activity. Okrent joked that at the time the Rotisserie League started, Robert Sklar's girlfriend, knowing how much he enjoyed the camaraderie of fantasy baseball, told him "their relationship was over" if he joined the league. On a more serious note, Okrent comments that he and his friends' participation for years in fantasy baseball "cemented some very deep friendships."[42]

In Judd Apatow's 2007 blockbuster hit comedy *Knocked Up*, Debbie (Leslie Mann) sneaks into a strange suburban house and catches her husband Pete (Paul Rudd) dressed in a Baltimore Orioles cap and jersey, participating in a fantasy baseball draft. After asking Pete "What the fuck is this?" he responds to her excitedly, "It's our fantasy baseball draft.... I told you all about this." *Knocked Up* creates most of its humor at the expense of the two male main characters, Pete and Ben (Seth Rogan), who seem unwilling to take on the responsibilities of relationship and family, but ultimately accept the idea that such commitments are worthwhile. As much as the scene of the baseball draft involves the stereotype of the socially maladjusted fan whose obsession creates problems with work and family, Apatow's film also shows clearly how Pete really enjoys his participation in fantasy baseball. In fact, it's exactly that Pete enjoys it so much that concerns his wife,

Debbie. After she storms out of the draft, Pete follows her to the street where they have the following exchange:

PETE   It's a fantasy baseball draft. I'm not cheating or anything.
DEBBIE   It's worse. . . . This is you wanting to be with your friends more than your family.

Sports fandom has traditionally offered people "a sense of identity and belonging."[43] For baseball fans that identity has often implied a shared history, knowing not only the great players of the game and their achievements, but also how baseball as the national pastime has functioned to unify this country around shared values of fairness, equal opportunity, and inclusion in the face of the challenges brought by its history of social division, in particular along lines of class, race, and immigration status. Unfortunately, at times such complex history has given way to nostalgia, "a regressive looking backwards . . . intent on recuperating an imaginary, illusory past."[44] In media representation of baseball in recent decades this nostalgic discourse has often railed against owner and free agent player greed and performance-enhancing drugs and pointed to the past as a time when baseball was "better."

Allison Burr-Miller notes that fantasy baseball inevitability relies on a convergence of media texts, from the internet and television primarily, that not only speed up the pace of baseball to fit modern life but also give fans the freedom to draw on information that fits their own interpretations of what the game means to them as well as connect with friends and other fans. This social dimension to fantasy baseball Burr-Miller describes as merging the online with the offline: "My experience with fantasy baseball participation has helped me maintain relationships with a group of friends who are now spread out across the country. While most of our discussion of baseball and updates on each other's lives are mediated, each year near the beginning of baseball season we get together and hold a draft party. At those parties we celebrate birthdays, concoct ritualized drinks and share news of big life events, all in the name of fantasy baseball. Such parties are not rare."[45]

Wall Street Journal columnist Sam Walker, in his book *Fantasyland*, comments that however competitive fantasy baseball may get, it is "at bottom, an elaborate excuse to hang out with your buddies."[46] Burr-Miller concludes that fantasy baseball therefore allows fans to empower themselves using their knowledge of the game, to connect with others rather than fall prey to nostalgic phobias. Seen this way, Burr-Miller regards fantasy as "a new way to watch baseball . . . to talk about baseball, and . . . to imagine baseball."[47] What Burr-Miller describes here is a social dimension to fantasy baseball that presents a potential response to the inherent isolation implied by the more nostalgic, backward-looking idea of the game as a celebration of an imagined and exclusive American past. Baseball fandom at its best is such an inclusive activity, offering a model for a civic life that could benefit us all.

6

Learning the Game

• • • • • • • • • • • • • • • • • • • •

> Little League baseball is a very good
> thing because it keeps the parents off
> the streets.
> —Yogi Berra

While most baseball films focus on adults demonstrating the skills that
make them heroes of the game, some instead tell the stories of young people
learning to play. Such movies about kids playing baseball inevitably involve
the influence of adults as parents and/or coaches and in the process show
the grown-ups teaching the young players more than just how to pitch, hit,
field, throw, and run the bases. *The Bad News Bears* (1976) is one such film
about youth baseball and its adult mentors. The movie concerns a group of
outsider kids who, in part because of their undeveloped skills and in part
because of where they come from, are looking for a chance to play Little
League baseball. But as much as *The Bad News Bears* is about the kids and
their opportunity on the field, it is also about the adults who want to stand
in their way or who claim to be guiding them.

The story opens with an extreme long shot of a lush, green park complex
in the San Fernando Valley north of Los Angeles, with mountains in the
background and a baseball practice taking place on the diamond in the

foreground. The camera pans left to show Buttermaker (Walter Matthau) arriving in his beat-up Cadillac convertible. After he parks, Buttermaker immediately reaches for a beer from the cooler in the back seat and spikes it with a shot of Jim Beam taken from the glove compartment. Whitewood (Ben Piazza), a liberal city council member with photos of Martin Luther King and the Kennedys on his office wall, arrives with his son Toby (David Stambaugh) and slips Buttermaker a check to coach the Bears. "It's a damn shame none of the fathers had the time for it," he laments. The Bears are made up of the kids no other team wants, and Whitewood, clearly as a political move to gain and retain supporters, has used a class-action suit to get them into North Valley Little League. Buttermaker is also an outsider. Having been a minor league pitcher when he was younger, he now gets by cleaning pools and drinks heavily. During a preseason practice with the Bears he passes out on the mound surrounded by a ring of empty beer cans.

In his book about the intersection of the 1960s counterculture and American athletics, David Zang calls *The Bad News Bears* "the most subversive sports film ever made."[1] In Zang's view, it rejects the narrative of most Hollywood sports movies about White and male protagonists who develop "character" from their achievement in competition. More specifically, the film subverts the assumptions about kids' recreational sports, in this case Little League baseball, as activities in which adults guide young people to the acquisition of self-confidence and the right values. The film shows the influence of the counterculture through its acceptance of social difference and by rejecting the competition central to a traditional sports ethos. In part because of the influence of that countercultural mindset, no baseball movies had been made from 1962 until 1973 when Paramount released a distinctly antiheroic adaptation of Mark Harris's novel *Bang the Drum Slowly*, in which Robert De Niro plays a backup catcher for the Yankees who dies of cancer. Vivian Sobchack explains this dry spell as due to the fact that the "'imagined community' and the utopian space previously figured by baseball on the screen were so completely at odds with the cultural upheavals in the America of the 1960s."[2]

The kids on the Bears represent the promise that opportunity is a fundamental right in American society. In contrast to the uniformly White male makeup of the other teams in North Valley Little League, the Bears include kids who got left out: an African American, Ahmad (Erin Blunt); two Mexican brothers, Jose (Jaime Escobedo) and Miguel (George Gonzales); a Jewish kid, Rudi (David Pollack); a girl, Amanda (Tatum O'Neal);

and Lupus (Quinn Smith), a shy blond boy whose lack of assertive masculinity makes many of the other kids and their parents uneasy. The Bears are such a catchall for those who have been marginalized that they even include an angry White kid, Tanner (Chris Barnes), who loudly voices the biases underlying the league's culture. Sounding like a miniature Archie Bunker, Tanner, when it becomes apparent that the Bears lack much skill on the baseball field, blurts out, "All we got on this team are a bunch of Jews, Spics, Niggers, pansies and a bugger-eating moron." Throughout the movie Tanner is so eloquent in his offensive statements that it's clear they aren't spontaneous but rather voice prejudices he has heard from adults.

As they purport to parent and coach the kids, the other main adult characters in the film repeatedly act and speak in a manner that shows the toxic thinking that Tanner articulates with his insults. Cleveland (Joyce Van Patten), who oversees the management of the league, rejects the presence of the Bears, complaining that "goddam class action suits are gonna ruin this country." When Kelly (Jackie Earle Haley), a defiant young man in sunglasses, biker boots, and jeans who later joins the Bears, rides on the field with his motorcycle, Cleveland chases him down and yells angrily: "You little punk. I'll deck that kid." Even Bears parents display a destructive anger driven by their obsession with success in competition. After his son lets a grounder get by him during the first practice, one of the Bears dads yells, "Damn it Reggie, attack that ball," and later, when his son misses an opportunity to get an out in the first game, the same dad calls out: "You gotta tag him dummy."

But among all the adult anger and bad behavior, the most destructive parenting in the film comes from another coach in the league, Turner (Vic Morrow), who leads the Yankees team. In a reference to the Sergeant Saunders character he played for five seasons (1962–1967) on the hit ABC World War II drama *Combat!*, Morrow as Turner barks out orders to the boys on his team as if they were solders fighting under his command. He also vents his frustration and anger toward Buttermaker and the Bears like they are the enemy trying to invade "his" league. After the Yankees beat the Bears in the season's first game 26-0, Turner rudely tells Buttermaker: "Your team has no right being on that field. . . . Do this league a favor . . . just drop out."

Although Buttermaker initially shows great patience with his players' insecurities and the overbearing coaches and parents, in reaction to Turner's provocations he too becomes obsessed with winning at all costs. He recruits Amanda, the eleven-year-old daughter of an ex-girlfriend whom he had previously taught to pitch, to join the team. Although Amanda initially dismisses Buttermaker's invitation, telling him that she is now more interested in modeling and dance and "I'm through with that tomboy stuff," he appeals to her pride by doubting she would be an effective pitcher and then seals the deal by offering to pay for ballet lessons if she'll join the Bears.

Another recruit, Kelly, Buttermaker also pursues more for how he will help the Bears win than to offer a positive sports experience. Zang sees the addition of these two ringer players, Amanda and Kelly, as further proof that the film rejects the conventional sports film narrative of likeable underdogs who outwork the competition and demonstrate their character in achieving success. Rather, he states, "Real underdogs . . . possess an aura of moral superiority. . . . The Bears have no special sense of . . . worthiness."[3] Yet beyond recruiting Amanda and Kelly, the most destructive manifestation of Buttermaker's message to the kids that all that matters is winning comes through the increasingly hostile and insulting statements he makes when they don't perform. To win a game he orders Kelly in center field to go after any ball he can get to, even if it requires taking plays away from his teammates. However, when Kelly hesitates to cut in front of Rudi in left field and the latter drops a fly ball, allowing a run to score, Buttermaker confronts his center fielder after the inning: "When I give you an order I expect you to follow it . . . grab yourself a god damn bat and let's get that run back." Clearly winning as a Little League coach for Buttermaker addresses some need for affirmation that his own mostly unsuccessful baseball career left unfulfilled, yet he seems unwilling to do what is required to mentor the kids to improve their baseball skills and teamwork to achieve that result.

After the game in which he chews out Kelly for not catching everything he can, Buttermaker has another ugly exchange, this time with Amanda. She suggests that they have dinner and see a movie with her mother, a clear sign that she wants Buttermaker to resume a fatherlike role in her life. He rejects the invitation, telling her, "You're a terrific kid. You shouldn't be hanging around with me . . . I like drinking too much . . . I'm a bum." But when Amanda persists, reminding him how he taught her to pitch, Buttermaker's patience runs out and he explodes. Throwing beer in her face he yells: "Goddamit! Can't you get it through your thick head I don't want your company!"

Yet as much as the adults' aggressive behavior and obsession with winning in *The Bad News Bears* undermine the idea of youth sports as a site of character building, what is even more subversive in the film is how the kids themselves rebel. As part of the counterculture's revision of the sports ethos, sociologist Jack Scott in his 1971 book *The Athletic Revolution* advocated for the players' interests to supersede those of coaches.[4] Throughout *The Bad News Bears*, a big part of the movie's humor comes from how some of the players speak with a vulgarity and bravado that mimics the selfish adults, but as the competition of the league reaches a climax in the championship game between the Yankees and Bears, the Little Leaguers reject the parents' influence with their actions. The big game starts badly, as Tanner and Kelly get in a fight during warm-ups over the latter hogging all the plays in the previous game. Buttermaker breaks up the scuffle and tells them sternly that it was his idea for Kelly to catch every ball. "We're in the championship aren't we? That's what you wanted wasn't it?," he tells the other kids.

As the tense championship game opens, both coaches reach new lows in their verbal abuse of their players. "You want to win don't ya? That's what you showed up for, every damn one of ya?," yells Buttermaker from the dugout. For his part, Turner is equally harsh in his criticism. When one of his players grounds out and doesn't run hard, he berates him: "What the hell's a matter with you. You come here to play ball?" As the coaches yell at their players, director Michael Richie gives us reaction shots of the kids, not responding but clearly disgusted with the men's misbehavior. Like Kelly the previous day, Rudi disobeys Buttermaker's order, in this case to let himself be hit by a pitch to get on base, and grounds out. Buttermaker angrily kicks the dugout wall and grabs the boy by the arm and shoves him to the bench while yelling, "I told you not to swing you idiot. . . . Next time I tell you to do something goddammit you do it or you're off this team!" The manager then caps off his tantrum by yelling at the whole team: "Don't you want to beat those bastards!" The dugout falls into shocked silence as Buttermaker realizes he has gone too far and is losing control of the kids. After an awkward pause, he lowers his voice and tells the players "Alright. Get out there and do the best you can."

Turner as well faces rebellion when his abusive behavior goes too far. Before the final game he had threatened his players that if they were to lose "you're gonna have to live with it." He later visits the mound to tell his son Joey (Brandon Cruz) not to give the Bears' catcher Engelberg (Gary Lee Cavagnaro) anything to hit. However, Joey, angered by the opposing hitter's taunts, aims a pitch at Engelberg's head. Turner rushes back to the mound and yells at his son, "You tried to hit him!" When the boy denies it, Turner slaps his son, knocking him to the ground. Just as with the Bears reaction in the dugout earlier to Buttermaker's tirade, this is a watershed moment and the entire field goes silent in shock. Joey proceeds to let Engelberg hit a home run despite the frustration of his father and then leaves the field, dropping the ball at the coach's feet. Not only does his son quitting make clear that Turner's parenting and coaching have failed, the beanball pitch that prompted the coach's loss of control also shows how he had taught his son the violent aggression he displayed by slapping the boy.

Seeing Turner's misbehavior confirms Buttermaker's realization that winning doesn't justify the terrible model of misbehavior such aggressiveness presents to the kids. He puts his four weakest players into the game, even though it may jeopardize the possibility of winning. After Buttermaker makes these substitutions Whitewood comes to the dugout and questions the move. When Buttermaker tells him that all the kids need a chance to play, the liberal politician betrays his commitment to opportunity for all by responding angrily: "Don't give me that righteous bullshit. We've got a chance to win!"

The rebellion started by the disobedience of Kelly, Rudi, and Turner's son reaches its climax after the Yankees win a close game 7-6. Buttermaker passes out beer to all his players, telling them they should be proud. As they hold a ridiculously large trophy for winning and the Bears receive a token award for second place, one of the players on Turner's team tells the Bears, "We treated you pretty unfair all season. We want to apologize. We still don't think you're all that good . . . [but] you got guts." Tanner speaks for the Bears when he responds, "Hey Yankees you can take your apology and your trophy and shove it straight up your ass!" The formerly shy Lupus punctuates Tanner's defiance by throwing the second place trophy at the Yankees players, adding, "And another thing, just wait till next year!" The irreverent baseball film then ends with the Bears' raucous celebration, pouring beer on each other in rebellion against the obsession with winning represented throughout the story by the adults. The movie's final image repeats the extreme long shot of the field with which it started, showing the Bears players celebrating their rebellion in the background and the American flag beyond the outfield fence in the left foreground, asserting its new idea of winning in the national pastime as about whom it includes rather than whom it excludes.

Like *The Bad News Bears*, *The Sandlot* (1993) is a film about kids playing baseball and in the process negotiating the influence of adults. Following the lead of the other grown-ups in *The Bad News Bears*, Buttermaker at first pushes on his team an all-consuming ethos of competition until he realizes that most of his players develop more confidence from the modest improvement gained by just playing and feeling part of a supportive group. Set in an earlier time, before the world of organized sports became so prominent in young people's lives, *The Sandlot* shows adults who are mostly removed from the world of baseball that is important to the preteen boys in the film, yet they still model ideas of gender that influence the kids' developing identities.

Rather than foregrounding the challenge of the counterculture to the values of the older generation, *The Sandlot* avoids such social critique and makes a nostalgic jump back in time to 1962. The narrative is presented as a flashback from thirty years later by the story's main character, Scotty Smalls (Arliss Howard), as an adult doing TV broadcasts for the Dodgers. He tells us in voice-over about the summer of 1962 when his friend Benny Rodriguez (Mike Vitar) taught him to play baseball. Coincidentally, or perhaps to offer a less subversive version of kids' baseball, the film then flashes back to the same San Fernando Valley that was the setting for *The Bad News Bears*, and we meet Scotty (Tom Guiry) as a eleven-year-old boy, just having moved there with his mom (Karen Allen) and stepfather Bill (Denis Leary).

Scotty's mom is concerned about his adjustment to a new neighborhood and encourages her son to get out, make friends, and have fun. The boy has developed an interest in baseball, but since his dad died when he was small and Bill has just become his stepfather, Scotty hasn't yet had anyone to help him learn the game. The mother clearly respects what sociologist Michael Messner calls the division between "kids knowledge" and "sports knowledge" that structures how many mothers and fathers approach their involvement with their children's participation in sports. Messner explains that using "kids knowledge" to support their children's experience "most women and some men . . . drawing on resources (or 'capital') that is culturally defined as 'feminine' . . . [act] as nurturing, as caring, as facilitating the kids to have 'fun.'"[5] By contrast, "sports knowledge" Messner defines as a set of skills about how to play the sports kids want to learn and how to be successful in competitive situations. In 1962, a decade before Title IX opened up access to participation in sports for many girls and women, Messner's statement that "since boys and men have had far more opportunities to play organized sports . . . adult men . . . serve in positions of knowledgeable authority, with women serving in a support capacity" describes the assumptions of Scotty's mom.[6] She supports Scotty's interest in baseball and urges him to play the sport and have fun, and it is her expectation that Bill will help her son learn how to play the game.

However, Bill seems more interested in work and career than in establishing a relationship with his stepson. When Scotty approaches Bill in his study soon after the move, we see a room filled with pennants and photos of ballplayers on the walls alongside trophies and a baseball signed by Babe Ruth displayed prominently. Bill agrees to play catch with the boy but shows no interest in doing so at the moment. When Scotty approaches him again in a later scene Bill initially claims he is too busy with work and only after the mom pushes does her husband agree to go out in the backyard and throw the ball. This first game of catch doesn't go well, however, as Scotty has had very little experience with either throwing or catching a baseball and Bill is noticeably impatient with the boy's lack of skills. When a throw drives Scotty's glove back into his left eye, their practice comes to a quick end and all Bill can say is "at least he caught it." Clearly Bill's disinterest in sharing his well-developed baseball knowledge with Scotty comes from his focus on work but also from his apparent doubt that the boy has the potential to learn the game. In describing the history of youth sports and how it required the participation of fathers looking for a way to parent kids that didn't undermine normative ideas of masculinity, Jay Coakley notes that such involvement of men in athletic skill building and coaching marked a break with previous ideas whereby "for most of the 20th century good fathers were good breadwinners" outside the home.[7] Bill clearly exemplifies the latter, more traditional idea of the role of a husband and father who will provide for his family but not play an especially prominent role in parenting at home.

In keeping with Bill's provider idea of masculinity and fathering, the film shows him escape the home to go off on a business trip to Chicago, while Scotty's mom also disappears into her domestic responsibilities. Luckily for Scotty, a boy from the neighborhood, Benny, generously invites him to join a group of boys who play baseball on the local sandlot field. The film then shifts its focus from Scotty's family to the daily activities of the boys centered around baseball and the summer spent hanging out together. As the influence of his mother and stepfather recedes from this point in *The Sandlot*, baseball with the other boys becomes an activity through which Scotty practices ideas of gender as well as how to play the game. Writing about the impact of youth sports on the formation of gender identity, Messner points out that the latter is not a role that people absorb during childhood and bring with them to their sports activity, it is "a multilayered social process that . . . is also a fundamental aspect of everyday group interactions."[8]

On the first day that Scotty visits the sandlot, he describes the other boys playing there as part of a "dream game" in which "they never kept score, never chose sides." Especially since Scotty is just learning the sport, this non-competitive environment appeals to him, and although some of the boys tease Scotty that he can't catch or throw the ball, luckily Bennie, the most skilled player on the field, helps him improve his technique and confidence and before long he is a regular member of the team. Baseball for the nine boys in *The Sandlot* exemplifies the kind of unstructured play that was more common for children in the United States until the 1970s, when, according to Coakley and Messner, the popularity of organized sports took off, prompted by ideas about how they benefitted kids in developing self-confidence and a work ethic, how parents saw them as safer than kids off playing on their own, and also how such structured athletic leagues gave fathers a way to parent their kids without challenging normative ideas of masculinity.[9]

Yet as both Coakley and Messner point out, organized sports in which fathers coach and mothers support based on the "sports knowledge/kids knowledge" division sends a message to children about gender difference. In *The Sandlot*, although adults are largely absent from the boys' daily baseball and time spent socializing together, when Scotty joins the team his parents have already communicated the gender division of labor relative to baseball: boys and men know about and play the game, and women—like Scotty's mom—can only support such participation. Messner notes that kids' baseball, even more than other sports such as soccer, is segregated by gender with boys playing against boys and girls channeled toward softball.[10] As an example of such gender segregation, the sandlot team is entirely made up of boys, and in several scenes in the film the relationship between their time together and baseball is explicitly linked to the construction of masculinity, in particular through contrasting its normative practices with things the boys regard as feminine. On one occasion Scotty arrives and tells the other boys that he was delayed because his mother asked him to wash the dishes, a comment that brings him ridicule for his willingness to do what the other boys regard as feminine work. In another scene a rival team, the Tigers, has the audacity to come on their bikes to the sandlot and challenge Benny's team to a game the following day. The leader of the visiting players, Phillips (Wil Horneff), and a member of the sandlot team, Porter

(Patrick Renna), trash talk back and forth, until the latter hurls the ultimate insult: "You play ball like a girl." In other words, for Phillips and his group to play like a girl is to not play baseball well.

Even the film's main subplot that takes the boys off the sandlot to the city pool on a day when it is too hot to play parallels baseball as a gendering activity. At the pool, the boys ogle an older girl, Wendy (Marley Shelton), who is a lifeguard, and one of the Sandlot team, Michael (Chauncey Leopardi), fakes drowning in the deep end to get her to pull him from the water and administer mouth-to-mouth resuscitation. This episode at the pool appears at first as a diversion from the boys' time together on the sandlot field that is the central activity of the movie, yet it connects by contrast to those games in that it is about femininity, represented here by the character of Wendy, who is discussed, looked at, even desired but not part of the boys' masculinity as it is constituted by baseball.

To its credit *The Sandlot* foregrounds the socially diverse makeup of the group as it includes two non-Whites, Benny and Kenny DeNunez (Brandon Adams), and also emphasizes how Scotty's access to diversity provides a learning experience for him. When Scotty borrows Bill's souvenir ball and it gets hit beyond the outfield fence of the sandlot into a yard guarded by a ferocious dog, the boys engage in a series of strategic plans to get the ball back, but without success. Finally they speak to the house's owner Mr. Mertle (James Earl Jones), a blind former Negro League player who retrieves the ball only to find it has been badly chewed by the dog. While his stepfather values his baseball signed by Babe Ruth as a precious consumer item that shows his ability to purchase it as well as his historically informed idea of fandom, to replace the one with Ruth's signature, Mertle gives Scotty an even more valuable ball, signed not just by Ruth but by the entire 1927 Murderers' Row Yankee team. Mr. Mertle tells the boys that he already has a lot of other memorabilia from his career as a professional ballplayer, including a photo of him with Ruth and Lou Gehrig. Besides how the Mertle character models kindness and generosity to the boys, he also defines baseball as a social activity that promotes friendship and enjoyable interaction more than competition. He tells the boys that he will give them the signed souvenir if they promise to come by once a week to talk baseball.

As Scotty from his time on the sandlot develops the ability to play baseball with confidence, this both relieves his mother about his development of such a marker of normative masculinity but also helps improve his relationship with Bill. The film concludes with Scotty and Bill playing catch again in the backyard, and we can see the stepdad is now much more comfortable with the activity as we hear Scotty's voice-over tell us that "things worked out between me and him." This scene of father and son playing catch recalls similar moments in other baseball films such as *The Natural* and *Field of Dreams*, showing what Messner calls "the deep emotional connection that many U.S. men attach to baseball—a connection that has much to do with nostalgia for their own boyhood and often with emotional ties to their own fathers."[11]

Games for My Father

The Disney biopic *The Rookie* and Clint Eastwood's *Trouble with the Curve* are both movies about adult main characters using baseball to repair strained relationships with their fathers. Mainly because he is the central character whose agency drives the narrative, Jimmy Morris (Dennis Quaid) in *The Rookie* succeeds in repairing his relationship with his father Jim Sr. (Brian Cox) by showing the older man the error of his authoritarian parenting. By contrast, in the Eastwood film his star image built on a gruff, controlling masculinity so defines his lead role as Atlanta Braves scout Gus Lobel that his grown daughter Mickey (Amy Adams) has to adjust to him to make their relationship work, in part through her ability to navigate the male-dominated world of professional baseball.

Because of his father's career in the navy, Jimmy Morris and his family move frequently. This creates problems for Jimmy's love of baseball and participation on teams. However, Jim Sr. pays little attention to his son's involvement with baseball, nor does he show much patience for the young man's frustration and tells Jimmy curtly: "It's my job to decide when we move. It's your job to make the best of it." Like the stepdad Bill in *The Sandlot*, Jim Sr. is more focused on his own career and providing for his family than with the concerns of his son. He shows no interest in seeing Jimmy play ball or in supporting his participation in the sport. When the family moves from Florida to Big Lake in West Texas and Jimmy's glove goes missing, Jim Sr. tells him impatiently: "There are more important things in life than baseball. The sooner you figure that out the better." Through such terse statements Jim Sr. in *The Rookie* exemplifies the kind of parenting that Nicholas Holt and Camilla Knight call "authoritarian . . . to shape and control their children's behavior."[12] Such authoritarian parents according to Holt and Knight "expect children to follow their rules and rarely explain the rationale for those rules. In other words, they expect their children to do as they are told without the need for further explanation."[13] Seen from the perspective of 2002 when *The Rookie* was released, rather than the 1970s when the Morris family's moves disrupt Jimmy's participation in baseball, Jim Sr. doesn't measure up to the assumption in youth sports that had become prevalent by that time, whereby, as Coakley states, "fathers are expected to actively promote their children's success. In the case of sports this means . . . to support and guide children as they learn to play."[14]

The move to Big Lake in particular is hard on young Jimmy because the high school there has no baseball team. Henry (Royce Applegate), the owner of a store in town where Jimmy orders a replacement glove, tells him that, in West Texas, football in the sport most people care about. Nonetheless Jimmy goes on to play baseball at a junior college after graduating from high school and is drafted by the Milwaukee Brewers, only to have a severe arm injury end his professional career. The film makes just brief reference to this part of Jimmy's involvement with baseball and instead quickly transitions from soon after the family arrives in Big Lake to Jimmy in his mid-thirties, teaching chemistry and coaching baseball at the Big Lake High School.

Jimmy and his wife Lorri (Rachel Griffiths), who also works at the high school as a counselor, have three small children, and their parenting style couldn't be more different from that of Jim Sr. In a quiet, confident scene typical of the film's tone, Jimmy and his eight-year-old son Hunter (Angus Jones) talk as they leave a local diner. When Hunter asks his dad "Does your arm ever hurt anymore?," Jimmy patiently explains that it never did in high school since there was no team to play on and in junior college he pitched well, prompting the Brewers to draft him, but the pain started after he began to play professionally. At that point Hunter has one more question for his dad: "Is that why you didn't make it [to the majors]?" Jimmy pauses and then tells his son quietly, "It's never just one thing." Hunter smiles at his father, and they get into the pickup to head home. The patience and respect that Jimmy shows his young son in this conversation fit Holt and Knight's statement that an important aspect of supportive parenting involves what they call "bidirectional (i.e., two-way) communication with their children," "with explanations for . . . actions."[15]

Holt and Knight cite a study of parenting and sports that showed that parental involvement, defined as "the extent to which a parent is interested in, knowledgeable about and takes a role in a child's life," is "generally better when parents provide children with resources and support that facilitate a sense of autonomy."[16] One way in which we see Jimmy involved with his son Hunter comes through the time they spend together with Jimmy coaching and Hunter given the responsibility of managing the equipment for the high school baseball team. Yet, when after one of the team's practices Jimmy throws a few pitches, his ensuing exchange with Hunter ironically recalls Jim Sr.'s controlling style of fathering, but only to make fun of such authoritarian parenting soon afterward. On their way home from the practice Jimmy tells his son not to say anything to his mother about the pitching. When the boy asks why, his dad responds: "Because I said so." Yet, at another practice soon afterward, when Jimmy speaks to his players, trying to support and empower them by emphasizing the need to pursue their dreams and play with greater effort and commitment, the boys respond that Jimmy also has to keep his dream of playing baseball alive. They have seen in practice that their coach can still pitch and they make a deal with him that if they play harder and win the district championship he has to try out for a major league team. When Jimmy reluctantly agrees and the boys leave for the locker room, Hunter takes the opportunity to poke gentle fun at his dad's earlier uncharacteristic unilateral order not to tell his mom about the pitching, asking, "I don't get to tell mom about this, do I?" Hunter's joke at his dad's expense, as well as his presence at the extended discussion that Jimmy has with his high school players, underscore how uncharacteristic the authoritarian "Because I said so" order was.

The Rookie gives Jimmy an opportunity to voice his displeasure with his father's style of parenting in a conversation with his mother. Noting how Jim Sr., now retired, got Hunter a baseball glove for his birthday, Jimmy's mother, Olline (Beth Grant), comments, "He's trying to be a good grandfather." Jimmy then asks with impatience: "What do you want, me to pretend everything was perfect?" Olline responds in an effort to defuse her son's frustration: "You been blaming your father for too many things for too many years. You got your shot at baseball. You got hurt. It had nothing to do with your father."

While The Rookie shows clearly the lack of involvement and communication by Jim Sr. and the frustration it causes Jimmy, the mother's comment that he stop blaming his father invokes the standard response in many sports films, and biopics in particular, to any barrier to achievement. Such films foreground the promotion of self-reliance central to classic Hollywood narrative when it uses what David Bordwell and Kristin Thompson call "individual characters as causal agents."[17] Stories about sports reinforce such a traditional American mythology in Hollywood movies that champions the promise of a unified self through individual achievement in order to deny the qualification by any kind of social factor, in this case the impact from authoritarian parenting. For sports in Hollywood and especially sports biopics, success depends primarily on determination and effort, not the contextual factors in one's life.

Success is exactly what Jimmy Morris finds as a coach, as a parent, and, even though he is now thirty-five years old, as a pitcher in professional baseball. Inspired by the deal with their coach, the Owls begin winning and become sectional champs. Fulfilling his part of the bargain, Jimmy attends a Tampa Bay Devil Rays tryout on a day when Lorri is working and he has to take the three children with him. As a striking image of Jimmy's commitment to being a hands-on dad, he is changing a dirty diaper on his youngest child when the Rays scouts call him to pitch at the tryout. After giving Hunter the responsibility of keeping an eye on his younger siblings, Jimmy takes the mound and impresses the scouts by throwing ninety-eight miles per hour.

Unsure whether he should take an offer from Tampa Bay to play in their minor league system, Jimmy goes to see his father to ask his advice. Although the glove he bought Hunter may suggest he is trying to be a good grandfather, Jim Sr.'s fathering style is still as top down as ever. When Jimmy tells him "I don't know what to do," rather than discuss weighing the opportunity Jimmy has dreamed about his whole life against the responsibility he also feels to help Lorri parent their three kids, Jim Sr. simply tells his son: "What you want matters less than what you are meant to do." It's ironic that Jim Sr. uses his authoritarian style of fathering to tell his son not to put career over parenting as he did. Lorri also has reservations about Jimmy's opportunity to return to professional baseball, remembering how difficult his failure was when he hurt his arm and wondering how they will get by on the $600 per month he will earn in the minors and how she will manage the three kids on her own. Ultimately, however, Lorri decides that Jimmy should go because of how inspiring his dad pursuing his lifelong dream will be for Hunter. "What are we telling him if you don't try now?" she asks Jimmy.

Jimmy pitches well and in September of that year the Devil Rays call him up. Coincidentally, when he arrives with the big team they are playing the

Texas Rangers in Arlington, and dozens of friends, family, and players from Big Lake drive to the game to support Jimmy. After a storybook ending in which he gets into his first game with Tampa Bay and strikes out the only hitter he faces on three fastballs, Jimmy sees his dad as he leaves the visitors' clubhouse. Their subsequent conversation acknowledges how the older Morris's style of parenting was a mistake, an error that Jimmy's success has helped the older man recognize:

JIMMY Sir. I didn't know you were here.

JIM SR. I wasn't going to miss this one. Watching you tonight. . . . I guess I let too many of these things get away.

Besides the patience and respect Jimmy shows his father in this difficult moment as the latter acknowledges his mistake, when he then gives his dad the ball from his major league debut it symbolizes how Jimmy understands the importance of the generosity and affection that the older man never displayed when he was growing up. Jim Sr. is left speechless by the gesture, and the scene concludes with Jimmy telling his dad, "Thanks for coming." Although the real Jimmy Morris who inspired this Disney biopic went on to have only a brief career pitching in Major League Baseball, his character in *The Rookie* endorses an idea of fathering that strikes a balance between career and hands-on involvement with kids and their sports activities, along with what Holt and Knight call the "bidirectional" communication about the issues and decisions that affect them.

In the decade prior to its release of *The Rookie* in 2002, Disney made an astonishing twenty-six sports films, nineteen of them after the studio purchased an 80 percent share of ESPN with its acquisition of ABC in 1996. One of these films, *Remember the Titans* (2000), earned $136 million, and *The Rookie* brought in a respectable $80 million.[18] Synergy with ESPN was part of the strategy for these sports movies, as it offered Disney a platform for advertising and showing them. The endorsement in *The Rookie* of a more progressive idea of parenting in which fathers are directly involved with raising their children, patiently communicate with them, and even change diapers seems to follow the revisionist direction that Disney embarked on in the 2000s with the positive portrayal of gay and lesbian characters and liberal feminism in the TV series *Glee* (2009–2015) and the *Frozen* franchise (2013–2019). Yet with its retention of the utopian sports narrative of self-reliance and what John Willis calls Disney's "insistence on the traditional nuclear family led by mother and father," *The Rookie* locates this idea of more gender-balanced parenting within a socially conservative context.[19]

Whereas Jimmy Morris makes a hero out of a hands-on dad, *Trouble with the Curve* uses Clint Eastwood's star image as an icon of tough-guy masculinity to tell the story of a more traditional provider father like Bill in *The Sandlot* and Jim Sr. in *The Rookie*. Like so many other roles he has played throughout his long career, Eastwood's performance here as Gus Lobel, a veteran scout for the Atlanta Braves, presents him as self-reliant and unwilling to follow the rules that most people abide by, an outsider attitude manifested by his grouchy, antisocial manner. Lucy Bolton's description of "the popular Eastwood persona" as "the independent male loner who is not particularly interested in women" summarizes well Gus's strained relationship in the film with his grown daughter Mickey (Amy Adams).[20] As Bolton notes, *Trouble with the Curve* exemplifies how "his relationships with his cinematic daughters are dysfunctional and damaged."[21] David Desser adds that "Gus is . . . one of a long line of fathers" in Eastwood films "with ambivalent relationships with their daughters."[22]

As the film opens we learn that Gus's job of traveling around to assess young players whom the Braves may want to sign is complicated by his declining eyesight. The annual amateur draft is coming up, and Gus is under the gun to look at a high school slugger in North Carolina named Bo Gentry (Joe Massingill) to decide if he is the player the Braves will select with their coveted first round pick. Besides the problem with his eyes, Gus also faces the challenge of being out of step with the ever-increasing use of computer analysis in evaluating young talent. Another scout for the Braves, Phillip (Matthew Lillard), mocks Gus's traditional approach in a meeting with general manager Vince (Robert Patrick) and the director of scouting Pete (John Goodman), stating, "These programs are essential tools to evaluation today. . . . Gus couldn't turn on a typewriter let alone a computer."

While Gus sets off to scout Atlanta's potential first round pick, Mickey is also under pressure as an attorney on a big case that will determine if she is promoted to partner in her firm. In the scene in which we first meet Mickey, three older male partners quiz her about her interest in the promotion. Sounding like her tough-talking father, she tells them plainly that she has been productive, "working [her] ass off" for seven years as an associate and deserves to become a partner. When one of the men comments that she would be the only woman partner in the firm, Mickey answers that her father is a baseball scout and that being in a male-dominated world doesn't intimidate her. "I grew up around men who swore, drank and farted," she explains.

To promote our identification with Gus despite his rough exterior, we see the Eastwood character show concern about Billy Clark (Scott Eastwood), a young player he signed who hasn't been hitting. Gus shows up at Billy's game and promises afterward to bring his family in to see him and help boost his spirits. When Gus later heads off to scout Gentry, he is happy to run into Johnny Flanagan (Justin Timberlake), another young man Gus signed and mentored, but who blew out his arm and now works as a scout for the Red Sox. Flanagan later tells Mickey that "when Gus scouted me we spent a lot of time together."

Yet despite how we get glimpses of Gus's nurturing side with these two young men, it's clear that his record as a father for Mickey has not been good. When the father and daughter are together they both seem impatient with the other and their communication is strained at best. At Pete's request, Mickey decides to take a couple of days off from work to go to North Carolina to help her father scout Gentry. Yet Gus is hardly welcoming when she arrives and they have a difficult conversation in which Mickey tells her dad that "I feel this dysfunctional sense of responsibility to make sure that you're okay." When Gus responds he can still do his job despite his bad eyes and that when he can't "I'll put a bullet in my head," the exchange ends with Mickey telling her father sarcastically, "As always it's been really great to talk to you." After speaking with Gus's doctor, Mickey approaches her dad again and brings up the problem of his sight. In response Gus tells her dismissively, "I'll figure out something," and Mickey impatiently responds, "I had this crazy idea that you and I could actually have a conversation about this rationally." Gus knows he needs to make a greater effort to communicate with his daughter but nonetheless resolves himself to his inability to do so. During a brief scene when he visits the grave of Mickey's dead mother, he tells the headstone: "I need you to talk to her. I have a hard time with that."

Nonetheless, the presence of Johnny seems to prompt Gus and Mickey to address the problems in their relationship. In a bar the evening after watching Gentry play, Gus explains that Mickey was six when her mother died and tells Johnny, "It should have been me. No kid should be without a mother." While this comment demonstrates Gus's love and concern for his daughter, it also implies that he regards women as more important than men in the process of parenting. As the conversation concludes, Gus acknowledges his rejection of his responsibility as a father. When Flanagan asks him "How'd you handle all that [being a single parent] by yourself?" Gus responds in his usual curt manner. "I didn't." Similarly, later in the film Johnny talks with Mickey about her dysfunctional relationship with her dad and gives her advice that fits with the older man's idea that it is the responsibility of women to make child/parent relationships work. When she tells him "He [Gus] never tells me anything," Johnny responds: "Maybe he wants to, you know, but doesn't know how. You might need to take the lead."

Despite the veteran scout's recommendation (developed with his daughter's help) that they pass on Gentry because he can't hit a curve ball, the Braves nonetheless make him their number-one pick. In a similar setback for Mickey, the law firm decides to promote a young male attorney instead of her. With Gus and Mickey both feeling vulnerable, they finally talk more openly about their dysfunctional relationship. Gus explains that he sent her off to live with an aunt and uncle soon after her mother died because of a traumatic incident that occurred at a ballpark in Mobile, Alabama. Gus was distracted speaking to a prospect and later found his young daughter in an equipment shed with a man about to sexually assault her. Yet despite this breakthrough in Gus's willingness to at last discuss his fear of the dangers and vulnerabilities of parenting, the two characters' shared knowledge of baseball is still required to bring them to a point of reconciliation.

After their watershed conversation Gus heads back to Atlanta, and Mickey the next morning observes a young man whose mother runs the motel where they have been staying pitching to his brother. The young man, Rigoberto Sanchez (Jay Galloway), is a tall, strong left-hander who has a very good fastball and an even better curve. Mickey immediately sees the young pitcher's potential and calls Pete, asking to get him a tryout with the Braves. In the film's climactic scene at the Braves' stadium, Rigoberto proves Gus and Mickey's theory about Bo Gentry's inability to hit a curve, making the first round draft pick look foolish. Gus proudly proclaims to Vince, Phillip, and Pete that Mickey "knows more about baseball than anyone in this room." Desser states correctly that such a resolution to *Trouble with the Curve* shows baseball as "no longer . . . the domain . . . solely of white men," and that "knowledgeable women . . . can become part of it as well."[23] Yet from Gus Lobel's perspective such knowledge of baseball makes Mickey less feminine in his eyes and therefore less of a threat as his parental responsibility put him in situations in which his control was compromised, he could

FIG. 12 Mickey (Amy Adams) meets her dad, scout Gus Lobel (Clint Eastwood), on his own terms in *Trouble with the Curve* (2012).

not always protect her, and she asked him to communicate his emotions. As Mickey points out to her father, the time they've spent together watching baseball has always been a more comfortable substitute for talking. Writing about *Trouble with a Curve*, Bolton notes that in response to Gus's "irresponsibility and [the] absenteeism [that] characterize his parenting," he and Mickey "are able to communicate through the world of work."[24] It is ultimately Mickey's ability to make her dad see her as less feminine and vulnerable and more a part of his masculine world of baseball that enables him to accept his role as a father.

In Sherri Grasmuck and Janet Goldwater's detailed and insightful ethnography of boys' baseball in Philadelphia, they make the point that some of the younger coaches that they observed have grown accustomed to a more patient, supportive style of parenting because of the simple fact that, with their female partners working outside the home, they need to raise their game as dads and do more to meet the needs of their kids. This is a good description of the scene in *The Rookie* when Jimmy takes his three small children to the Devil Rays tryout while their mom is at work. The movie may be adding to our admiration of Jimmy's ability to perform for the scouts under such a pressurized situation, yet it is also representing a fact of family life in the world of two-career households. Grasmuck and Goldwater's observation also helps explain the more dysfunctional fathers, Bill in *The Sandlot*, Jim Sr. in *The Rookie*, and Gus in *Trouble with the Curve*. The idea of parenting they follow dates to a time when fathers weren't expected to nurture kids, offer emotional support, or even spend much time with them. As Grasmuck and Goldwater explain, the expression of emotional vulnerability that old-school macho coaches and dads tell their players to suppress, famously invoked by Jimmy Dugan (Tom Hanks) in *A League of Their Own* when he proclaims that "There's no crying in baseball!," represents avoidance of the fact that fearlessness is probably impossible to fully attain and experiencing emotion helps one be more generous and compassionate, two qualities that are certainly useful to any parent.[25]

Conclusion

• • • • • • • • • • • • • • • • • • • •

The Show for the Thinking
Fan and Going Online

The year 2011 saw the release of *Moneyball* and 2012 *Trouble with the Curve*, both baseball movies built around established male stars but beyond that very different in the opposing perspectives they offer on the state of the sport. *Moneyball* explained to the general public the growing trend in professional baseball toward the use of sabermetrics, data-based analysis of on-the-field performance relying on computer technology and a new set of statistical measurements. The film makes heroes of Brad Pitt in the role of Oakland general manager Billy Beane and his assistant Peter Brand (Jonah Hill), the latter armed with a laptop for doing the careful interpretation that helps an underresourced small-market team like the A's compete with the New York Yankees and Boston Red Sox of the baseball world. As Ben Lindbergh and Travis Sawchik explain in *The MVP Machine: How Baseball's New Nonconformists Are Using Data to Build Better Players*, in the time since the film made its impact there has been a shift in the use of new data from a prior emphasis on finding and appreciating the contribution of undervalued players to applying that information to better develop talent. They quote Chris Long, who has worked as a quantitative analyst for the San Diego Padres, summing up this shift by stating, "You can identify value," what

Beane and his team succeeded at, "or you can create value," although Lindbergh and Sawchik acknowledge, "Ideally, you'd do both."[1]

In Clint Eastwood's *Trouble with the Curve*, the attitude toward the sabermetric revolution couldn't be more different, or more disparaging. While the film ostensibly focuses on Eastwood's Gus Lobel character trying to hang onto his job as a scout for the Atlanta Braves as he ages and the unresolved bad feelings built up from years of neglect in his relationship with his grown daughter Mickey, a major subtext of the movie is its rejection of how the new technology has changed player evaluation. That sabermetrics get aligned with a careerist scout Phillip, who doesn't put in the work required to do his job well and disrespects his colleagues, helps the film demonize the new forms of evaluation. Yet by reaffirming Lobel's ability, despite his age and the loss of his sight, to evaluate prospects by just watching them play or—in Gus's case with a player the Braves are scouting—*listening* to how the ball comes off his bat and talking with Mickey, who with her better eyes *watches* the young man hit, *Trouble with the Curve* also has the ulterior motive of asserting the centrality of White masculinity in the sport. What is especially insidious about *Trouble with the Curve* is how the movie hides its sexism by using the Mickey character, a thirtysomething woman with an impressive knowledge of the game, to save the day, but in doing so has her risk her law career to affirm the greater importance of her father's job that only men are allowed to do. *Moneyball* also wants to appear socially progressive by presenting its celebration of the new advanced metrics as leveling the playing field and allowing hard work and intelligence to offset the advantage of money. Yet, like the Eastwood film, it ultimately affirms the centrality of White men in the baseball world.

One of the data-driven innovators celebrated in Lindbergh and Sawchik's book, Kyle Boddy, may ask, "Why is there [still] so little data and so much 'feel' involved in player development?" Yet a strong indication of how sabermetrics has in fact become the new orthodoxy can be found in the *MLB Now* television program featured on MLB Network, launched in January 2009 and two-thirds owned by Major League Baseball with the other third controlled by media companies such as AT&T, Cox, and Comcast. It was the last of the twenty-four-hour cable networks to be set up by the four major U.S. professional sports, but it had grown to 56 million subscribers by 2019.[2] MLB Network shows a mix of live games, highlights, and analysis shows, with *MLB Now* fitting in the third category. *MLB Now* debuted in 2013 with the format of Kristina Fitzpatrick moderating a debate between journalist Brian Kenny, representing the sabermetrics viewpoint, and former player Harold Reynolds, offering a more traditional perspective. In its second season in 2014, however, Reynolds and Fitzpatrick left the program and Kenny took over to lead a discussion of that day's baseball news with three guests who represent a mix of sabermetric analysts, former players or team executives, and veteran sportswriters. Since Kenny became the host of *MLB Now* his prominence as one of the main media voices advocating for the sabermetric perspective has grown significantly. In 2016 he published a well-received book, *Ahead of the Curve: Inside the Baseball Revolution*, that Sarah Trembanis described as making "a passionate case for the use of sabermetrics in baseball decision making."[3]

Brian Kenny begins each episode of *MLB Now* by describing it as "the show for the thinking fan." The emphasis on sabermetric analysis that this tagline previews exemplifies Neil Weinberg's assertion that "to keep the sport relevant and competitive in a world with so many leisure options," baseball must "deliver the game in a way that speaks to the modern fan."[4] Yet Weinberg recognizes that "sabermetrics aren't for everyone," and therefore the best way to add it to media coverage of baseball is with a balance of new statistics and more traditional ways of talking about the game that reassure longtime fans. As Weinberg puts it, "The challenge lies in creating a broadcast that is informative for statistically minded fans while also remaining accessible and compelling for people who don't wish to think about the game through that lens."[5] *MLB Now*, with its mix of analytics and the better-known discourse of former players and veteran sportswriters, aims for that balanced approach. Kenny himself has acknowledged that "the key [is] to speak the language of the mainstream fan while bringing 'our way of thinking' (i.e., sabermetrics) into the discussion."[6]

Along with its assumption about the need to increase the appeal of the sport by adding the new discourse of analytics, *MLB Now* shows some awareness of how more inclusion of social diversity would also expand the fan base. An unscientific sample of ten episodes of the program from the COVID-19-shortened 2020 season included six women and non-White men as panelists. Recognition of the need for diversity dates to the beginnings of the program in 2013, when Reynolds, who is African American, and Kristina Fitzpatrick were featured with Kenny. Yet diversity in just six of forty panelists who appeared in the aforementioned ten 2020 episodes, and that only six women and ten Latino, Asian, or African American men are included within the forty-six regular on-air personalities on MLB

Network, reaffirm a larger pattern in which White men still dominate media representation of baseball.

Since MLB Network is two-thirds controlled by team owners, it's not surprising that Kenny defends the idea that sabermetrics has worked to limit free agent salaries. While justifying the practice that only a few younger stars like Bryce Harper, Manny Machado, and Mike Trout "still in their mid-20s and . . . all big time producers" get multiyear, big-money deals to "carry the brand" for teams and establish "an emotional investment" with fans in a highly competitive media marketplace, Kenny also asserts that "in the new analytical world of baseball, big-time free agent spending" is "in a slowdown, and at the most, doomed." Writing in 2019 Kenny argued that "in recent years, just below half of those deals are worth it to the club when they are all done."[7]

Despite how the new advanced metrics may not be in the best interest of player compensation, Weinberg still argues that as such discourse gains a greater profile in media coverage of baseball, it could nonetheless still have a positive social impact: "There's a broader value in welcoming more scientifically rigorous thinking onto television. We live in a society that isn't great at working through problems scientifically. In some cases, evidence is ignored and people doubt things that should be obvious. Sport has an important place in our culture and moving the needle on small things [like how to evaluate the performance of a baseball player] can lead to progress on larger issues."[8] Weinberg makes a valid point here. A 2019 Pew Research Center poll showed that while six-in-ten Americans believe "scientists should play an active role in policy debates about scientific issues," there is also division along political party lines about whether to trust their research.[9] The Pew poll, however, also shows that the more those asked have had access to research data, the more confidence they report in the positive impact of such information on their lives. At a time when a global pandemic and climate change are especially pressing issues that affect us all, if an analytic, evidence-based approach to better understanding baseball can reassure people about the value of scientific knowledge, then maybe we should all be interested in the show for the thinking fan.

But as important as film and especially television have long been for representing baseball, the challenges that the sport faces moving forward make the necessity of collaboration with new media forms all the more clear. Commissioner Rob Manfred claimed that MLB owners lost as much as $3 billion in 2020. Mike Ozanian, writing in *Forbes* in December 2020, noted that MLB saw total revenue drop from $6.5 billion in 2019 to about $4 billion in 2020, although he admits that those figures don't include money teams made from their ownership stakes in regional sports networks that show their games. Even with that additional TV revenue added in, however, Ozanian estimates that baseball still lost at least $1 billion in 2020.[10]

The drop in revenue because of the pandemic has exacerbated labor conflict in MLB. Players don't trust owner claims of big losses, have for years been concerned about the use of sabermetrics to roll back salaries, and don't want the percentage of their pay they got in 2020 for the shortened season to set a precedent.[11] Certainly lost attendance was a major part of the MLB decline in revenue in 2020. In 2019, 39 percent of baseball's revenue came from attendance and in-park purchases.[12]

MLB teams are hoping that vaccination will unleash pent-up demand for going to entertainment events like ballgames. Historians Johnny Smith and Randy Roberts, in *War Fever: Boston, Baseball, and America in the Shadow of the Great War*, note that soldiers returning from World War I brought Spanish flu back with them and reduced attendance for the 1918 World Series between the Red Sox, led by their young star left-handed pitcher Babe Ruth, and the Chicago Cubs. For game 5 just 24,694 of Fenway Park's 35,000 seats were sold. After a warning the next day about the danger of the flu from a public health official, there were just 15,238 spectators in the stands for game 6. Smith and Roberts conclude that World War I together with the flu cut MLB attendance in 1918 by more than 50 percent.[13]

Yet by the following year, the war and pandemic had ended and attendance at MLB games bounced back from 2,830,613 in 1918 to 6,532,439 in 1919. NPR journalist Greg Rosalsky calls this a classic example of what economists term "pent-up demand," and MLB owners now are hoping that vaccination will unleash a similar return to their ballparks.[14] But regardless of how well MLB attendance rebounds, in response to the double challenge of the pandemic and the long-standing need to appeal to younger and more diverse fans, owners are looking to expand baseball's online presence. CNBC sports business reporter Jabari Young has reported that while MLB still counts on ESPN and AT&T-owned TBS to continue to pay billions for TV rights, they are also looking to increase streaming of their games. Young speculated this might come through partnerships with Amazon, Hulu, and Disney+ to stream games to fans MLB is not currently reaching. Young also conjectured that MLB wants to develop its involvement in Esports so as "to appeal to kids playing video games."[15]

Beyond streaming and gaming to expand its online presence, MLB is also aware of its need to engage new fans on social media. Sports business journalist Eddie Moran notes that baseball has a long way to go in this domain. As of January 2020, MLB had just 6.1 million followers on Instagram, compared to 16.4 million for the NFL and 43.7 million for the NBA.[16] As part of is social media effort, MLB has begun to focus its attention on growing its presence on the popular video-sharing social network TikTok. In early 2020 only fourteen MLB teams used TikTok, whereas all but one of the NFL teams had at least 100,000 TikTok followers and the NBA's Golden State Warriors had over one million. Attesting to owners' interest in getting more video content on the internet, Barbara McHugh, senior vice president of marketing for MLB, commented in 2020 that "unique, authentic content stands out to fans. That's especially true of content featuring our players . . . that tells their personal stories to generate positive attention with our fans." Involving individual players and getting them to engage fans is a big part of MLB's stepped-up social media campaign. At the time of the All-Star Game in 2019 MLB had 219 players involved in its Player Social Media Program, a number that was up to 481 by the end of the 2019 season.[17]

While films about baseball mix nostalgia for White masculinity with occasional stories of greater inclusion, and television coverage focuses on innovative technologies to bring fans closer to the action and give them statistical insights, online media may help baseball reach a broader cross section of American society that will both give MLB an economic boost as well as support its claim to being the national game.

List of Baseball Films
and Television Shows

The Busher (1919), Jerome Storm
Headin' Home (1920), Lawrence C. Windom
Babe Comes Home (1927), Ted Wilde
Elmer the Great (1933), Mervyn LeRoy
The Pride of the Yankees (1942), Sam Wood
The Babe Ruth Story (1948), Roy Del Ruth
The Stratton Story (1949), Sam Wood
The Jackie Robinson Story (1950), Alfred E. Green
The Pride of St. Louis (1952), Harmon Jones
Bang the Drum Slowly (1973), John D. Hancock
The Bingo Long Traveling All-Stars and Motor Kings (1976), John Badham
The Bad News Bears (1976), Michael Ritchie
The Comeback Kid (1980), Peter Levin
Blue Skies Again (1983), Richard Michaels
Tiger Town (1983), Alan Shapiro
The Natural (1984), Barry Levinson
The Slugger's Wife (1985), Hal Ashby
A Winner Never Quits (1986), Mel Damski
Bull Durham (1988), Ron Shelton
Stealing Home (1988), Steven Kampmann and William Porter
Eight Men Out (1988), John Sayles

Field of Dreams (1989), Phil Alden Robinson
Major League (1989), David S. Ward
Mr. Baseball (1992), Fred Schepisi
The Babe (1992), Arthur Hiller
A League of Their Own (1992), Penny Marshall
The Sandlot (1993), David Mickey Evans
Baseball (1994), Ken Burns
Cobb (1994), Ron Shelton
Soul of the Game (1996), Kevin Rodney Sullivan
The Fan (1996), Tony Scott
For the Love of the Game (1999), Sam Raimi
61* (2001), Billy Crystal
The Rookie (2002), John Lee Hancock
Mr. 3000 (2004), Charles Stone III
Fever Pitch (2005), Bobby and Peter Farrelly
Kokoyakyu (2006), Kenneth Eng
Sugar (2008), Anna Boden and Ryan Fleck
Roberto Clemente (2009), Bernardo Ruiz
Time in the Minors (2010), Tony Okun
The Tenth Inning (2010), Ken Burns
Fernando Nation (2010), Cruz Angeles
Moneyball (2011), Bennett Miller
The Curious Case of Curt Flood (2011), Ezra Edelman
Trouble with the Curve (2012), Robert Lorenz
42 (2013), Brian Helgeland
MLB Now (2013–present), MLB Network
The Battered Bastards of Baseball (2014), Maclain Way and
    Chapman Way
I Throw Like a Girl (2014), Spike Lee
Jackie Robinson (2016), Ken Burns
Brockmire (2017–2020), Tim Kirby
The Catcher Was a Spy (2018), Ben Lewin
Jessica Mendoza: The First Female Analyst in Major League Baseball (2019)
    Katie Couric Media
A Secret Love (2020), Chris Bolan

Acknowledgments

First and foremost I would like to thank Les Friedman for asking me to participate in the Screening Sports series and to do this book. Les provided encouragement, guidance, and helpful feedback throughout the process of writing it. Nicole Solano believed in this project, answered many questions and supported me in moving it along. Noah Cohan, Montye Fuse, Paul Harasha, Guy Harrison, Vicky Johnson, Rich King, Jennifer McClearen, Keith Miller, Josh Rosenthal, Samantha Sheppard, and Travis Vogan all contributed to a group of researchers who take sports studies seriously and have inspired me to as well.

An earlier version of chapter 1 was published as "Hollywood Baseball Films: Nostalgic White Masculinity or the National Pastime?" in the *Quarterly Review of Film and Video* and was improved by the comments of its readers.

Finally, the biggest thanks goes to my partner, María, and my son, Matteo, for their willingness to watch and discuss baseball with me. Dialogue with them has been very helpful in thinking through and writing this book.

Notes

Introduction

1 Ken Burns and Lynn Novick, *Baseball, Inning Three* (Florentine Films and WETA, 1994).
2 Vivian Sobchack, "Baseball in the Post-American Cinema, or Life in the Minor Leagues," in *Out of Bounds: Sports, Media, and the Politics of Identity*, ed. Aaron Baker and Todd Boyd (Bloomington: Indiana University Press, 1997), 179.
3 Sobchack, "Baseball in the Post-American Cinema," 193.
4 Sobchack, "Baseball in the Post-American Cinema," 187.
5 Mitchell Nathanson, *A People's History of Baseball* (Urbana: University of Illinois Press, 2012), 23.
6 Nathanson, *People's History of Baseball*, 29.
7 Hua Hsu, "The End of White America?," *Atlantic*, January/February 2009, 5.
8 Jules Tygiel, *Baseball's Great Experiment: Jackie Robinson and His Legacy* (New York: Oxford University Press, 1997), 132, 205.
9 Dana Jennings, "The Superhero Who Leapt Color Lines," *New York Times*, April 5, 2013. https://www.nytimes.com/2013/04/07/movies/jackie-robinson-the -hero-in-42.html.
10 Jennifer Ring, "Invisible Women in America's National Pastime . . . or, 'She's Good. It's History, Man,'" *Journal of Sport and Social Issues* 37, no. 1 (2013): 59–60.
11 Kwame Anthony Appiah, "The Case for Capitalizing the B in Black," *Atlantic*, June 18, 2020, https://www.theatlantic.com/ideas/archive/2020/06/time-to -capitalize-blackand-white/613159/.
12 Appiah, "Case for Capitalizing the B in Black"; Richard Dyer, *White* (New York: Routledge, 1997), 3.

Chapter 1   Hollywood Baseball Films

1 Benjamin G. Rader, *American Sports: From the Age of Folk Games to the Age of Televised Sports*, 5th ed. (Upper Saddle River, NJ: Prentice Halle, 2004), 259.

2 Robert Elias, "A Fit for a Fractured Society: Baseball and the American Promise," in *Baseball and the American Dream: Race, Class, Gender, and the National Pastime*, ed. Elias (Armonk, NY: M.E. Sharpe, 2001), 18.

3 Lawrence R. Samuel, *The American Dream: A Cultural History* (Syracuse, NY: Syracuse University Press, 2012), 2, 5.

4 Samuel, *American Dream*, 3.

5 Samuel, *American Dream*, 4.

6 Jennifer L. Hochschild, *Facing Up to the American Dream: Race, Class and the Soul of the Nation* (Princeton, NJ: Princeton University Press, 1995), 28.

7 Hochschild, *Facing Up to the American Dream*, xi.

8 Robert Sklar, *Movie-Made America: A Cultural History of American Movies* (New York: Vintage Books, 1994), 357.

9 Samuel, *American Dream*, 9.

10 Jim Cullen, *The American Dream: A Short History of an Idea That Shaped a Nation* (New York: Oxford University Press, 2003), 136.

11 Samuel, *American Dream*, 145.

12 Samuel, *American Dream*, 153.

13 Elias, "Fit for a Fractured Society," 5.

14 David Quentin Voigt, *America Through Baseball* (Chicago: Nelson Hall, 1976). Harold Seymour, "Baseball: Badge of Americanism," in *Cooperstown Symposium on Baseball and the American Culture,* ed. Alvin L. Hall (Westport CT: Meckler, 1990), 1–22. Both Voigt and Seymour cited in Elias, "Fit for a Fractured Society," 11.

15 Elias, "Fit for a Fractured Society," 9.

16 Svetlana Boym, *The Future of Nostalgia* (New York: Basic Books, 2001), xiii.

17 Boym, *Future of Nostalgia*, xiv.

18 Barzun quoted in Gerald Early, "Birdland: Two Observations on the Cultural Significance of Baseball," *American Poetry Review*, July/August 1996, 9.

19 Susan Jacoby, *Why Baseball Matters* (New Haven, CT: Yale University Press, 2018), 22.

20 Jacoby, *Why Baseball Matters*, 23.

21 Elias, "Fit for a Fractured Society," 22.

22 Elias, "Fit for a Fractured Society," 19.

23 Elias, "Fit for a Fractured Society," 20.

24 Paul Grainge, "Nostalgia and Style in Retro America: Moods, Modes and Media Recycling," *Journal of American & Comparative Cultures* 23, no. 1 (Spring 2000): 29; Frances Smith, "Smoke Gets in Your Eyes: Re-Reading Gender in the 'Nostalgia Film,'" *Quarterly Review of and Video* 35, no. 5 (2018): 464.

25 Grainge, "Nostalgia and Style," 28.

26 Institute for Diversity and Ethics in Sports, "The 2021 Racial and Gender Report Card: Major League Baseball," https://43530132-36e9-4f52-811a-182c7a91933b.filesusr.com/ugd/a4adoc_b6693f8943394f2785328f1a992249a1.pdf; Bob Nightengale, "It's a Baseball Problem: MLB Redoubles Its Efforts as Sport's Black Population Remains Low," *USA Today*, April 14, 2019, https://www.usatoday.com/story/sports/mlb/columnist/bob-nightengale/2019/04/14/african-american-mlb-players-baseball-jackie-robinson/3465999002/.

27 "Chris Rock's Take on Blacks in Baseball" (HBO Sports, April 17, 2015), https://www.youtube.com/watch?v=oFFQkQ6Va3A.

28 Gerald Early, "Why Baseball *Was* the Black National Pastime," in *Basketball Jones*, ed. Todd Boyd and Kenneth Shropshire (New York: New York University Press, 2000), 39.

29 "Chris Rock's Take."

30 Jennifer Ring, *Stolen Bases: Why American Girls Don't Play Baseball* (Urbana: University of Illinois Press, 2009), 15.

31 Ring, *Stolen Bases*, 17.

32 Ring, *Stolen Bases*, 18.

33 Ring, *Stolen Bases*, 18.

34 Ring, *Stolen Bases*, 19.

35 Ring, *Stolen Bases*, 19–20.

36 Elias, "Fit for a Fractured Society," 26.

37 Elias, "Fit for a Fractured Society," 26.

38 Elias, "Fit for a Fractured Society," 26.

39 R. W. Connell, *Masculinities*, 2nd ed. (Berkeley: University of California Press, 2005), 54.

40 Martha M. Lauzen, "It's a Man's (Celluloid) World: Portrayals of Female Characters in the Top Grossing Films of 2019" (Center for the Study of Women in Film & Television 2020), https://womenintvfilm.sdsu.edu/research/.

41 Aaron Baker, *Contesting Identities: Sports in American Film* (Urbana: University of Illinois Press, 2003), 49.

42 Rob Edelman, "Eddie Waitkus and *The Natural*: What Is Assumption? What Is Fact?" (Society for American Baseball Research, 2013), https://sabr.org/journal/article/eddie-waitkus-and-the-natural-what-is-assumption-what-is-fact/.

43 David J. Leonard, "Is This Heaven? White Sporting Masculinities and the Hollywood Imagination," in *Visual Economies of/in Motion Sport and Film*, ed. C. Richard King and David J. Leonard (New York: Peter Lang, 2006), 167.

44 Marjorie D. Kibby, "Nostalgia for the Masculine: Onward to the Past in the Sports Films of the Eighties," *Canadian Journal of Film Studies* 7, no. 1 (Spring 1998): 17.

45 Kibby, "Nostalgia for the Masculine," 18–19.

46 Kibby, "Nostalgia for the Masculine," 20.

47 Leonard, "Is This Heaven?," 173.

48 Quoted in Leonard, "Is This Heaven?," 174.

49 Richard Dyer, *White* (New York: Routledge, 1997), 1.

50 Elias, "Fit for a Fractured Society," 21.

51 Leonard, "Is This Heaven?," 190–191.

52 Richard Sandomir, *The Pride of the Yankees: Lou Gehrig, Gary Cooper and the Making of a Classic* (New York: Hachette, 2017), 140.

53 Sandomir, *Pride of the Yankees*, 236.

54 Robert Burgoyne, *Film Nation: Hollywood Looks at U.S. History* (Minneapolis: University of Minnesota Press, 2010), 9.

55 Burgoyne, *Film Nation*, 9.

56 Sandomir, *Pride of the Yankees*, 80.

57 Sandomir, *Pride of the Yankees*, 219.

58 Charles Eckert, "The Carole Lombard in Macy's Window," in *Fabrications: Costume and the Female Body*, ed. Jane Gaines and Charlotte Herzog (New York: Routledge, 1990), 108.

59 The comments here on *Pride of the Yankees* as part of a cycle of wartime biopics and representing the gender roles of the Gehrig family are adapted from my earlier book, *Contesting Identities: Sports in American Film* (Urbana: University of Illinois Press, 2003), 62–66.

60 Susan K. Cahn, *Coming on Strong: Gender and Sexuality in Women's Sport*, 2nd ed. (Urbana: University of Illinois Press, 2015), 141.

61 Cahn, *Coming on Strong*, 142,144.

62 Cahn, *Coming on Strong*, 140–141.

63 Cahn, *Coming on Strong*, 149.

64 Cahn, *Coming on Strong*, 150–151.

65 Cahn, *Coming on Strong*, 149.

66 Cahn, *Coming on Strong*, 152.

67 Cahn, *Coming on Strong*, 155.

68 Cahn, *Coming on Strong*, 152–153.

69 All-American Girls Professional Baseball League, "League History," https://www.aagpbl.org/history/league-history.

70 Cahn, *Coming on Strong*, 161.

71 Cahn, *Coming on Strong*, 163.

72 Arnold Rampersad, *Jackie Robinson* (New York: Knopf, 1997), 225.

73 Todd Boyd, *The New HNIC: The Death of Civil Rights and the Reign of Hip Hop* (New York: New York University Press, 2002), 10–11.

74 Dave Zirin, "A Review of *42*: Jackie Robinson's Bitter Pill," *The Nation*, April 17, 2013.

75 "MLB Taking Students to See *42*," ESPN, April 22, 2013, https://www.espn.com/mlb/story/_/id/9199496/mlb-teams-taking-students-see-film-42.

76 David J. Leonard, "Saving/Staging Whiteness: Racial Reconciliation in *42* and FIFA 2017/2018," *Black Camera* 10, no. 1 (Fall 2018): 178–179.

77 Leonard, "Saving/Staging Whiteness," 181–182.

78 Joseph Sobran, "The Republic of Baseball," *National Review*, June 11, 1990, https://www.theamericanconservative.com/repository/the-republic-of-baseball/.

79 Nathan Abrams, *The New Jew in Film* (New Brunswick, NJ: Rutgers University Press, 2012), 42.

80 Abrams, *New Jew in Film*, 20.

81 Boyarin is quoted in Abrams, *New Jew in Film*, 21.

82 Deborah Moore, *GI Jews: How World War II Changed a Generation* (Cambridge, MA: Harvard University Press, 2009), 9.

83 Moore, *GI Jews*, 9.

84 Nicholas Dawidoff, *The Catcher Was a Spy* (New York: Pantheon, 1994), 346.

85 Dawidoff, *Catcher Was a Spy*, 32–33.

86 Dawidoff, *Catcher Was a Spy*, 41.

87 Dawidoff, *Catcher Was a Spy*, 117.

88 Dawidoff, *Catcher Was a Spy*, 118.

89 Harry M. Benshoff and Sean Griffin, *Queer Images: A History of Gay and Lesbian Film in America* (Lanham, MD: Rowman & Littlefield, 2006), 249.

90 Benshoff and Griffin, *Queer Images*, 3, 7.

91 Walters quoted in Benshoff and Griffin, *Queer Images*, 261.

92 Benshoff and Griffin, *Queer Images*, 260.

93 Benshoff and Griffin, *Queer Images*, 261.

94 Benshoff and Griffin, *Queer Images*, 155.

95 Will Leitch, "25 of the Best Baseball Movies Ever," MLB.com, March 15, 2020, https://www.mlb.com/news/best-baseball-movies-of-all-time-c301609142.

Chapter 2   The Business of Baseball

1 Robert Elias, "A Fit for a Fractured Society" in *Baseball and the American Dream: Race, Class, Gender, and the National Pastime,* ed. Elias (Armonk, NY: M.E. Sharpe, 2001), 21.

2 "A Conversation between Eric Foner and John Sayles," in *Past Imperfect: History According to the Movies,* ed. Mark C. Carnes (New York: Henry Holt, 1995), 14–15.

3 Doug Rossinow, *The Reagan Era: A History of the 1980s* (New York: Columbia University Press, 2015), 280.

4 Rossinow, *Reagan Era*, 281.

5 Bob Hoie, "1919 Baseball Salaries and the Mythically Underpaid Chicago White Sox," *BaseBall* 6, no. 1 (Spring 2012): 17–34.

6 For 1919 attendance figures, see https://www.baseball-reference.com/leagues /MLB/1919-misc.shtml; Benjamin Rader, *Baseball: A History of America's Game* (Urbana: University of Illinois Press, 2002), 112.

7 Eliot Asinof, *Eight Men Out: The Black Sox and the 1919 World Series* (New York: Henry Holt, 2000), 15.

8 Jacob Pomrenke, "1919 American League Salaries," in *1919 Chicago White Sox Essays*, https://sabr.org/journals/1919-chicago-white-sox-essays/.

9 Hoie, "1919 Baseball Salaries," 30–31.

10 Rader, *Baseball*, 118.

11 Rader, *Baseball*, 118.

12 Rader, *Baseball*, 117.

13 "Conversation between Eric Foner and John Sayles," 14.

14 "Conversation between Eric Foner and John Sayles," 13.

15 Rader, *Baseball*, 116.

16 Rader, *Baseball*, 122.

17 Jules Tygiel, *Past Time: Baseball as History* (New York: Oxford University Press, 2000), 67.

18 "Conversation between Eric Foner and John Sayles," 27.

19 Jim Hemphill, "'We Got over 90 Setups One Day': John Sayles on *Eight Men Out*," *Filmmaker Magazine*, November 15, 2015.

20 Daniel Nathan, *Saying It Ain't So: A Cultural History of the Black Sox Scandal* (Urbana: University of Illinois Press, 2003), 179.

21 Gabe Zaldivar, "Power Ranking the 11 Highest Grossing Baseball Movies of All Time," *Forbes,* May 31, 2016, https://www.forbes.com/sites/gabezaldivar/2016/03 /31/power-ranking-the-11-highest-grossing-baseball-movies-of-all-time/?sh =3788ca907138; *Eight Men Out* https://www.imdb.com/title/tt0095082/?ref_=fn _al_tt_1.

22 1920 American League Attendance, https://www.baseball-reference.com/leagues /AL/1920-misc.shtml; Ken Burns, *Baseball*, episode 4 (Public Broadcasting Service, 1994).

23 Rader, *Baseball*, 142.
24 Leigh Montville, *The Big Bam: The Life and Times of Babe Ruth* (New York: Anchor, 2007), 13–14.
25 Robert Creamer, *Babe: The Legend Comes to Life* (New York: Fireside, 1974), 220.
26 Rader, *Baseball*, 138.
27 Thomas Sowell, *Migrations and Culture* (New York: Basic Books, 1996), 82.
28 Rader, *Baseball*, 138.
29 Creamer, *Babe*, 424.
30 Bosley Crowther, "*The Babe Ruth Story*, Starring William Bendix as Baseball Hero Opens at the Astor," *New York Times*, July 27, 1948, https://www.nytimes.com/1948/07/27/archives/the-screen-the-babe-ruth-story-starring-william-bendix-as-baseball.html.
31 Crowther, "*The Babe Ruth Story*."
32 Jane Leavy, *The Big Fella: Babe Ruth and the World He Created* (New York: Harper, 2018), 391.
33 Leavy, *Big Fella*, 390.
34 Leavy, *Big Fella*, 389.
35 Creamer, *Babe*, 384–391.
36 Andrew Zimbalist, *May the Best Team Win: Baseball Economics and Public Policy* (Washington, DC: Brookings Institution, 2003), 75.
37 Zimbalist, *May the Best Team Win*, 84.
38 Leavy, *Big Fella*, 76.
39 Leavy, *Big Fella*, 75.
40 Leavy, *Big Fella*, 77.
41 Leavy, *Big Fella*, 78.
42 Leavy, *Big Fella*, 60.
43 Leavy, *Big Fella*, 81.
44 Leavy, *Big Fella*, 80.
45 Rader, *Baseball*, 175.
46 Leavy, *Big Fella*, 72.
47 Leavy, *Big Fella*, 72.
48 Leavy, *Big Fella*, 72.
49 Richard Sandomir, *The Pride of the Yankees: Lou Gehrig, Gary Cooper and the Making of a Classic* (New York: Hachette, 2017), 33.
50 Hal Erickson, *The Baseball Filmography* (Jefferson, NC: McFarland, 2002), 63.
51 Leavy, *Big Fella*, 108–109.
52 Tygiel, *Past Time*, 68.
53 Tygiel, *Past Time*, 68.
54 Tygiel, *Past Time*, 69.
55 Rader, *Baseball*, 175.
56 Tygiel, *Past Time*, 71.
57 Tygiel, *Past Time*, 72.
58 St. Louis Media History Foundation, "St. Louis Cardinals Radio History" (2012), https://www.stlmediahistory.org/index.php/Radio/RadioArticles/st.-louis-cardinals-radio-history; "History of WIL" (2021), https://www.route56.com/pioneer-radio-history/wil/.
59 James R. Walker and Robert V. Bellamy Jr., *Center Field Shot: A History of Baseball on Television* (Lincoln: University of Nebraska Press, 2008), 45.

60 Walker and Bellamy, *Center Field Shot*, 50.
61 Walker and Bellamy, *Center Field Shot*, 50.
62 Rader, *Baseball*, 176.
63 Sandomir, *Pride of the Yankees*, 43.
64 Sandomir, *Pride of the Yankees*, 30.
65 Sandomir, *Pride of the Yankees*, 162.
66 Walker and Bellamy, *Center Field Shot*, 42.
67 Walker and Bellamy, *Center Field Shot*, 51.
68 Walker and Bellamy, *Center Field Shot*, 26.
69 Walker and Bellamy, *Center Field Shot*, 67–68.
70 Walker and Bellamy, *Center Field Shot*, 34, 287.
71 Walker and Bellamy, *Center Field Shot*, 87.
72 Walker and Bellamy, *Center Field Shot*, 94.
73 Walker and Bellamy, *Center Field Shot*, 94.
74 Walker and Bellamy, *Center Field Shot*, 91–92.
75 Walker and Bellamy, *Center Field Shot*, 107.
76 Walker and Bellamy, *Center Field Shot*, 133–134.
77 Walker and Bellamy, *Center Field Shot*, 142–143,
78 Walker and Bellamy, *Center Field Shot*, 148, 169, 314.
79 Walker and Bellamy, *Center Field Shot*, 312.
80 Walker and Bellamy, *Center Field Shot*, 287, 291.
81 Walker and Bellamy, *Center Field Shot*, 285.
82 Walker and Bellamy, *Center Field Shot*, 286.
83 Walker and Bellamy, *Center Field Shot*, 291, 277.
84 Walker and Bellamy, *Center Field Shot*, 292.
85 Walker and Bellamy, *Center Field Shot*, 144.
86 Bill Nichols, *Introduction to Documentary*, 2nd ed. (Bloomington: Indiana University Press, 2010), xi.
87 Nichols, *Introduction to Documentary*, 7, 10.
88 Allen Barra, "How Curt Flood Changed Baseball and Killed His Career in the Process," *Atlantic*, July 12, 2011, 4, www.theatlantic.com/entertainment/archive/2011/how-curt-flood-changed-baseball-and-killed-his-career-in the process/241783/.
89 Nichols, *Introduction to Documentary*, 31.
90 Bruce Markusen, "Cooperstown Confidential: Dick Allen," *Hardball Times*, December 18, 2009, https://tht.fangraphs.com/cooperstown-confidential-dick-allen/.
91 Barra, "How Curt Flood Changed Baseball," 9.
92 Benjamin Baumer and Andrew Zimbalist, *The Sabermetric Revolution: Assessing the Growth of Analytics in Baseball* (Philadelphia: University of Pennsylvania Press, 2014), 21.
93 Rob Neyer, "Revisiting Curt Flood's Legacy," *SB Nation*, July 13, 2011, 3.
94 Neyer, "Revisiting Curt Flood's Legacy," 3.
95 *Moneyball*, directed by Bennett Miller, https://www.imdb.com/title/tt1210166/?ref_=fn_al_tt_1.
96 Baumer and Zimbalist, *Sabermetric Revolution*, 21–22.
97 Baumer and Zimbalist, *Sabermetric Revolution*, 22.
98 Baumer and Zimbalist, *Sabermetric Revolution*, 2.

99 Baumer and Zimbalist, *Sabermetric Revolution*, 7.
100 Steve Slowinski, "What Is War?," https://library.fangraphs.com/misc/war/.
101 Baumer and Zimbalist, *Sabermetric Revolution*, 4.
102 "Conversation between Eric Foner and John Sayles," 13.
103 Robert Rosenstone, *Visions of the Past: The Challenge of Film to Our Idea of History* (Cambridge, MA: Harvard University Press, 1995), 22.
104 Baumer and Zimbalist, *Sabermetric Revolution*, 19.
105 Baumer and Zimbalist, *Sabermetric Revolution*, 21.
106 Baumer and Zimbalist, *Sabermetric Revolution*, 21.
107 Tyler Drenon, "Do MLB Owners Wield Sabermetrics as a Hammer?," *Hardball Times*, December 16, 2014, www.fangraphs.com.
108 Mike Ozanian and Kurt Badenhausen, "Despite Lockdown, MLB Teams Gain Value in 2020," *Forbes*, April 9, 2020, 7, https://www.forbes.com/sites/mikeozanian/2020/04/09/despite-lockdown-mlb-teams-gain-value-in-2020.
109 Ozanian and Badenhausen, "Despite Lockdown, MLB Teams Gain Value," 3.
110 Mike Axisa, "The Average MLB Salary Dropped in 2018 for Only the Fourth Time in the Last 50 Years," CBS Sports, December 23, 2018, 3, https://www.cbssports.com/mlb/news/the-average-mlb-salary-dropped-in-2018-for-only-the-fourth-time-in-the-last-50-years/.
111 Justin Terranova, "Brian Kenny Talks Gerrit Cole's Mega-worth, Working with Joe Girardi," *New York Post*, November 15, 2019, https://nypost.com/2019/11/15/brian-kenny-talks-gerrit-coles-mega-worth-working-with-joe-girardi/.
112 Jimmy Traina, "This Fact about MLB Salaries May Surprise You," *Sports Illustrated*, May 27, 2020, https://www.si.com/extra-mustard/2020/05/27/mlb-2020-player-salaries.
113 Axisa, "Average MLB Salary Dropped," 4.
114 Axisa, "Average MLB Salary Dropped," 4.
115 Ben Lindbergh and Travis Sawchik, *The MVP Machine: How Baseball's New Nonconformists Are Using Data to Build Better Players* (New York: Basic Books, 2020), 3.
116 Michael Baumann, "Baseball Is Broken: Can Anything Short of a Strike Fix It?," *The Ringer*, January 14, 2019, 4, https://www.theringer.com/mlb/2019/1/14/18181665/mlb-mlbpa-player-power-labor-strike-machado-harper-murray.
117 Baumann, "Baseball Is Broken," 4–5.
118 Baumann, "Baseball Is Broken," 3.
119 Kurt Badenhausen, "Baseball's Highest-Paid Players 2019: Mike Trout Leads with $39 Million," *Forbes*, April 1, 2019, https://www.forbes.com/sites/kurtbadenhausen/2019/04/01/baseballs-highest-paid-players-2019-mike-trout-leads-with-39-million/#22ec8f3c6cc7.
120 Badenhausen, "Baseball's Highest-Paid Players 2019," 2–3.
121 Rader, *Baseball*, 91, 147.
122 James Wagner, "Minor League Baseball Season Is Canceled for the First Time," *New York Times*, June 30, 2020, https://www.nytimes.com/2020/06/30/sports/baseball/minor-league-baseball-season-canceled.html.
123 Jared Wyllys, "MLB Might Be Increasing Minor League Pay, and That's a Good Thing," *Forbes*, March 19, 2019, https://www.forbes.com/sites/jaredwyllys/2019/03/19/mlb-might-be-increasing-minor-league-pay-and-thats-a-good-thing/#105c00343248.

124 Dirk Hayhurst, "An Inside Look into the Harsh Conditions of Minor League Baseball," *Bleacher Report*, May 14, 2014, 12, https://bleacherreport.com/articles /2062307-an-inside-look-into-the-harsh-conditions-of-minor-league-baseball.

125 Tom Goldman, "Fight Against Low, Low Pay in Minor League Baseball Continues Despite New Obstacles," NPR, August 3, 2018, 3.

126 Goldman, "Fight Against Low, Low Pay," 6.

127 Goldman, "Fight Against Low, Low Pay," 7.

128 Hayhurst, "An Inside Look," 2.

129 Hayhurst, "An Inside Look," 2.

Chapter 3   Screening Who Gets to Play

1 Mitchell Nathanson, *A People's History of Baseball* (Urbana: University of Illinois Press, 2012), 23.

2 Nathanson, *People's History of Baseball*, 29.

3 Institute for Diversity and Ethics in Sports, "The 2021 Racial and Gender Report Card: Major League Baseball," https://43530132-36e9-4f52-811a-182c7a91933b .filesusr.com/ugd/138a69_0fc7d964273c45938ad7a26f7e638636.pdf.

4 Ian O'Connor, "The Commissioner and His Quest," ESPN, April 15, 2010, https://www.espn.co.uk/new-york/mlb/columns/story?id=5095255.

5 "MLB Says Percentage of Black Players Highest since 2012," *USA Today*, April 10, 2018, https://www.usatoday.com/story/sports/mlb/2018/04/10/mlb-says -percentage-of-black-players-highest-since-2012/33696133/.

6 Paul P. Murphy, "Baseball Is Making Black Lives Matter Center Stage on Opening Day," CNN, July 24, 2020, https://www.cnn.com/2020/07/23/us /opening-day-baseball-mlb-black-lives-matter-trnd/index.html.

7 James Wagner, "On Opening Day, a Rarity for MLB: Support for Black Lives Matter," *New York Times*, July 23, 2020, https://www.nytimes.com/2020/07/23 /sports/baseball/mlb-black-lives-matter.html.

8 Hua Hsu, "The End of White America?," *Atlantic*, January/February 2009, 5.

9 Jules Tygiel, *Baseball's Great Experiment: Jackie Robinson and His Legacy* (New York: Oxford University Press, 1997), 132, 205.

10 Dana Jennings, "The Superhero Who Leapt Color Lines," *New York Times*, April 5, 2013, https://www.nytimes.com/2013/04/07/movies/jackie-robinson-the -hero-in-42.html.

11 Benjamin Rader, *Baseball: A History of America's Game* (Urbana: University of Illinois Press, 2002), 107.

12 Rader, *Baseball*, 107.

13 Rader, *Baseball*, 108.

14 Steve Tripp, "'The Most Popular Unpopular Man in Baseball': Baseball Fans and Ty Cobb in the Early 20th Century," *Journal of Social History* 43 (Fall 2009): 70.

15 Tripp, "'Most Popular Unpopular Man in Baseball,'" 71.

16 Tripp, "'Most Popular Unpopular Man in Baseball,'" 71.

17 Tripp, "'Most Popular Unpopular Man in Baseball,'" 72.

18 Tripp, "'Most Popular Unpopular Man in Baseball,'" 75.

19 Tripp, "'Most Popular Unpopular Man in Baseball,'" 78.

20 Robert Rosenstone, "The Historical Film as Real History," *Film-Historia* 5, no. 1 (1995): 5.

21 Arnold Rampersad, *Jackie Robinson* (New York: Knopf, 1997), 223.

22 Tygiel, *Baseball's Great Experiment*, 334.

23 Rampersad, *Jackie Robinson*, 224.

24 Rader, *Baseball*, 160.

25 Henry Louis Gates, "Beyond the Culture Wars: Identities in Dialogue," *Profession* 1993 (1993): 6, 9.

26 Ken Burns and Lynn Novick, "About the Film," in *Baseball*, https://www.pbs.org/kenburns/baseball/about/.

27 Nathanson, *People's History of Baseball*, 94.

28 Peter Dreier, "Jackie Robinson's Legacy: Baseball, Race and Politics," in *Baseball and the American Dream: Race, Class, Gender, and the National Pastime*, ed. Robert Elias (Armonk, NY: M.E. Sharpe, 2001), 51.

29 Rob Ruck, *Raceball: How the Major Leagues Colonized the Black and Latin Game* (Boston: Beacon, 2011), 27.

30 Ruck, *Raceball*, 28.

31 Robert Nowatzki, "A Dream Deferred: African Americans in Baseball," in *African Americans and Popular Culture*, vol. 2, ed. Todd Boyd (Westport, CT: Praeger, 2008), 38.

32 Nathanson, *People's History of Baseball*, 83.

33 Nathanson, *People's History of Baseball*, 100.

34 Nathanson, *People's History of Baseball*, 81.

35 Nathanson, *People's History of Baseball*, 69.

36 Paul Petrovic, "'Give 'Em the Razzle-Dazzle': The Negro Leagues in *The Bingo Long Traveling All-Stars and Motor Kings* and *Soul of the Game*," *Black Ball* 3, no. 1 (Spring 2010): 62.

37 Benjamin Rader, *American Sports: From the Age of Sports Games to the Age of Televised Sports*, 5th ed. (Upper Saddle River, NJ: Prentice Hall, 2004), 319.

38 Adrian Burgos Jr., *Playing America's Game: Baseball, Latinos and the Color Line* (Los Angeles: University of California Press, 2007), 3.

39 Ruck, *Raceball*, 33; Nowatzki, "Dream Deferred," 39.

40 "The Negro Leagues," MLB.com, https://www.mlb.com/history/negro-leagues/teams/indianapolis-clowns.

41 Petrovic, "'Give 'Em the Razzle-Dazzle,'" 65.

42 Petrovic, "'Give 'Em the Razzle-Dazzle,'" 65, 68.

43 Ruck, *Raceball*, 28.

44 Ruck, *Raceball*, 45.

45 Ruck, *Raceball*, 44.

46 Ruck, *Raceball*, 45.

47 David Levering Lewis, "The Segregated North," *New York Times*, January 11, 2013, 13.

48 Derrick A. Bell, "Who's Afraid of Critical Race Theory?," *University of Illinois Law Review* 893 (1995): 5.

49 Catherine Squires, *The Post-Racial Mystique: Media and Race in the Twenty-First Century* (New York: New York University Press, 2014), 12.

50 Jennifer Ring, "Invisible Women in America's National Pastime . . . or 'She's Good. It's History, Man,'" *Journal of Sports and Social Issues* 37, no. 1 (2013): 59.

51 Ring, "Invisible Women in America's National Pastime," 60–61.

52 Ring, "Invisible Women," 61.

53 Ring, "Invisible Women," 61–62.

54 Ring, "Invisible Women," 62.

55 Anna Wade, "#Shortstops: Maria Pepe Changes the Face of Little League" (National Baseball Hall of Fame, n.d.), https://baseballhall.org/discover/short -stops/nothing-little-about-it.

56 Jennifer Ring, *Stolen Bases: Why American Girls Don't Play Baseball* (Urbana: University of Illinois Press, 2009), 16.

57 Susan K. Cahn, *Coming on Strong: Gender and Sexuality in Women's Sport*, 2nd ed. (Urbana: University of Illinois Press, 2015), 152.

58 Amira Rose Davis, "No League of Their Own: Baseball, Black Women and the Politics of Representation," *Radical History Review* 125 (May 2016): 74.

59 Samantha N. Sheppard, *Sporting Blackness* (Los Angeles: University of California Press, 2020), 108.

60 Karen Given, "75 Years After the Women's Pro League, Bring Baseball Back to Girls," WBUR, August 17, 2018, https://www.wbur.org/onlyagame/2018/08/17 /women-baseball-mone-davis.

61 Ring, "Invisible Women," 67.

62 Ring, "Invisible Women," 74.

63 Ring, "Invisible Women," 74.

64 Betsy Morais, "The Girl of Summer," *Atlantic*, September 2016, 18.

65 Morais, "Girl of Summer," 19.

66 Guy Harrison, "We Want to See You Set It Up and Be Slutty: Post-feminism and Sport Media's Appearance Double Standard," *Critical Studies in Mass Communication* 26, no. 2 (2019): 143.

67 Alexandra Bruell, "ESPN's New Pitch to Advertisers: 'We Reach Women,'" *Wall Street Journal*, January 8, 2018, https://www.wsj.com/articles/espns-new-pitch-to -advertisers-we-reach-women-1515409200.

Chapter 4 The Glocalized Game

1 Manfred B. Steger, *Globalization: A Very Short Introduction*, 4th ed. (New York: Oxford University Press, 2017), 1.

2 Walter LaFeber, *Michael Jordan and the New Global Capitalism* (New York: Norton, 2002), 55–57.

3 Major League Baseball, "MLB International" (2021), https://www.mlb.com /international.

4 Barrie Axford, *Theories of Globalization* (Cambridge: Polity, 2013), 92.

5 Steger, *Globalization*, 2.

6 Habibul Haque Khondker and Roland Robertson, "Glocalization, Consumption, and Cricket: The Indian Premier League," *Journal of Consumer Culture* 18, no. 2 (2018): 282.

7 William W. Kelly, "Is Baseball a Global Sport? America's National Pastime as Global Field and International Sport," *Global Networks* 7, no. 2 (2007): 188, 191.

8 Kelly, "Is Baseball a Global Sport?," 189.

9 Maury Brown, "MLB Sees Record 10.7 Billion in Revenues for 2019," *Forbes*, December 21, 2019, https://www.forbes.com/sites/maurybrown/2019/12/21/mlb -sees-record-107-billion-in-revenues-for-2019/#1dbc65b65d78; "Average MLB Salary Drops for Second Straight Year," ESPN, December 20, 2019,

https://www.espn.com/mlb/story/_/id/28341983/average-mlb-salary-drops
-second-straight-year.

10 Kelly, "Is Baseball a Global Sport?," 199.

11 Alan M. Klein, *Growing the Game: The Globalization of Major League Baseball* (New Haven, CT: Yale University Press, 2006), 11.

12 Interview with Burgos, November 10, 2017.

13 Nikil Saval, "Globalisation: The Rise and Fall of an Idea That Swept the World," *Guardian*, July 14, 2017, 4, https://www.theguardian.com/world/2017/jul/14 /globalisation-the-rise-and-fall-of-an-idea-that-swept-the-world.

14 Michael Real and Diana Beeson, "Globalization and Diversity in American Sports," in *Bodies of Discourse: Sports Stars, Media, and the Global Public*, ed. Cornel Sandvoss, Michael Real, and Alina Bernstein (New York: Peter Lang, 2012), 155.

15 Agustin Bertran, "Altice and Multimedios Del Caribe Take MLB 2019 to the Dominican Republic," *Nextv News Latin America*, April 1, 2019, https//en .nextvlatam.com; Andrei S. Markovits and Lars Rensmann, *Gaming the World: How Sports Are Reshaping Global Politics and Culture* (Princeton, NJ: Princeton University Press, 2013), 84.

16 Ezequiel Kitsu Lihosit, "Major League Baseball's Latin American Connection: Salaries, Scouting, and Globalization" (MA thesis, University of San Diego, 2016), 9, https://digital.sandiego.edu/theses/9.

17 Mark Armour and Daniel R. Levitt, "Baseball Demographics, 1947–2016" (Society for American Baseball Research), https://sabr.org/bioproj/topic/baseball -demographics-1947-2016/.

18 "Record 110 Players from Dominican Republic on MLB Rosters," ESPN, July 24, 2020, https://www.espn.com/mlb/story/_/id/29531510/record-109-players -dominican-republic-mlb-opening-day-rosters.

19 See Samuel O. Regalado, *Viva Baseball? Latin Major Leagues and Their Special Hunger* (Urbana: University of Illinois Press, 1998) and Klein, *Growing the Game*.

20 Lihosit, "Major League Baseball's Latin American Connection," 4.

21 Ruck is quoted in David Lagesse, "Baseball Is a Field of Dreams—and Dashed Hopes—for Dominicans," NPR, April 3, 2016, https://www.npr.org/sections /goatsandsoda/2016/04/03/472699693/baseball-is-a-field-of-dreams-and-dashed -hopes-for-dominicans.

22 Bill Brink, "Two Systems, Two Pools of Money Lead to Inequality for Would-Be Professional Baseball Players," *Pittsburgh Post-Gazette*, July 8, 2019, https://www .post-gazette.com/business/bop/2019/07/08/Business-of-Pittsburgh-Major -League-Baseball-Starling-Marte-Gregory-Polanco-draft-bonus-pool -international/stories/201907070009.

23 Statista Research Department, "Average Player Salary in the NPB 2019, by Team" (April 8, 2020), https://www.statista.com/statistics/675557/average-npb-salary-by -team/.

24 L. Jon Wertheim, "Have It Both Ways," *Sports Illustrated*, April 17, 2017, 92–97; Pedro Moura, "Shohei Ohtani Agrees to Sign with Angels," *Los Angeles Times*, December 8, 2017, https://www.latimes.com/sports/angels/la-sp-angels-sign -ohtani-20171208-story.html.

25 Klein, *Growing the Game*, 165.

26 Klein, *Growing the Game*, 165.

27 Klein, *Growing the Game*, 143; Wayne G. McDonnell, "Ichiro Suzuki's Negotiating Success Is Just as Impressive as His Extraordinary Career," *Forbes*, May 22, 2019, https://www.forbes.com/sites/waynemcdonnell/2019/03/22/ichiro-suzukis-negotiating-success-is-just-as-impressive-as-his-extraordinary-career/#1c22561c5fae; "Top Major League Baseball Salaries for 2001," https://www.thebaseballnexus.com/top_salaries/2001.

28 Baseball Reference, "MLB Attendance," https://www.baseball-reference.com/leagues/MLB/2000-misc.shtml, https://www.baseball-reference.com/leagues/MLB/2001-misc.shtml; Angelo Bruscas, "Ms Lead Majors in TV Ratings," *Seattle Post-Intelligencer*, June 3, 2003, https://www.seattlepi.com/news/article/M-s-lead-majors-in-TV-ratings-1116264.php.

29 Kelly, "Is Baseball a Global Sport?," 188.

30 Kelly, "Is Baseball a Global Sport?," 194.

31 Kelly, "Is Baseball a Global Sport?," 195.

32 Quoted in Kelly, "Is Baseball a Global Sport?," 196.

33 Kelly, "Is Baseball a Global Sport?," 197.

34 Klein, *Growing the Game*, 126, 164.

35 Klein, *Growing the Game*, 128.

36 Klein, *Growing the Game*, 126.

37 Steven R. Weisman, "Studio: Japanese Didn't Force Script Changes," *Chicago Tribune*, November 20, 1991, https://www.chicagotribune.com/news/ct-xpm-1991-11-20-9104150193-story.html.

38 "*Kokoyakyu*, Filmmaker Interview," *POV*, July 4, 2006, http://archive.pov.org/kokoyakyu/interview/.

39 Dan Gordon, "Japan: Changing of the Guard in High School Baseball," in *Baseball without Borders: The International Pastime*, ed. George Gmelch (Lincoln: University of Nebraska Press, 2006), 16–17.

40 Adrian Burgos, *Playing America's Game: Baseball, Latinos and the Color Line* (Los Angeles: University of California Press, 2007), 225.

41 Gustavo Martínez Contreras, "Clemente bateó contra la injusticia," *El Diario*, December 30, 2014, https://eldiariony.com/2014/12/30/clemente-bateo-contra-la-injusticia/.

42 David Maraniss, "No Gentle Saint: Roberto Clemente Was a Fierce Critic of Both Baseball and American Society," *The Undefeated*, May 31, 2016, https://theundefeated.com/features/roberto-clemente-was-a-fierce-critic-of-both-baseball-and-american-society/.

43 Rob Ruck, *Raceball: How the Major Leagues Colonized the Black and Latino Game* (Boston: Beacon, 2011), 168.

44 Contreras, "Clemente bateó contra la injusticia."

45 "Pop Hit One for the Family," *New York Times*, October 18, 1979, https://www.nytimes.com/1979/10/18/archives/pops-hit-one-for-the-family-sports-of-the-times.html.

46 Real and Beeson, "Globalization and Diversity in American Sports," 156.

Chapter 5 Fanball

1 Henry Jenkins, *Textual Poachers: Television Fans and Participatory Culture* (New York: Routledge, 2013), 12.

2 Jenkins, *Textual Poachers*, 10.
3 Warren Goldstein, "Fiction," *Washington Post*, July 9, 1995, https://www
   .washingtonpost.com/archive/entertainment/books/1995/07/09/fiction
   /b02baedo-4a86-4913-b230-921c71ce60b3/.
4 Noah Cohan, *We Average Unbeautiful Watchers: Fan Narratives and the Reading
   of American Sports* (Lincoln: University of Nebraska Press, 2019), 125, 122–123.
5 Cohan, *We Average Unbeautiful Watchers*, 132.
6 Cohan, *We Average Unbeautiful Watchers*, 141.
7 Cohan, *We Average Unbeautiful Watchers*, 123.
8 Matthew A. Cabot, "Barry Bonds vs. the Media," *Journal of Mass Media Ethics* 26
   (2011): 67.
9 Andrew Zimbalist, *May the Best Team Win: Baseball Economics and Public Policy*
   (Washington, DC: Brookings Institution, 2003), 88–89.
10 Zimbalist, *May the Best Team Win*, 90–91.
11 Hannah Keyser, "A Look at Fan Rage from 1994 Strike, and Those Who Never
   Really Came Back," Yahoo Sports, August 11, 2019, https://sports.yahoo.com/a
   -look-at-fan-rage-from-1994-mlb-strike-and-those-who-never-really-came-back
   -054158066.html.
12 Fred Stein, *A History of the Baseball Fan* (Jefferson, NC: McFarland, 2005), 194.
13 Alan Siegel, "Unrequited Love Story: *Bull Durham* at 30," *The Ringer*, June 14,
   2018, https://www.theringer.com/movies/2018/6/14/17451268/bull-durham-30
   -anniversary-kevin-costner-ron-shelton-susan-sarandon.
14 Siegel, "Unrequited Love Story."
15 Cohan, *We Average Unbeautiful Watchers*, 127.
16 Cohan, *We Average Unbeautiful Watchers*, 127.
17 Cohan, *We Average Unbeautiful Watchers*, 126.
18 Cohan, *We Average Unbeautiful Watchers*, 148.
19 Cohan, *We Average Unbeautiful Watchers*, 150.
20 Jenkins, *Textual Poachers*, 18.
21 Jenkins, *Textual Poachers*, 23.
22 Jason Turbow, "In 1981, an Unknown Pitcher from Mexico Changed the Game
   for the Dodgers," *Los Angeles Magazine*, June 3, 2019, https://www.lamag.com
   /culturefiles/fernando-valenzuela-they-bled-blue/.
23 Turbow, "In 1981."
24 Turbow, "In 1981"; Samuel O. Regalado, *Viva Baseball! Latin Major Leaguers and
   Their Special Hunger* (Urbana: University of Illinois Press, 1998), 172.
25 Joseph Durso, "Valenzuela (7-0) Tops Mets by 1-0 for His Fifth Shutout," *New
   York Times*, May 9, 1981, https://www.nytimes.com/1981/05/09/sports/valenzuela
   -7-0-tops-mets-by-1-0-for-his-fifth-shutout.html.
26 Patrick J. McDonnell, "A Pitcher Who Told the Future: The Craze Surrounding
   Fernando Valenzuela's Success with the Dodgers 20 Years Ago Hinted at the
   Emerging Power of Latinos in L.A.," *Los Angeles Times*, July 9, 2001, 2.
27 McDonnell, "Pitcher Who Told the Future," 3.
28 Fiske quoted in Cornel Sandvoss, *Fans: The Mirror of Consumption* (Malden, MA:
   Polity, 2005), 29.
29 Jenkins, *Textual Poachers*, 23.
30 Alan Klein, *Growing the Game; The Globalization of Major League Baseball* (New
   Haven, CT: Yale University Press, 2006), 83.

31 Gary Pomerantz, "Valenzuela: The Holdout Holds Fast in 1st Victory," *Washington Post*, April 11, 1982, https://www.washingtonpost.com/archive/sports/1982/04/11/valenzuela-the-holdout-holds-fast-in-1st-victory/f83ca424-a66f-4cf1-9c1a-13377645829a/.
32 McDonnell, "Pitcher Who Told the Future," 3.
33 Jonathan Kelly, "Q&A: Fantasy Baseball Creator Daniel Okrent," *Vanity Fair*, March 21, 2008, https://www.vanityfair.com/news/2008/03/qa-fantasy-base; Morty Ain, "We Had No Idea," ESPN, February 23, 2010, https://www.espn.com/mlb/insider/news/story?id=4939543.
34 *USA Today*, "About USA Today," https://static.usatoday.com/about/timeline/.
35 Kelly, "Q&A."
36 Todd Nesbit and Kerry King-Adzima, "Major League Baseball Attendance and the Role of Fantasy Baseball," *Journal of Sports Economics* 13, no. 5 (2012): 495.
37 Nesbit and King-Adzima, "Major League Baseball Attendance," 496.
38 Darren Heitner, "The Hyper Growth of Daily Fantasy Sports Is Going to Change Our Culture and Our Laws," *Forbes*, September 16, 2015, 1, https://www.forbes.com/sites/darrenheitner/2015/09/16/the-hyper-growth-of-daily-fantasy-sports-is-going-to-change-our-culture-and-our-laws/#4795dbce5aca.
39 Heitner, "Hyper Growth," 4–5.
40 Todd M. Nesbit and Kerry A. King, "The Impact of Fantasy Sports on Television Viewership," *Journal of Media Economics* 23, no. 1 (2010): 39; Heitner, "Hyper Growth," 5.
41 Heitner, "Hyper Growth," 5.
42 Ain, "We Had No Idea"
43 Allison C. Burr-Miller, "What's Your Fantasy? Fantasy Baseball as Equipment for Living," *Southern Communication Journal* 76, no. 5 (2011): 448.
44 Fiona Allon, "Nostalgia Unbound: Illegibility and the Synthetic Excess of Space," *Continuum: Journal of Media and Cultural Studies* 14 (2000): 284.
45 Burr-Miller, "What's Your Fantasy?," 458–459.
46 Sam Walker, *Fantasyland: A Sportswriter's Obsessive Bid to Win the World's Most Ruthless Fantasy Baseball League* (New York: Penguin, 2006), 145.
47 Burr-Miller, "What's Your Fantasy?," 460.

Chapter 6 Learning the Game

1 David W. Zang, *Sports Wars: Athletes in the Age of Aquarius* (Fayetteville: University of Arkansas Press, 2001), 141.
2 Vivian Sobchack, "Baseball in the Post-American Cinema, or Life in the Minor Leagues," in *Out of Bounds: Sports, Media, and the Politics of Identity*, ed. Aaron Baker and Todd Boyd (Bloomington: Indiana University Press, 1997), 183.
3 Zang, *Sports Wars*, 145.
4 Jack Scott, *The Athletic Revolution* (New York: Free Press, 1971).
5 Michael Messner, *It's All for the Kids: Gender, Families and Youth Sports* (Los Angeles: University of California Press, 2009), 19.
6 Michael Messner, *Out of Play: Critical Essays on Gender and Sport* (Albany: State University of New York Press, 2007), 19.
7 Jay Coakley, "The Good Father: Parental Expectations and Youth Sports," *Leisure Studies* 25, no. 2 (April 2006): 155.

8 Messner, *It's All for the Kids*, 22.
9 Coakley, "Good Father," 154–155; Messner, *It's All for the Kids*, 9–13.
10 Messner, *Its All for the Kids*, 15–16.
11 Messner, *Its All for the Kids*, 14.
12 Nicholas L. Holt and Camilla J. Knight, *Parenting in Youth Sport: From Research to Practice* (New York: Taylor & Francis, 2014), 42.
13 Holt and Knight, *Parenting in Youth Sport*, 42.
14 Coakley, "Good Father," 154.
15 Holt and Knight, *Parenting in Youth Sport*, 43.
16 Holt and Knight, *Parenting in Youth Sport*, 47.
17 David Bordwell and Kristin Thompson, *Film Art* (New York: McGraw-Hill, 1997), 108.
18 *Remember the Titans,* directed by Boaz Yakin, https://www.imdb.com/title/tt0210945/?ref_=fn_al_tt_1; *The Rookie*, https://www.imdb.com/title/tt0265662/?ref_=fn_al_tt_2.
19 John Willis, *Disney Culture* (New Brunswick, NJ: Rutgers University Press, 2017), 128.
20 Lucy Bolton, "'You Ain't Ugly Like Me: It's Just That We Both Got Scars': Women in Eastwood's Films," in *Tough Ain't Enough*, ed. Lester D. Friedman and David Desser (New Brunswick, NJ: Rutgers University Press, 2018), 137.
21 Bolton, "'You Ain't Ugly Like Me,'" 150.
22 David Desser, "'I Know I'm as Blind as a Slab of Concrete, but I'm Not Helpless': The Aging Action Hero," in Friedman and Desser, *Tough Ain't Enough*, 165.
23 Desser, "'I Know I'm as Blind as a Slab of Concrete,'" 166.
24 Belton, "'You Ain't Ugly Like Me,'" 141.
25 Sherri Grasmuck and Janet Goldwater, *Protecting Home: Class, Race, and Masculinity in Boys Baseball* (New Brunswick, NJ: Rutgers University Press, 2005), 112–113.

Conclusion

1 Ben Lindbergh and Travis Sawchik, *The MVP Machine: How Baseball's New Nonconformists Are Using Data to Build Better Players* (New York: Basic Books, 2019), 12.
2 Andrew Bucholtz, "April Cable Coverage Estimates Show Further Sports Drops, Especially at NFL Network and MLB Network," *Awful Announcing*, April 1, 2019, https://awfulannouncing.com/league-networks/april-cable-coverage-estimates-nfln-mlbn.html.
3 Sarah Trembanis, "*Ahead of the Curve: Inside the Baseball Revolution* by Brian Kenny (Review)," *Journal of Sport History* 44, no. 3 (Fall 2017): 512.
4 Neil Weinberg, "It's Time for the Sabermetric Revolution to be Televised," *The Hardball Times*, June 30, 2016, https://tht.fangraphs.com/its-time-for-the-sabermetric-revolution-to-be-televised/.
5 Weinberg, "It's Time for the Sabermetric Revolution."
6 Weinberg, "It's Time for the Sabermetric Revolution."
7 Brian Kenny, "MLB Network Insider: Big Time Contrasts Have an Impact Off the Field Too," *Hollywood Reporter*, April 2, 2019, https://www.hollywoodreporter

.com/live-feed/mlb-network-insider-big-time-contracts-have-an-impact-field-guest
-column-1198509.

8 Weinberg, "It's Time for the Sabermetric Revolution."

9 Cary Funk, Meg Hefferon, Brian Kennedy, and Courtney Johnson, "Trust and
   Mistrust in Americans Views of Scientific Experts" (Pew Research Center,
   August 2, 2019), https://www.pewresearch.org/science/2019/08/02/trust-and
   -mistrust-in-americans-views-of-scientific-experts/.

10 Mike Ozanian, "MLB Teams Lost $1 Billion in 2020 on $2.5 Billion Profit
   Swing," *Forbes*, December 22, 2020.

11 Bob Klapisch, "MLB's 2nd Round with COVID-19: Delayed Spring Training and
   Opening Day Likely as Labor War Looms; No Line-Cutting for Vaccine," *NJ.com*,
   December 20, 2020, https://www.nj.com/yankees/2020/12/mlbs-2nd-round-with
   -covid-19-delayed-spring-training-and-opening-day-likely-as-labor-war-looms-no
   -line-cutting-for-vaccine-klapisch.html.

12 "Report: MLB Projects $640K Per Game Loss with No Fans," *USA Today*,
   May 16, 2020, https://www.usatoday.com/story/sports/mlb/2020/05/16/major
   -league-baseball-revenue-loss-report/5207671002/.

13 Greg Rosalsky, "What 1919 Teaches Us about Pent-Up Demand," NPR.org,
   January 12, 2021, https://www.npr.org/sections/money/2021/01/12/955617983
   /what-1919-teaches-us-about-pent-up-demand.

14 Rosalsky, "What 1919 Teaches Us."

15 Jabari Young on MSNBC Power Lunch program, December 17, 2019, https://
   www.cnbc.com/video/2019/12/17/how-major-league-baseball-is-innovating.html.

16 Eddie Moran, "Baseball Tries to Boost Its Social Media Efforts," *Front Office
   Sports*, January 28, 2020, https://frontofficesports.com/baseball-social-media/.

17 Moran, "Baseball Tries to Boost Its Social Media Efforts."

Index

Note: Page numbers in *italics* indicate film stills.

of, 53; the media and, 57–63; off-the-field activities of, 54, 81; owners' exploitation of, 3, 55–57, 77; popularity of, 16, 53, 55, 156; struck out by a woman, 16; in World Series, 53, 62–63, 171
Ryan, Nolan, 140

sabermetrics, 72–78, 167–171
Samuel, Lawrence, 10–12
Sanada, Hiroyuki, 40
Sandlot, The (film), 6, 36, 42, 152–157, 165
Sandomir, Richard, 26, 61, 63
San Francisco Giants, 130
Sanguillén, Manny, 123
Sarandon, Susan, 42, 132, 134
Saturday Evening Post (magazine), 29
Sawchik, Travis, 76, 167–168
Sayles, John, 45–52, 73
Schalk, Ray, 49
Schofield, Bobby, 40
Schrager, Harley, 79–80
Schrager, Tony, 79–80
Schwab, John, 40
science, sociocultural role of, 170
Scott, Jack, 151
Scott, Tony, 128
Seattle Mariners, 113–114
Secret Love, A (documentary), 42
self-reliance, as American value, 3, 4, 11, 17, 18, 19, 22, 23, 24, 35, 41, 57, 89–90, 159–160, 162. *See also* individualism
Selig, Bud, 84, 131
Selleck, Tom, 115
Sewell, Omer, 140
sexuality: in *The Catcher Was a Spy*, 40–41; in *42*, 33–34; gay/lesbian, 40–41
Seymour, Harold, 12
Sheen, Charlie, 51, 66, *67*
Shelton, Marley, 156
Shelton, Ron, 87, 88, 132–134
Shepard, Samantha, 103
Shioya, Toshi, 116
simplification, in film narratives, 48, 73–74
*61** (film), 42
Sklar, Robert, 11, 142–144
Slugger's Wife, The (film), 23
Smith, Frances, 14
Smith, Jimmy, 171

Smith, Quinn, 149
Smith, Reggie, 115
Smith, Wendell, 92
Smits, Jimmy, 120, 121
Snipes, Wesley, 128
Snyder, Brad, 71
Sobchack, Vivian, 2, 3, 148
Sobran, Joseph, 35–36
social diversity: in baseball, 2, 12, 14–18, 43, 83–86, 91, 95; economic impact of, 4–5, 86, 141; fan outreach and, 4–5, 15, 83–84, 91, 169; in the media, 84, 169–170; media representations of, 3, 4, 9–10, 36, 41–43, 148–149, 152, 156; MLB and, 83, 85–86, 100; owners and, 43, 170
social media, 172
Society for American Baseball Research (SABR), 72
softball, 28–29, 30, 101, 105–106, 155
Sony, 77
Sotomayor, Sonia, 131
Soul of the Game (film), 36, 93–96, 99–100
Spalding, Albert, 101
Speedy (film), 59
Sporting News (newspaper), 16, 60
Sports Illustrated (magazine), 132
Springside Chestnut Hill Academy, 105
Squires, Catherine, 100
Stambaugh, David, 148
Stargell, Willie, 123
Star Wars films, 23
statistical analysis. *See* sabermetrics
Stealing Home (film), 23
Steger, Manfred, 108, 110
Stein, Fred, 132
Steinhagen, Ruth Ann, 20
Stern, Bill, 63
Stewart, Riley, 90
St. Louis Cardinals, 53, 60, 68, 74
Strathairn, David, 30
Strathairn, Tay, 49
Stratton Story, The (film), 36
strikes, 56, 128, 131
Strong, Mark, 40
Stump, Al, 87–88
Sugar (film), 5, 36, 42, 124–125
Sullivan, Joseph "Sport," 47
Sullivan, Kevin Rodney, 94, 96

About the Author

AARON BAKER is a professor of Film and Media Studies at Arizona State University. His writing focuses primarily on sports culture and film authorship. He is the author of *Contesting Identity: Sports in American Film* and the editor of *Out of Bounds: Sports, Media, and the Politics of Identity.*